MY SHOUT

AT THE

DALY WATERS PUB

BY MARK VENABLE

This book is dedicated to Leonie, my wife and best friend.

Without you, our adventure at Daly Waters Pub would only been a dream.

First Published 2017

PREFACE

This book is my recollection of actual events between 1986 and 1988, when I was publican of The Daly Waters Pub in the Northern Territory. In reality, I commenced this book the day I left the pub by telling and re-telling these stories for the last thirty years to family, friends and anyone who would listen.

For years I dreamt of one day of writing this book, however the demanding years of pub life ensured there was no time. Now, in semi-retirement and with encouragement from family and friends, "My Shout at Daly Waters Pub" isn't a dream anymore.

Conversations with "quotation marks" are for literary effect to help describe an event.

Thankyou to everyone mentioned in this book. Without you, there would be no story to tell. I feel incredibly privileged to have owned such an important piece of Australian outback history and I pray the historic pub forever remains fundamentally as it is today.

1987 sketch of the Daly Waters Pub by Les Wood, our yardie Grant's dad.

Table of Contents

Daly Waters

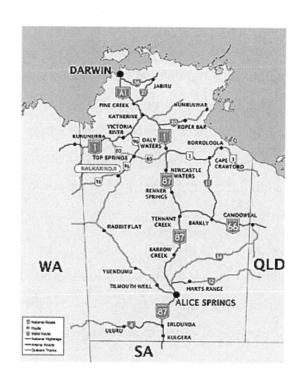

Chapter 1. INTRODUCTION

It's approaching midnight on our first day as publicans of the historic Daly Waters Pub. Rodeo weekend is in full swing and the old corrugated iron pub is bursting at the seams with jackaroos, jillaroos and cattle station owners plus a handful of tourists, wide eyed at the scene confronting them.

I know it's almost midnight because Mataranka policeman Bob shows me his watch and tells me for the third time tonight "Mark, there's far too many people in here, and they're still drinking on road. Shut the pub. Now"!!

I reckon Bob has it in for the pub, but I don't know why. He's been driving to town throughout day, begging me to close the pub early, before retreating back to the Hi-Way Inn roadhouse, several kilometres south. I think he wants the rodeo crowd to go to the roadhouse so he doesn't have to come here ... but why? I don't care, I'm too busy serving drinks and don't have the time to get my head around it.

The rodeo goers are rough, tough and rowdy but generally a well behaved lot. Sure, there's been a few fights as the jackaroos, from all parts of the Northern Territory and beyond, reacquaint and sort out lingering personal differences, whilst remedying their insatiable thirsts with copious amounts of beer or rum and coke. We struggle to keep up with the demand and I continually yell "more cans" to the over-worked lad stocking the bar fridge. I only met him today but I've already forgotten his name, what an induction.

Another fight begins with "I'll kill you, you bast..." and I reluctantly start to head out from behind the bar. A huge hand grabs my shoulder and local cattle station owner Roy Beebe says slowly in a deep voice "you stay behind there where it's safe son. Let the copper sort it out. No harm will be done to you or your pub. I'll see to that".

The juke-box belts out the hit song "True Blue" and everyone is shouting John Williamson's famous lines "Hey True Blue. Is it me and you. Is it mum and dad, or a cockatoo, Is it standin' by your mate, WHEN HE'S IN A FIGHT ... or just Vegemi-ite" as loud as they possibly can. The atmosphere inside is buzzing as the two fighters are pushed outside onto the street. I'm only thirty years old but have been drinking in outback pubs for years and I have never witnessed anything like this. I love it.

I spin around to see the open till drawer bulging with dirt and booze stained notes of all denominations. Most are crumpled beyond recognition but all have been gratefully accepted with a big smile and "thanks mate". My wife Leonie has been regularly emptying the till drawer throughout the night and I think "How much have we taken. It must be thousands". A pretty little jillaroo shouts "four rum and cokes thanks mate" and I am quickly ordered back into reality.

Earlier in the day, I opened the gates to our camp ground and waived the normal overnight fees, just for the rodeo goers. They applauded me. Leonie and the girls in the kitchen, cook endless steak sandwiches, fries and beef burgers ... for hour after hour and well after last meal orders are normally taken. They applaud the girls too. I dare to think they might like their new publicans.

At exactly midnight, with Sergeant Bob staring at me, I ring the cowbell behind the bar. The crowd quietens a decibel or two and I hear someone say "the bloody new publican is closing the damn bar" and Bob smiles for the first time today. "So much for them liking me" races through my mind. I stretch to beyond my full six foot height, cup my hands to my mouth and yell out, as loud as I can, "it's midnight and that means it's ... MY SHOUT". One hundred jackaroos scream with delight as an angry policeman disappears, yet again.

I'm handing out free beers, as fast as I can, when I see Leonie with yet another tray of her wonderful beef burgers and fries, struggling to make her way through the boisterous drunken crowd. She glances towards me with a nervous tired smile and I melt, as I think to myself ... "how the hell did the two of us end up here".

Chapter 2. THOSE WHO CAME BEFORE US

In 1862 John McDougall Stuart successfully crossed the Australian mainland from south to north, after finally breaking through the Northern Territory lancewood scrub that thwarted his previous attempts. At a place where a creek entered a large swamp Stuart and his team, who were all parched, discovered fresh water. It saved their lives and to mark the spot he carved a large "S" into a tree. The tree became known as "Stuart's Tree" and still stands today. The area was given the name Daly Waters, to honour Sir Dominic Daly the governor of South Australia and the life-saving waters Stuart discovered. By completing his epic journey Stuart became the first man to lead a party across the continent and return. His experience, care and fierce determination ensured he returned with his full party and his feat is still regarded as one of the most successful and well run expeditions in Australia's early exploration history.

From 1871 to 1872 the Overland Telegraph Line from Adelaide to Darwin was constructed. It linked Australia to the rest of the world and followed Stuart's route north but the harsh conditions caused the project to fall well behind schedule and so, for a time, a Pony Express was used between Daly Waters and Tennant Creek 400kms to the south. From 1872, an Overland Telegraph Station, consisting of a telegraph building and several thatched roof sleeping huts existed at Daly Waters, from where the signals were received and forwarded. An original telegraph pole from approximately 1872 stands outside the pub.

Fresh water was vital for droving cattle through the Northern Territory and as Daly Waters was the last watering hole before the perilous Murranji Stock Route it became an important stopping point. In 1881, when the famed Durack brothers drove their entire herd from Queensland to the West Australian coast, Daly Waters was a landmark stop on their journey. From then on, drovers used the permanent waters at Daly Waters as their stopping point when moving cattle.

In the early 1900's, as drovers were moving cattle through Daly Waters in Australia, across the seas in England a farmer's son, Bill Pearce met a young local girl, Henrietta. In the ensuing years Henrietta moved to Canada to live with a millionaire family whilst Bill moved to the Riverina in Australia, where he worked on Sir Samuel McCaughey's sheep stations. After a time Bill moved to the Northern Territory, getting a job as chauffeur #1 for the NT Administrator. Bill didn't enjoy life in Darwin and so he packed his bag and drifted 300km south-east of Darwin to the lonely remote mining settlement of Marranboy.

Sixteen years after meeting Henrietta, Bill sent a letter asking her to marry him and come to Australia and join him at Marranboy, where, he wrote, he was a partner in a tin-mine. Henrietta, still smitten with Bill after all these years, desperately wanted to return to England and so she suggested he meet her in England to convince her why she should move to outback Australia, hoping he would stay with her in England and forget his outback mine. Instead Bill, in his typical cavalier fashion, jumped on a ship and immediately went to Henrietta in Canada, where he laid out his plan for their life together in the remote Northern Territory.

Bill was honest and painted a bleak picture of life at Marranboy, describing her future in the bush as a lonely existence with no female company, in a very hot climate making bread daily. Henrietta, after seven years of living in luxury, needed more than a little persuasion to go to Australia.

In 1929 after a decade of harsh years living at the mine and raising their young daughter Rita, Bill decided, against Henrietta's wishes, to purchase several blocks in a new Government land release at Daly Waters where he said he "would open a wayside store". At this time, the only residents of Daly Waters were a handful of men operating the Overland Telegraph Office. Henrietta was not impressed but as always, she went with Bill.

Rumours abound of a "sly grog shop" operating around Daly Waters from 1897 to 1929 selling liquor from the telegraph station and tents by a series of opportunists, until about 1930 when Bill and Henrietta built the corrugated iron Daly Waters Store at the merging of several stock routes. The Pearce's store possibly sold the odd illegal tipple until it was granted an official "public house" liquor license in 1938 and named the Daly Waters Pub. At this stage there was no major north-south road, as exists today but instead the territory consisted of a maze of tracks and stock routes joining the stations and towns to each other.

According to locals, Daly Waters never hosted a permanent aboriginal population but there is plenty of evidence of temporary camps near the Daly Waters lagoon and further upstream on Daly Creek at the beautiful horseshoe waterfall, with its permanent water-hole in the rocks. It is said the aboriginals avoid the area as it is inhabited by aboriginal executioner spirit, the Kurdaitcha Man (sometimes known as the feather-footed man). Several aboriginals told me the tribes in the region only used Daly Waters as a temporary resting place, so as to not upset the bad spirit.

I also heard, from a reliable source, the Kurdaitcha Man only appeared and harassed the local aboriginals after 1975, when Smiley Burnett purchased the pub. This left me wondering, did Smiley "take on" the persona of the Kurdaitcha Man late at night to force the aboriginals to leave the area.

In 1926 the rudimentary landing strip near the Telegraph Station at Daly Waters was a pivotal stop during the London to Sydney air race and in 1934 the Daly Waters Airstrip received an upgrade and became the site of the first International Airport in Australia. Planes were refuelled and passengers took a break, whilst heading to or from Singapore and eventually onto London. In 1935 the full trip cost 275 pounds, with the passengers enduring 31 stops over 12 tortuous days! This seemed an expensive and incredibly long trip, as today the same flight can be done for 275 pounds, only 1 stop and in 20 hours.

Bill and Henrietta Pearce made superb mine-hosts, with Henrietta feeding the passengers alongside the plane and providing overnight accommodation at the house for the first class passengers. Bill was responsible for refuelling and mechanically servicing the planes. Bill quickly became proficient in his duties and proudly demonstrated, to the Qantas bosses, he could refuel and plane and transfer the mail in twenty-five minutes whilst Henrietta looked after them on the ground.

Bill and Henrietta Pearce hosted many famous guests during their time at Daly Waters. The Pub visitor's book contained many signatures, including the first Qantas passenger to enter Australia, Lady Louis Mountbatten as well as the world famous pianist Arthur Rubenstein, female NZ aviator Jean Batten, the fabulously wealthy Mr Louis Rothschild and Governor General Lord and Lady Gowrie.

As Australia entered World War Two, Daly Waters played an important role in defending Australia. During this time the Pearce's recently completed home and pub were taken over by the USA for their first Australian office for war administration and later it was used as an RAAF hospital. During the war the Pearce's were forced to live in the laundry on their verandah but they didn't mind. Beaufort and Mitchell Bombers, Kitty Hawks and a fighter squadron were based at Daly Waters and the remains of a couple of crashed aircraft can still be found around the airfield. During our time at Daly Waters we found small pieces of wreckage when wandering in the scrub and around the pub.

Bill and Henrietta Pearce sold the Daly Waters Pub in 1950, after twenty years. Their vision and Bill's hard work produced a truly unique pub, destined to become as famous as any pub in Australia and they are my heroes of Daly Waters Pub.

Nowadays, the Daly Waters aerodrome is in semi-retirement with private aircraft, mining exploration companies and Air-Med (Remote Area Medical Service) constituting the bulk of the traffic. However some things never change, as the Daly Waters Pub continues to refuel planes and accommodates their passengers.

At a remote place in Australia, where Stuart found life-saving water and the Durack's rested their cattle and quenched their thirst and where the Overland Telegraph Station stood, still stands the historic Daly Waters Pub where tourists and locals alike, can rest and quench their thirst.

The Daly Waters Pub is an irresistible destination for travellers from around the world. It has been written up in many overseas tabloids and magazines and is famous for its colourful history, the nightly Beef and Barra BBQ, friendly bush hospitality and ice-cold beer. Memorabilia adorns the walls and wherever you look there is more to read and photograph. Local station workers and territory legends are often found having a coldie in the bar and tourists, including world famous entertainers, business people and politicians as well as sportsmen and women, continue to visit the pub.

In a 2005 interview, Ted Egan, famous musician and Administrator of the Northern Territory at the time, publically declared Daly Waters Pub to be the best pub in the Territory and that's from a man who knows his pubs. The Daly Waters Pub has won too many hospitality awards to list and has been showcased in many Australian and international travel documentaries. In 2016, the Pub featured in the highly acclaimed movie "Last Cab to Darwin".

To demonstrate the pub's fame is keeping up with the times, The Daly Waters Pub is more searched on Google than any other outback pub in Australia … including the Birdsville Hotel.

Chapter 3. BE CAREFUL WHAT YOU WISH FOR

For as long as I remember, I wanted to be a publican.

My first memories of life in a pub came from when I was a snotty nosed kid. My dad Richard (Dick) Venable was a sign-writer and automotive spray painter and in the 1960's dad's best mate Rex Harris and his wife Mary were the managers at the glamorous Hotel Victor at Victor Harbor in South Australia. Rex was a great publican and the locals loved him. We regularly stayed upstairs in the beautiful rooms and my sister Jules and I revelled in some of the best times of our childhood at that huge hotel. We swam in the pool every day and ate breakfast at our own private table in the superb dining room, where Chef Mark would spoil us with the thinnest French toast and eggs for breakfast and later, great grilled flounder and chips for lunch or dinner. We were invited to ring the dinner xylophone at 6pm to announce meal time for the hotel guests and we regularly sat at the top of the stairs, where we would watch the adults dance and party on Saturday nights. We felt like children of royalty but as Rex and Mary didn't have kids of their own, we must have driven them mad. Not having children myself, I occasionally appreciate that now. Unfortunately Rex was a big drinker and in the end, the drinking killed him. For that reason I don't think dad wouldn't have approved of my dream career.

I was employed as an Assistant Surveyor by the South Australian Department of Lands in the Survey Section from 1974 to 1985 and I worked in most areas of South Australia, staying in over fifty country pubs and meeting many wonderful publicans. At the time I didn't fully appreciate these experiences would shape my future pub life as I keenly observed publicans like Greg Fahey in Peterborough, Kevin Gregg in Clare and later in Keith, Bud Goldsworthy in Waikerie and Jake Anderson in Innamincka go about their craft. I learned much about the industry and occasionally I helped behind the bar. I was fully hooked on one day becoming a publican.

Apart from dad enjoying a quiet frothy in the Morphett Arms front bar and dad's mum Vivian managing a country hotel, before I can remember, there is a little family history in the hotel industry. My sister and I called our grandmother Nanma. She was from the Black family in Port Lincoln and I adored her. In the 1920's Nanma met a seafaring American engineer in Port Lincoln and continued to join him each time he visited to our waters. She eventually sailed around the world with him and married. As ship's engineer, he enjoyed similar privileges as the Captain and was permitted to take his wife on board. Nanma then moved to San Francisco, where she gave birth to my father and spent all her time waiting for her seafaring husband to return from sea, which wasn't often enough. Tired of waiting, Nanma bundled up her five year old son, boarded a ship and came home. After taking various jobs, Nanma and new husband Sandy, moved south to manage the Commercial Hotel in Naracoorte. After ten years they returned to Adelaide where Nanma worked as the live-in housekeeper for Mr Vic Staines, a Northern Territory sheep station owner. As a three or four year old, I remember visiting Nanma in that huge home at St Peters and being very scared of the grumpy old man.

I clearly remember Nanma, in her later years, telling me some hilarious stories about her time in the Commercial Hotel. One particularly popular yarn was of a pub clean-up when numerous false teeth were found in the bottom of the Commercial Hotel's septic tank. Nanma didn't have a clue what to do with these clackers but she knew the owners would want them back. So she strung a clothes-line beside the outdoor men's toilet and hung out the sets of teeth with pegs, leaving them to be claimed by their toothless owners.

When telling the story Nanma would always finish with "and for the love of Mary they were all gone within a week", before doubling up with laughter.

In 1981, soon after meeting my future wife Leonie at a Glenelg hotel, I told her of my dream to own a bush pub. To my surprise, she didn't baulk or run away but instead showed interest and asked many questions about where, when and how. Her response came as a huge relief as my first wife hated the idea and never would have done it with me. Leonie not only accepted it but together we dreamt of one day buying a small country pub. Our relationship flourished and in 1983 we were married. Our joint desire to own a bush pub also grew and even though Leonie worked as an insurance manager for the AMP, with her office high up in the city, her desire to be part of a pub in the country was obvious.

Our dream of owning a bush pub started to become real in 1983 and 1984 when I was involved in one of the last great outback surveying jobs in South Australia. Our job was to resurvey the couple of hundred kilometres of South Australian and Queensland border, from Cameron Corner to Haddon Corner. The survey was required due to errors in the original 1880's survey resulting in a royalty (tax) dispute between both state governments, over what state should get the tax funds from the lucrative Jackson Oil fields (Qld) and the Cooper Basin oilfield (SA). Both oilfields were very close to the disputed border and so a team of four or five of us spent a year and a half doing four to six week trips into the desert to re-establish the border in its original position. The team was Surveyor Jack Kean and assistants Ross Cole, Phil Thurnam, Peter Rose and myself.

On this epic job we spent quite a bit of time in the remote historic towns of Innamincka, Noccundra, Betoota and Birdsville, where we had some wonderful and unique experiences. On the Cooper Creek near Inamincka, the most north-easterly of all South Australian towns, I shot a duck, which we cooked and ate that night and we enjoyed plenty of cold beers in the pub with publicans Jake and Denny Anderson. We camped on the verandah of the Betoota Pub in Queensland, with its population of two where we got to know the crazy publican Simon (Ziggy) and his permanent house-guest George. We witnessed the publican at Noccundra blacking out all swear words in the graffiti on his walls, because a prudish politician was about to pay him a visit. We ate freshly caught yellow-belly near Birdsville, where we camped on the Diamantina River. We became geographically embarrassed (lost) in the desert for three days and whilst lost we discovered an amazing aboriginal site at a crystal clear waterhole, complete with grinding stones and spear heads. In all, we shared some amazing experiences in the outback and we became close mates.

Map showing Innamincka and Betoota

We camped out in the desert most of the time and it was my best working experience ever. Every day was a challenge and keeping food fresh was near to impossible. Nightly pre-dinner snacks were smoked oysters on Jatz biscuits with a can or two of tepid beer, "chilled" in a water bag hanging from the front of the truck. As there was no refrigeration, a diet of spuds and onions with canned steak and onion or Fray Bentos pies was the main fare. Scurvy was a constant worry and I suffered a minor dose on one occasion. To moisten my dried flaking skin I liberally applied Ole cooking oil. It tanned me so black in the constant sun, Leonie almost didn't recognise me on my return. Water was for drinking, not washing and so we smelled really bad. Visits to the outback towns were for a shower as much as a beer, a cooked meal and different company. We camped wherever we worked and it wasn't uncommon for dingoes to visit our camp during the night to lick our dinner-plates clean. One morning I found my plate clean but a baked onion was next to it, in the sand. Obviously, dingoes don't like onions. On one trip I threw a stone at a rabbit, knocked it out and ate it for dinner. Another day we walked into the bar of the Innamincka Pub and were introduced by publican Jake to Aussie legend Dick Smith. He asked us for advice on the bush tracks around the area as he was planning the first ever Variety Bash. We carried excellent maps and aerial photography and happily gave him the advice with payment in cans of West End beer. The more advice we gave him the more beers he bought us and after quite a few hours we were quite drunk and still un-showered.

Our survey team in the Innamincka Hotel from left is
Phil, Ross and boss Jack

After spending so much time in these outback pubs I
thought I'd be very happy owning any of these hotels and
when I mentioned this to Phil he agreed. We talked about it
every day. When the job was almost over we talked about
our dream to Jake and Denny at Innamincka and Simon at
Betoota. Jake wasn't interested in selling our first choice,
Innamincka Hotel but Simon's reaction was slightly
different. He said he would consider it and if we were still
interested in a few months we should return with our wives
and talk.

In the 1980's Simon, who was a WW11 refugee from
Poland, lived out the back of the pub and an old retired

drover George Nor-West lived on a camp stretcher next to the front door on the pub's front verandah. George's drinks and meals were recorded by Simon in a ledger book in neat copperplate handwriting. At the end of the month this would be tallied up against his pension cheque and the difference either banked for George by Simon, or deducted by Simon to be accrued for the next month.

Our survey vehicles in front of the Betoota Hotel (circa 1983)

Simon only opened the pub for locals and workers as he despised tourists. On the first day we were in the bar, having a warm beer, Simon spotted two four-wheel drives with caravans coming into town. He told us to shut up and promptly closed the front door. We hid in silence whilst they tried to gain entry before driving off. When asked "why" Simon replied, "all they will want is petrol and a cup of tea and it'll cost me more to turn the generator on for the pumps and kettle than I'll make from those bastards". He then added, "sometimes, it happens many times a day". Phil and I looked at each other, I said "is that so" and both of us gave a look, translating to "we may have found our pub".

Simon only turned the generator on after you arrived and therefore our beers went from hot on arrival to warm then to tepid and finally, when we were drunk, too cold. He was a rotten surly old bastard but in amongst all that he was a legendary character with some great stories. You could tell he loved telling yarns but he reserved them for a chosen few. Fortunately, we were included in those few, along with the lads from neighbouring Mt Lindsay station who we got to know well. But Simon certainly didn't spoil us and so we camped on the verandah next to George Nor-West and cold-showered in the public toilets. One day we stopped and made camp just out of town where we came across a beautiful waterhole. We went to the pub that night and asked Simon why he never told us about it and he said "you never asked" but I'm sure it was because he knew we wouldn't spend anywhere near as much over the bar if we were camped out of town.

After the border survey was completed any future survey work we did seemed mundane and boring as the fuel glut of the early 1980's saw an end to petroleum exploration survey work. In 1985 at 29 years of age I resigned from the Lands Department and with my best mate Dave Taylor we started Sou-West Lawn and Garden Service. It was bloody hard work but we were young, playing footy and loved the physical nature of our business. Importantly we were our own bosses for the first time in our lives and we made a few bucks.

When I resigned from the Lands Department my boss Bill Haylock said to me he couldn't understand why anyone would throw a secure government career away to go lawn-mowing but Bill didn't see the bigger picture. For me, the bigger picture, was to find a bush pub. I've always wanted to come across Bill and say "what do you say now, old-timer" but the meeting has never happened.

The survey work taught me many life lessons but nothing at school or the Lands Department prepared me for hard work better than what my parents taught me at home. My dad worked incredibly hard. He did extra studies when working, as well as doing extra paint jobs at home on weekends. As the "young man" of the family, I was expected to help after school on Friday evenings and sometimes on weekends with rubbing down trucks and cars for dad to paint. I'm the first to admit I didn't throw myself into it and probably let dad down more than I helped. Dad would go over my work and fix it every weekend but subconsciously it sunk in and, when I finally found myself as my own boss, the hard work and attention to detail came naturally to me.

The thought of finding an outback pub never left my mind and several months after asking Simon if he'd sell us the pub, Phil and I returned to Betoota, with our wives. We arrived and immediately ordered two beers and vodka and squashes for the girls. The beers were typically hot and as Simon doesn't use glasses nor does he measure anything he handed the girls a can each of squash and said "drink". Leonie looked at me and I quietly said, "just take a sip and hand it back". The girls did as instructed and Simon then poured a healthy slug of vodka direct into each can. Only at Betoota ...

Leonie and publican Simon in the Betoota Hotel in 1985

Simon refused to talk about "the sale" by changing the subject each time it was raised, until finally, he suggested we go out the back to the dining room to talk. Phil and I were invited to this huge room once before, when we were told it was used for the local dances when Betoota was "on the map". At one end of the hall-like room was a large wooden table and six old chairs. In the far corner was a pile of boxes of unopened new electrical appliances. Apparently, Simon took a "shine" to a travelling salesman. Every time he came through town, Simon would buy something. Because, in Simon's words, "he felt sorry for him".

Unfortunately and unexpectedly, the meeting didn't go well. Simon said "the outback is no place for ladies and you shouldn't drag them out here" and added "besides, what would I do with my goats. I have to live here to look after them". We didn't know Simon was so attached to his thousand or so head of starving wild goats and after some failed attempts at changing his mind, we decided it was over. We decided to try, once more, to get Jake and Denny to sell Innamincka. The next morning we all took frightfully cold showers at the pub and almost killed poor old George Nor-West when he accidentally walked into the shower whilst Leonie was in there. He came out blubbering and staggering around saying "oh my God, sorry, sorry, oh my Lord Jesus, I simply wanted to fill my billy" soon followed, by a dripping wet Leonie, saying "I'm just making sure George hasn't suffered a heart attack".

Legendary drover George Nor-West on his bed.

It was off to Innamincka on a big drive along a very basic track winding through Sturt Stony Desert, that Burke and Wills described as "possibly the most inhospitable place on this earth". We arrived into Innamincka later the next day and didn't beat around the bush by saying, as soon as we walked in the door, "Jake and Denny we want to buy the pub". Jake and Denny thought all night about our offer and started talking about maybe leasing the pub to us ... in a few years. After two fun filled days with these great friends we left for home, unsure of our immediate future in pubs.

A few months later, I arrived home after a hard days gardening and Leonie said, "I found this ad in the paper this morning". The small ad simply read "Historic Pub in the NT for Sale" and included a phone number. I said, "you bloody ripper. This sounds great, I think you may have found our pub".

The next morning I rang the agent and he told me it was the Daly Waters Pub. I'd never heard of it and as these were the days before the internet, there was no way to fully research it at home. The agent normally sold fish and chip shops and was unable to offer little information on the pub, other than the price and a casual mention it was a "walk in walk out deal". This, he said "means what you see is what you get. Nothing leaves the place when you buy it." It sounded great to me and even though I didn't know the pub, I was excited. I immediately rang Phil and said "the Daly Waters Pub was on the market, do you know it". Phil quickly said "do I bloody know it. The Daly Waters Pub! Toni and I have been there mate. We loved it". Again, I thought we may have found our pub.

When I told my dad we were considering buying the Daly Waters Pub he went grey and I thought he was having a stroke. He gasped "oh no, not that pub mate". I didn't know dad would have even heard of Daly Waters. It would have been the last thing I expected but he went on and related a story to me from 1949, when he was a young bus sign-writer at Bonds Tours. He was only seventeen years of age, working in Alice Springs for Mr Bond, painting buses at his depot. Whilst there, he was invited to take a tour through the Northern Territory, north to Darwin. On the long slow trip they stayed overnight at the Daly Waters Pub. Dad said he was scared the entire time he was there. Apparently, the driver, Laurie, became very drunk in the bar with a few locals and lost all his money, in a card game. He came into the motel late at night and wanted dad to lend him money to gamble and drink some more. Dad pretended he was asleep and refused to give him a penny.

Dad went on to describe Daly Waters as Dodge City and said he didn't sleep a wink that night.

Dodge City was a name I heard from more than a few others in the ensuing months, mainly due to a couple of well publicised shoot-outs that occurred in town. What were we thinking?

A Bonds Tours bus in front of the Daly Waters Pub in 1949

Incredibly, this photo may have been taken on my dad's NT trip

(Bill Watts Collection. Courtesy NT Library)

I called the agent back, said we were interested and immediately we decided to drive to the Territory and perform a pub inspection. As Toni couldn't get time off from work, three excited prospective publicans drove 2,450km to Daly Waters to check the pub out.

I remember little of this trip. It was a blur of the excitement of the unknown and then the fear of the same. I do remember a beautiful rustic old tin shed pub with colourful bougainvillea flowers on the outside and I clearly remember walking into a living breathing character of a hotel complete with a bar covered in stickers, a wall of money left by visitors, a concrete floor, a museum with relics in a corner, a fuel bowser across the road with sign "fuel, pay at pub", metal frame bar chairs and bar stools, a small dirt floor beer garden with a few tables and chairs, an old motel with concrete floors, some tin shed outdoor toilets, a 44 gallon drum hot water system and a big lady Ruth and a bigger man Bill as owners and their teenage son Stuart. I remember it being bloody hot, camping in our tent in a dirt campground and enjoying the coldest beers ever … oh and I remember being introduced to a few locals.

Incredibly, I don't remember the actual buying of the pub. We didn't negotiate on the price or the conditions whilst we were there and this was probably because it was our first time and we were too excited and scared. I can't remember if we agreed to buy it before we received Toni's approval but none of it mattered, as when we arrived home we were contracted to purchase the freehold of an incredibly historic outback hotel, for a big price that appeared reasonable to us. Even though we would need to quickly sell our houses with pretty much everything else we owned and take out a large loan, it didn't faze us or put us off. I engaged a mate Greg to sell our house. It was all moving so fast. Fortunately, Phil's house sold quickly and ours sold only a week or two later. It was a mad rush but everything started to fall into place as I sold my half of the landscaping business to business partner and good mate Dave, whilst Leonie quit her job, of fifteen years, at the AMP. It was such an exciting but hectic time as we sold some furniture and moved the rest into a secure storage shed. We didn't know anyone who had done anything resembling our change of life and therefore couldn't take advice from anyone on how we should be prioritising our tasks. We just got on with it but we weren't stressed. We didn't have time for stress.

Leonie and I were sitting at home one night and heard a knock on the door. It was quite late. We opened the door and standing on the verandah, was Jake and Denny from the Innamincka Pub. Without coming in they said "we've decided to sell Innamincka to you". The look of shock, not excitement on our faces, probably told them we weren't going to buy. We invited them in and told them our story. They left, disappointed. Unfortunately, we never saw Jake again, as in terribly sad circumstances he died in the outback. We did, however, see Denny again and actually employed their son Troy, during a hotel stint in Port Pirie in the 1990's.

We engaged a local Adelaide accountant who, after paying him large sums to set up our company Daly Waters Property Pty Ltd, we never heard from again. Years later I read he was accused of "bottom of the harbour tax avoidance schemes" ... so probably just as well.

Phil and I flew to Darwin during this period to set up credit with breweries and other suppliers as well as getting our liquor license transfer completed and meeting with the bank. In addition to using all of our own funds, we borrowed, what seemed to us, a princely sum of money. It was all falling into place now and the fact nothing had gone wrong, started to worry me. "Something is going to ruin this dream", I kept telling myself. I'm such a positive person, the negativity alarmed me.

I was terribly saddened when Nanma passed away, just before we purchased the Daly Waters Pub but one piece of advice she gave me, just before her passing, I've always tried to honour. It showed her complete understanding of what I would endure in pub life, when she said "I think you're mad, you brute. But forget that, now listen to me, I know you will drink, its part of the job but promise me you'll have one alcohol free day per week and drink huge amounts of water and you will be okay". I've tried to honour my promise for all of these years. I certainly inherited some of her genes and those genes have a big influence on the way I am. I feel her around me all the time and when it happens, like right now as I type, I look toward the sky, thank her for being there and send her my love. She has been my guardian angel ever since she left us and I still miss her.

During this hectic period, Leonie somehow found time to search local second-hand book shops for a book "Two at Daly Waters", the name of a book a friend had casually dropped into a conversation. The book was a series of stories of Bill and Henrietta Pearce at Daly Waters Pub, as told to the author Elisabeth George by Henrietta, during a rare visit to Adelaide in the early 1940's. Somehow, incredibly, Leonie managed to find a hardcopy 1945 first edition and together we read the book, over and over. It described in detail, the Pearce's terribly tough existence at Daly Waters, with no comforts and extreme hardship. We

44

both looked at each other and thought "what are we thinking".

With only one week to go, before we would leave on our adventure, we held a large and emotional going away party at our house. It was exciting but terrifying to say our last goodbyes to friends and family and it was tinged with sadness. Whilst everyone said "we will come and visit", most friends wouldn't but thankfully, family would. One week later our house sale settled and within a few days we left, on what we hoped would be the adventure of a lifetime.

Leonie and I somehow crammed our treasured possessions of clothing, photos of family and a few kitchen items, into a 1974 VW Combi van and drove north out of Adelaide. Phil and Toni performed the same exercise at their end. In our Combi van we also took our beautiful cat Max, our two Burke parrots Burke and Wills and our two cockatiels. We towed one of Phil's trailers but I have no recollection of what was in it. Tools and building equipment maybe. As we left Port Augusta and entered the barren outback landscape of the north, Max was crying, Leonie was crying and I was shitting myself, thinking "well Mark, it's too late to turn back now lad". Mum and dad were probably thinking the same thing at home and I know mum would have been crying her eyes out. We led the way and held our breath.

Getting ready to leave Adelaide in our Combi van in 1986

We drove all day, until dusk. Our first stop was a roadside camp somewhere in the remote north of South Australia. I remember the four of us sitting around a campfire, talking about what role we were each going to play and how much fun it was going to be. It was the first time in months we could be together with no-one else. I think we were all excited but at the same time scared out of our wits, mainly as none of us were experienced in business or a pub. In recent years I'd worked a few hours behind bars in a few country pubs and certainly spent plenty of time behind the bar at the footy club but Leonie was an office worker with no hospitality experience, whilst Phil was experienced in only surveying and Toni was a teacher in a suburban school.

What were we thinking?

Chapter 4. MORE THAN THE PUB ...

The Daly Waters Pub ... from left the pub, beer-garden, motel and caravan-park.

When we purchased Daly Waters Pub we received far more than we bargained for. Even our initial inspection didn't prepare us for what was included in this incredibly varied business. Nor did it prepare us for the huge amount of work we were in for.

PUB ... short for Public House. Our Public House license conditions stipulated we needed to provide food to anyone who wanted a meal ... at any time. On top of this we were required to offer stabling facilities for the traveller's horses and we could stay open for 24 hours a day every day, if we wished.

MOTEL ... our old tin shed motel housed seven bedrooms with one shared bathroom but none of us realised the amount of work required for the daily tiresome chore of changing bed linen and washing same, sweeping and mopping floors and cleaning toilets. Fortunately, I was stuck in the bar.

FUEL and WORKSHOP ... in addition to supplying vehicular fuel, we were required to refuel planes landing at the airstrip 2km away and helicopters, that landing next to the pub. This entailed ensuring sufficient aviation fuel was available at all times as well as having aircraft-approved pumping equipment and storage facilities. In the garage, we ended up fixing punctures, change tyres, sell and fit new and second-hand tyres, do towing and basic mechanical repairs.

GENERAL STORE ... the general store, whilst small, needed to carry as many useful daily items as possible. Thinking back we should have expected the pub to be the supplier of more than beer and rum. The store was in a tiny little room at the end of the bar. Think toilet and bathroom needs and think of basic consumables such as long life milk, frozen bread, margarine, salt and pepper but we only sold vegetables and meats in emergencies.

HOUSES ... we purchased the pub with two houses and an extra block of land. None of our property wasn't pegged and we had no real idea where our land finished and the cattle station land started. One house was opposite the pub and was built for the workers at the airfield sometime in the 1950's. The other house was actually an Atco transportable shack at the back of the hotel and fortunately it was air-conditioned. Phil and Toni won the toss of a coin and it became their house at the start.

BANK ... we were now bankers. Leonie became the registered CBA branch manager. She took deposits and gave withdrawals from her little teller station at the end of the bar in the general store. This was years before ATM's or EFTPOS so everyone still carried bank books. The bank did random inspections and they were very strict.

POST OFFICE ... Daly Waters lost its real post office some years before and so the pub took on the job of selling stamps and clearing the post box every day. The mail would then be placed in a large canvas mail bag, padlocked and sent by Greyhound Coach to Katherine. We also held the locked mail bags (called Private Mail Bags) for the cattle stations surrounding the pub.

FREIGHT DEPOT … trucks would regularly drive into town and after driving around for ten minutes would come into the pub and ask something like "hey mate, I have a parcel for Nutwood Downs and I can't bloody find it anywhere" to which we'd say "leave it here mate, they'll be in through the week to get it". Parcels ranged from replacement parts for machinery to RM Williams clothing the local station lads ordered from the RM Williams catalogue, every jackaroo's magazine of choice and even ahead of Playboy.

TELSTRA ... the local public phone needed daily clearing of money and weekly cleaning. We purchased the pub pre-invention of mobile phones, this ensured almost every tourist travelling in the outback wanted to phone home to let the family know they hadn't been eaten by a crocodile or bitten by a snake. This busy phone often saw long queues of patient callers waiting for their turn. Some nights, I'd run a few beers down to the thirsty tourists in the line.

CARAVAN PARK ... the hotel included a small, predominantly unpowered campground near the motel. Over time this grew in size and capacity. The park was resplendent with many shady trees including the magnificent flame trees. These trees were beautiful with their vibrant red flowers but they held huge seed-pods (see on the left of the photo). When they fell onto a caravan roof the occupant would swear the sky may have fallen on them.

MUSEUM ... over the years each publican, locals and tourists donated museum pieces to the pub. Jars, bottles, tools and war artefacts are displayed in a corner of the pub and on the walls. We even found a few of our own. Phil discovered several whilst at the dump and a couple of others were found when wandering in the bush.

EMERGENCY FIRST AID STATION ... the government supplied the pub with a large white first aid kit containing all the regular first aid items plus some extra strong painkillers. This kit was a registered first aid station and needed to be fully stocked at all times in case of an emergency in the area. Unfortunately, the painkillers were missing when we eventually saw inside it and whilst I have no evidence, I strongly suspect they were previously used for the most common injury we witnessed ... hangovers. The second most useful and most used items were bandages. These were dispensed regularly to tourists for an array of cuts and abrasions ... most were incurred late at night and most required a painkiller in the morning.

AMBULANCE ... on more than one occasion we needed to urgently drive injured tourists to meet an ambulance coming from Katherine. As publican, we were the first point of contact between the ambulance service and the police. They would ring us requesting help and naturally we would provide any help we could. On one occasion this almost ended in disaster when I took an injured man to meet an ambulance and I almost hit a bull, asleep in the middle of the highway. Normally cattle are relatively easy to spot at night due to the reflection from their eyes but when asleep the beast simply disappears and looks like the road.

BARBER SHOP ... if anyone needed a haircut they asked at the bar and either Leonie or Toni would cut their hair. After the girls decided they weren't cut out for this (sorry) we organised, once a month, for a hairdresser to drive 100km from Larrimah and set up her barber shop on the pub verandah. The locals (anyone living within 100km) would know the date in advance and would arrive for a chin wag and a haircut. It was also a good time for the cattle station owners to collect their mail from the pub.

Leonie performing her first haircut … appropriately on a bald man

BUREAU OF METEOROLOGY … the front door of the pub displayed a sign reading "TODAY'S WEATHER". I thought we would need to change it every day but it quickly became evident the weather in our remote part of the Northern Territory suffers from few daily variations. In fact, in our first three weeks, the temperature only varied by two degrees from 31degrees C (88F) to 33 degrees C (92F). Each day saw little or no wind, clear skies and therefore nil chance of rain and you may have guessed the sign remained unchanged. If there was an easier job it would be hard to imagine what it was. The NT News would phone us when strange weather events occurred in our area and ask what it was like at Daly Waters and we often made the news.

COMMUNITY NOTICES ... it was our role in the community to distribute community notices and display important notices at the Pub and there was a sign on the Store door reading "COMMUNITY NEWS" where notices would be placed. Notices could include such information as "water meters will be read on the 14th. Please ensure your meter is still there ... and is clear of crocs, snakes and spiders".

POWER STATION ... Daly Waters was not on the NT grid but instead, our electricity was provided from a power generation station, located about 1km out of town. The station was owned by the government but the pub held the contract of running and maintaining the generators. This included monthly meter readings of the six houses and the pub and it also entailed us performing regular 200 hour servicing of the two huge diesel generator motors. We filled out daily logs of their performance and so now, we were diesel mechanics and meter readers.

WATER SUPPLY ... obviously, someone needed to look after the water supply but we didn't even consider it would be us. The pub contracted the job of ensuring the town bore ran properly and the town tank was always full. This task also involved daily log reads, weekly servicing and monthly meter reads of each house.

POLICE OFFICER ... in the 1980's for any town in the NT with a pub but no police officer it was common practice for the publican to be formally investigated for suitability and then informally sworn in as a police officer. Phil and I both attended a briefing in Darwin and we're both given informal police powers for our town. We were allowed to arrest and hold. Fortunately, we weren't given a gun but I was disappointed we didn't get a real shiny police badge. Although if we needed a police badge we only needed to reach up above the bar to grab one of the thirty or so police arm badges given to the pub by police officers from all over the world including one American badge, so big it would have just about covered my back.

JAIL ... the Daly Waters jail could be found behind the old post office. We held the keys at the pub and were informed "to use it if we needed to hold anyone whilst waiting for the *real* police to arrive". Fortunately, we were never forced to use it ... but we did come close a couple of times.

The Daly Waters jail

TAXI ... on a Saturday night, during our first month, a few of the aboriginal station hands, from nearby Kalala Station, were dropped into the pub. At about midnight they stocked up on take-away booze and said they wanted to go home. One of them said "hey boss, Mr Bill always drove us home in his taxi. Can you take us home now boss"? I thought about it and even though Bill hadn't told me of this, I considered it was better to continue this arrangement and not disappoint them. Eight drunken station hands, with heaps of beer and rum, fell into the pub ute and off we went on the ten-kilometre drive to the station. At about the half way mark, a few of the boys started fighting and the not so pretty, ebony coloured housekeeper Chloe put her hand on my knee and said, "I been liking you Maaark" ... I screeched to a halt and threw them all out of the car and raced back to the pub. Later I found out I was conned. Bill always refused to take them and made them walk home every Saturday night. After that night, the only time I drove them home was when we needed to shut the pub early, so we could attend an event somewhere else.

We did however, offer a taxi service to and from the airport. In the Australian Pilots Handbook, the instructions for Daly Waters airstrip read "do a low pass over the hotel, to let the publican know you need fuel or to be collected and taken to the pub". Low flyovers occurred regularly. One of us would always jump in a car and go to the airport, pick up a few passengers and take them to the pub for a drink and meal. All part of the service.

I've probably forgotten a few of the tasks we inherited when we purchased the pub but I'm sure you'll pick them up through the story.

Chapter 5. JUST A TIN SHED

The Daly Waters Pub in 1986 just after we moved in.

"It's just a bloody tin shed" exclaimed many tourists, when first arriving at the Daly Waters Pub. Well, I suppose it is a bit like a tin shed but it's actually corrugated iron and there is something very special about Bill and Henrietta's old homely store and pub, as it looks great and oozes atmosphere even before you walk inside. With its peaked red iron roof, magnificent flame trees and colourful bougainvillea across the front, almost always in flower, it is a sight to behold. The shady verandah is a great spot to sit and relax with a cold beer and the windows across the facade afford great views from inside the bar. Within weeks of purchasing the pub, we reconstructed the old horse trough out front, attracting birds and station horses and occasionally a kangaroo or emu would be seen drinking from it. There was a simple but unmissable sign on the facade simply announcing you are at the "DALY WATERS PUB Est 1930".

In 1930, original owner Bill Pearce built the pub by carting all the cement and iron from Darwin and structural timber from the Maranboy region. Maranboy Pine was used as it contains an oily resin termites hate and will avoid eating it as long as there is better tasting timber in the vicinity. Bill Pearce knew this from his tin-mining days at Maranboy and cut it all himself. Almost any other timber would have been eaten by the ever present voracious termites within weeks. On one occasion, I left a pallet on the ground behind the pub and not more than one month later, it was gone and a half formed termite mound sat in its place. When we arrived, the original timbers were approaching sixty years of age and were as good as new. Station owner Roy Beebe told Phil and me very early on to always ensure there was a ready source of softer more palatable timbers out the back of the pub for the termites to feast on. These Daly Waters termites didn't only eat timber, over time we discovered beer cartons were top of their list followed by newspaper and books. No one said they were dumb.

The galvanised iron used for the roof and walls was soft and thick as it contained more lead than normal. It needed to be flexible to handle the extreme weather with its hot cyclonic conditions in the wet season and August chill in the dry. We endured several storms where at least 360mm of rain fell in twelve hours and not a drop came in through the roof, it did, however, come in through the front door and up through the concrete motel floor.

The pub floor was a simple concrete slab making cleaning very easy. We'd bring the fire-hose in each morning and hose the pub out. A blend of ring pulls, stubby tops, food scraps, cigarette butts, dead bodies and blood were washed out the front door. The hose-out could be a rewarding job as the cleaner regularly found money, cigarettes, lighters, car-keys, lost girl-friends and jewellery at the exit point and this occurred with ridiculous regularity.

Incredibly there was no glass in the windows of the pub and there never was. In 1930, Bill Pearce built the "house" with a wide verandah and a three foot window all around, fitted only with bronze gauze wire and the only door lock was a simple slide bolt latch similar to those you will find in public toilets. No-one ever broke in whilst we were in the pub, surprising me as we saw some very suspicious looking characters, who I'm sure were guilty of worse crimes than a simple pub break and enter. The Territory was full of people with no name and it was an oft-told tale, at census time every town in the Territory half emptied, for obvious reasons and so I consider we were lucky.

Once inside you were immediately confronted by a long bar covered with stickers and the walls and the ceiling were adorned with old bottles, flags, business cards, jackaroo hats, baseball caps, coasters, tea spoons, coins and notes, frescos, leather, stubby coolers, police and armed forces badges, photos, handwriting, graffiti, photos, souvenirs, the me-an-you and cattle station branding irons. The only relief from the heat was a few ceiling fans and more often than not, they wobbled as if they were about to fly away and maim the tallest person in the bar. The fans did claim quite a few unwary patrons who raised their arms too high and more than once an overly excited young girl on the shoulders of her boyfriend took an injury from the blades.

We became the proud publicans of the Daly Waters Pub in 1986

The only source of entertainment was a pool table and jukebox. Unfortunately, the pool cues became weapons and on more than a few occasions a cue became a spear or a club and a pool ball became a missile. When we purchased the pub a dart board was on the wall but for obvious reasons we didn't keep it for very long. The jukebox was full of the outback favourite stars including Willie Nelson, Johnny Cash and John Williamson as well as a few Top 20 hits. One day I heard a girl loudly shriek "Oh My God, there is cockroaches in the juke-box". The bar was full of tourists who instantly stopped what they were doing and went silent and I thought to myself I needed to calm everyone down. So I started to explain to her cockroaches are an insect in the Territory and not a pest but she looked

65

at me as if I was stupid and said "the Cockroaches are a great Australian rock band you idiot. Your jukebox has their latest hit". It broke everyone up laughing, at my expense.

The bar area was surprisingly bigger than it looked. It comfortably held about fifty people but we regularly squeezed in many more. If we couldn't fit more drinkers inside we let the crowd spill onto the street. We didn't care, we were in a big city. To the left of the bar was the little general store and bank and to the right rear was the museum and immediately outside the door was the shady beer garden where I cooked the famous Beef and Barra BBQ every night.

When we purchased the pub, the beer garden was a simple unattractive open area with a few chairs and tables. It was too small and far too hot in the midday sun and it very quickly became full when coach loads of tourists arrived or at night for the Beef and Barra BBQ. We needed to quickly fix the space issue, so Phil and Grant demolished the walls of the old shed between the motel and the pub leaving only a frame and roof. They then went into the bush to collect timber from Amungee Mungee Station where Lancewood trees are found. These trees were used for the posts and rafters as they are long and straight and so hard they blunt a chainsaw or a drill in minutes and termites can't eat them but you cannot hammer a nail into a lancewood post, as Phil demonstrated to me when he came into the bar with the first of many broken hammers. So the cut timber was bought back in the trailer and then the guys assembled the framework without a nail or screw. They tied the posts together with fencing wire using a common "figure-eight" fencing knot and then covered the framework with a layer of wire-netting. Then they went out bush again to cut eucalyptus branches complete with their leaves. These leafy branches were then layered overlapping on top of the wire netting to create a wonderful natural shade. Lastly, more wire netting was laid over the top of the boughs and leaves to hold it all in place. Once this was complete Phil and Grant then constructed the timber tables and bench chairs and finally our "Bough Shed Beer Garden" was complete. Phil was a dab hand at the building side of the business but wasn't so at home behind the bar and as I loved the hospitality and bar work, the partnership worked well.

The bough shed beer garden under construction

The beer garden was a great area for events and over the next couple of years in addition to the nightly Beef and Barra BBQ we staged bands, held Christmas parties for the locals, showed movies, held a fashion parade, re-created TV show Blind Date and even hosted an official Country Liberal Party meeting.

The finished Bough Shed Beer Garden in all its glory at
night.

Next door to the outback beer garden was the motel, an
old Stanley Williams hut, once used for housing passengers
from aircraft landing at the airstrip not far from the hotel.
These buildings once covered Northern Australia and were
used as shearer quarters and railway housing and they
numbered in the thousands. Our hut was divided into seven
bedrooms with one shared bathroom. We named one room
the honeymoon suite because it contained a double bed.
My dad stayed in the motel in 1949 when the walls didn't
go to the roof, privacy didn't exist and I'd be bloody certain
there wasn't a honeymoon suite.

There were three outside galvanised iron toilet and
shower blocks. These facilities were only ever designed to

cater for a few visitors at a time and quickly failed to meet the demands we put on them. So we paid a bulldozer driver who was passing through town a few cartons of beer to excavate a huge septic drain and holding tank and we threw a dead kangaroo into it to start the biological process ... exactly as we were instructed by a plumber on his way to Darwin. It kept up for a few months and then it overflowed and caused a bit of a stink. The septic excavation and extension work was the worst job you could imagine. It involved getting into the old septic system and literally lifting the old crap out by scooping it into 44 gallon drums and taking it to the dump on a trailer. Fortunately, for me, two couples Steve and Michelle and Lofty and Liz were staying at the pub looking for work. So Steve and Lofty, working for two days on their hands and knees, gave me a hand to dig the shit out. I was ignorant of the serious sickness you can get from raw sewerage in open cuts and suffice to say, we all suffered from plenty of them. Maybe it was the copious quantities of rum we drank after work that protected us from illness.

Up to our knees in raw sewerage

Next to one of the shower blocks was our hot water system "donkey". Not a normal "hee-haw" donkey, though. In the outback, a donkey is also a hot water contraption and is so named because from the side it looks a bit like a donkey. Our donkey consisted of an WWII galvanised 44 gallon drum laying on its side raised about 50cm above the ground on blocks and having an inlet pipe coming into one end and an outlet pipe out of the other. It then branched out to form a closed plumbing system from the water supply to the hot water taps in the showers and to the kitchen. Underneath the drum was a blazing wood fire.

The Daly Waters donkey. Flames and smoke at sunrise, heating the water for the day

The donkey is a rather simple hydraulic principle that determines the cold water coming in the bottom at one end will come out the top at the other end hotter than when it arrived. It's about here the principle gets a bit tricky. When water is constantly flowing, because taps are turned on, you can expect a reasonably constant temperature of the water coming out the "hot end" to the tap. The temperature of the water depends on the incoming water temperature, the volume of water flowing and the heat of fire underneath. Still with me? There is probably a formula for this but in reality what I just said never happens. What happens is either there is no one using any hot water taps or there is one person using a hot water tap or everyone wants to use a hot water tap at the same time and the scenario changes by the minute. So firstly imagine the scenario where no-one is using a tap, which is most of the time. The fire is blazing and the drum is full of water. The water is initially cold and gradually heats up until ... you guessed right, it's boiling. So where does all the pressure go? Remember this is a closed system so without a pressure release device something will blow. Stories abound of donkey drums exploding and taking lives, pipes bursting and showering anyone nearby with scalding water and one reliable story I heard of a basin tap becoming a missile and flying through the roof of a cattle station dunny. Our donkey incorporated a standard hot water system pressure release valve and in case it failed we installed a small section of garden hose in the line of copper plumbing. It is called "soft plumbing" and our thinking was if the pressure release valve failed then the garden hose would burst instead of a tap going into orbit and decapitating a tourist brushing their teeth. This single 44 gallon drum, and constant fire fed about ten hot water taps AND as long as the fire was going it amazingly never ran out of water. The Daly Waters donkey became a tourist attraction in itself.

Most visitors would not believe it was our only source for hot water. But it was the only source from the time we arrived at Daly Waters until we left. I hope it still is.

On the far side of the motel, and the first part of the pub property visitors come across, is the Caravan Park. It starts opposite Doug Young's house and is now quite large, certainly much larger than when we purchased the pub. What we initially acquired was a small unpowered campground where the first arriving campers and vanners pulled up under the shady flame trees. After they were taken, it was try to find a spot wherever you could find bare flat ground. The first arrivals were offered nearby power, but when they were taken, the only electricity available was if the camper used their own power lead. And it needed to be more than 50 metres long. We left a few powers leads running in all directions across the ground with four point Kambrook power boards on the ends to enable more campers to connect to electricity. Some industrious campers would even use double adapters to increase the number of users but it doesn't take much imagination to realise this eventually would cause us many problems. We warned the campers the power was only for lighting and fridges and most certainly NOT to use electric toasters, kettles and stoves but of course, they did exactly the opposite. This resulted in our yardie Grant having to station himself on a bar chair at the circuit breaker board clicking the breakers back in as they cut out. He looked like an organ player in an outback church. Whilst the power boards worked well most of the time they did have a tendency to overheat and some suffered meltdowns. One day an unfortunate user ran into the pub complaining "I have no idea what happened but I was blow drying my hair and suddenly we all lost power". So we needed to add "NO hair dryers" to the list.

As the pub became busier it became obvious the campground needed expansion and upgrading. We needed more sites with access to decent reliable power and therefore we needed a grader to create a flat usable surface. The tourists were arriving, by car, caravan and bus, from the four corners of Australia. A glance at the registration plates in the caravan park showed most were from South Australia but in time the averages shifted to a more even spread.

The extension to the caravan park, dirt at this stage, can
be seen in the foreground

Noel Davis came to the rescue and graded the park for
the standard outback payment of a box of beer and
somehow we convinced the grumpy old hermit Doug
Young to do the first major slash of the weeds and light
scrubby bushes with the airport tractor slasher, stored in his
shed. As he didn't drink I can't remember how we paid
Doug. Maybe we didn't pay him enough as he certainly
didn't offer his service again.

We sourced a few old telegraph poles, dug a few holes
and used insulators from the original telegraph line on the
top of the poles to string power lines overhead. Our
travelling electrician "Sparky" provided us with a couple of
pre-wired distribution boards and within a few months of

purchasing the pub, we were seriously into the Caravan Park business.

Houses 6 Inhabitants 9. It sounds like a football score but from it, you can correctly assume Daly Waters was a very small town. When we arrived we added four, to make it Houses 6 Inhabitants 13.

From the left : Doug Young house, Our Pub house, Dean Ottens house, the pub with red roof, Tony Moran's (Pat Barry's) house above the red pub roof, town hall to the left of it, Noel Davis house to the right and lastly Mollie Hartig's house on the far right almost out of shot

To get to Daly Waters you depart from the Stuart Highway near the end of the Daly Waters Airfield. From here you get an excellent view along the full length of the magnificent runway and as you head towards Daly Waters you will find the old plane hangar on your right.

After passing the hangar you cross the Daly Creek which feeds into Daly Waters lagoon. The first house you came across when entering Daly Waters from the Stuart Highway was a typical raised and shuttered territory home owned by the government and rented by a hermit dwarf-like man named Doug Young. We only saw Doug when he would limp up the road to collect or deliver his mail. Most of the time he was an unhappy little man and the rest of the time he was angry. His only real friend was his dog. The locals put up with him. Doug rarely washed and always wore the same brown pants with braces and a dirty orange shirt, with thick glasses that were always smeared. Doug spied on everyone from his shuttered window and diligently reported his findings to the authorities, who for the most part simply filed the report in the appropriate place. I think Doug believed in aliens and thought anyone who went to a pub was possessed by the devil ... and he is probably with him now.

Next to Doug was a thin vacant block and then the second house in town belonged to the pub. Leonie and I along with Max, our cat, started living there. It was another raised territory home surrounded by shutters and without air-conditioning. For most of the time it didn't matter too much. We only slept there and it was always very late at night by the time we reached our bed. We would be so tired after an eighteen hour day we would collapse then wake to do it all again.

Next door to us was another raised house owned by Dean Ottens and rented by Andy Hind. Andy ran a crocodile Dundee type tourist business and from this house, he would take tourists on fishing trips in his four wheel drive to Borroloola. Andy eventually left town and local cattle station manager Steve Atwell from Hidden Valley station moved in with his girlfriend Bronwyn and his beast of a dog Boss. His loyal station hand Lockie McKinnon slept on a camp stretcher under the house.

The next building was the little store and mechanic shed for the outback fuel servo. A sign declared "FUEL - ASK AT THE PUB". This sign was photographed by almost every tourist that came to town. Opposite this servo was the pub.

If you turned left here you would find the community hall on your left. This hall was rarely used but did receive a grant in the bicentennial year 1988 to get a clean-up and refurbishment. To celebrate its completion we partied late but it was the only time we saw it used for a large function. Once every couple of months we would hold the community meeting here to discuss procedural matters and plan events for the future.

Opposite the hall was the old police station. In 1986, it was the large stately home of the local stock inspector Tony Moran. Tony moved on after a few months and another stock inspector, the interesting Pat Barry with lovely wife Anna and kids moved in. Pat held a couple of memorable backyard parties in that house. At one party I remember station manager Billy Tapp brandishing a Colt 44 and shooting into the darkness with flames coming from the barrel with each bang. It was a scary experience.

So now we go back to the corner and diagonally opposite the pub to the Steptoe and Sons yard of Noel Davis. Noel was an earthmoving contractor and his yard was full of the oldest earthmoving machinery you could imagine. He owned dozers and graders and many old trucks including an ancient brown Mack Series 1 that he adored. Noel was forever attired in black stubby work shorts, thongs and an open to the waist brown body shirt (it was once possibly white). He wore scratched glasses that he would continuously wipe with a greasy rag from his back pocket, this caused a permanent facial grease smear. The Davis family would be away for weeks grading some distant station track and then he'd return to town with a bit of money and another piece of machinery and then head out of town again. Noel Davis and his wife Sue, with their two kids, travelled everywhere together in a shaky old incredibly long caravan. The kids were as tough as nails but they were a happy go lucky family and we liked them.

Next to Noel lived Mollie Hartig and sons George and Brett along with Brett's wife Vanetta. Brett worked as a road train driver on Kalala Station. Most of the time Brett was with his best mates Dave and Dallas. Vanetta was lovely, she dressed well and always wore a signature smile … unless Brett was playing up.

Mollie Hartig was a lovely little woman who seemed to be the matriarch of the town. She always voiced her an opinion, never held her thoughts back and she would stand her ground in front of anyone. I don't think she fully approved of us blokes but as the pub held her mail and did her banking I think she put up with us. Leonie spent many happy times with Mollie enjoying a cup of tea at her house and really appreciated her kindness. Mollie's son George was a nice lad. He didn't have full-time station work but regularly did odd jobs for Val and Barry Utley on Sunday Creek Station or Roy Beebe at Kalala and always displayed a smile on his face.

Daly Waters was so small I could almost see every house from the bar … and everyone could see who was in the bar from their house. Therefore, everyone knew where everyone was and what they were up to, at all times. It was great for security but very ordinary for privacy.

Chapter 7. AND A SIX PACK AWAY

The Northern Territory is vast. Distances are measured in hours, not miles and many measure them in stubbies not hours. Take-away beers are called travellers and in the 1980's few Territorians went anywhere without a few travellers on the front seat. The cattle stations surrounding the pub are huge and are measured in square miles, not acres and the people who lived on them were considered next-door neighbours even if they lived two beers or fifty miles away. Metres, square kilometres, kilograms and hectares are unheard of, as it is feet and inches and pounds.

The pub is situated within the boundaries of Kalala Station and is 5 miles (8km) to the east of the station homestead. In 1986 Kalala was around 1,600 square miles or 1,000,000 acres and was owned by the giant gentleman Roy Beebe. Roy walked and talked slowly and whilst I never heard him raise his voice, I would never say he didn't. I felt Roy respected us, as he knew our job was difficult being new in a tough area, full of tough men. Roy lived on Kalala with his sister Nita and about a dozen station hands. We saw Roy weekly when he would drop in for a chat and a beer and we generally saw Nita on her way to or back from shopping in Katherine, or from the horse races in Darwin. Nita dressed up for these events in colourful dresses and fascinators and she always returned to the pub after having partied hard, still having a wonderful time. Roy and his brother Mick were the first cattlemen to introduce Brahman cattle to the Northern Territory and they stocked them on several stations they owned. Roy and Mick commenced their working lives operating heavy machinery on Uckaronidge, the family cattle station. Roy told me, in the early days he was on a meatworks run to Tenant Creek when he blew the truck motor and needed to change the engine bearings to get it going again. As they couldn't afford to buy bearings, he made them from a Brahman hide he cut from one of the beasts he was carrying in the truck. Roy and Mick worked incredibly hard and went on to purchase Kalala Station and Tanumbrini Station and expand their empire.

Further out from Kalala was Sunday Creek Station owned by the incredibly hard working Barry and Val Utley. It was the Utley dream to improve the land with diversification, and cropping, and thus much experimenting with different crops, feeds and livestock was done on Sunday Creek. Unfortunately, I think, the climatic conditions tested the Utley's, and whilst they worked the land hard, I don't think it lived up to their full expectations. Their daughter Bev married stock inspector Tom

Stockwell, who went on to be head of the Cattlemen Association. Both worked tirelessly with the Utley's to make Sunday Creek successful. The Utley's were interesting people to talk to, and we enjoyed their company. When we returned to Daly Waters, after we sold the pub, we had a wonderful lunch at Sunday Creek.

Several kilometres south, on the corner of the Stuart and Carpentaria Highways lay the Hi-Way Inn Roadhouse, nicknamed by locals Hi-Way Sin. It was run by the tough and uncompromising Val Miller. From our very first day, Val and I never hit it off. When I first met Val she could see we were serious about making our business successful. I think she was worried about the competition and whilst we were civil to each other, I could see her concern.

To the north was Maryfield Station, owned by the legendary William Tapp Snr, who lived on the iconic Killarney Station. His son Billy (William Jnr) lived on and managed Maryfield with his partner Donna. We saw plenty of Billy and his station hands. They were great people and we were fond of them.

Northeast was Nutwood Downs owned by Rod Dunbar. Rod wanted nothing to do with us ... or anyone. It was said to me he disliked the government and refused to let stock inspectors on his land. He vehemently disagreed with their stance on de-stocking the land to eliminate disease and fought it tooth and nail. We only saw anyone from Nutwood when they collected mail or parcels. The next town, ninety kilometres to the north of Daly Waters was Larrimah. The hotel was owned by the father and son team of Carl and Ray Drummond. We liked their company and when we went north we'd always drop in for a beer and chat and they'd do vice versa. It was a pretty old pub complete with a pet donkey, plenty of peacocks in the trees and a stuffed toy Pink Panther fishing in a puddle out the front. Larrimah Pub was originally located at the end of the old railway line running south from Darwin. It was several kilometres away at Birdum but was moved on a truck to the highway and re-named Larrimah when the railway line closed.

Just off the Carpentaria Highway, to the east of Daly Waters, lay Amungee Mungee owned by brothers Carl and Tom. These boys were regulars at the pub and hardly ever missed coming in on Saturday nights for the action. Unfortunately, being territory lads, they were prone to getting into trouble and I was constantly on their watch.

Sixty kilometres south from Daly Waters was Dunmurra Roadhouse and Wayside Inn owned by Bob and Raelene Knight. These wonderful people were the first neighbours we met. It was the day we took over the pub and they drove up from their wayside-inn to introduce themselves. Raelene took the girls aside and offered them some womanly advice whilst Bob talked about the locals and advised us on some of the men we needed to watch out for on our first weekend, which was Daly Waters Rodeo weekend. They also advised us on how to do our banking. Their son Robbie became a good mate and visited us regularly.

Not far north of Dunmurra was Hayfield station owned by John and Val Dyer John was a well-respected station owner and became President of the Cattleman's Association of the NT. John occasionally would bring his station hands into the pub to reward them for a job well done. He would line up the beers for the boys and then they'd sit down on the concrete pub floor backs against the wall and drink beers whilst talking amongst themselves. His boys never caused us any trouble and the always immaculately presented John was a complete gentleman.

To the south-west of us, and only directly driveable in the dry, lay Hidden Valley Station owned by Dean and Margot Ottens. Dean was an ex SANFL football champion and a huge man. After shaking hands with Dean you needed to check yours still existed. Their sons, Brad and Luke, both went on to play AFL footy in Melbourne. Dean was a great bloke who eventually fell for the lure of easy money, by growing a marijuana crop and for this he went to jail. Prior to the crop opportunity, Dean and Margot moved to Adelaide and appointed a manager Steve Atwell and his sidekick, legendary drover Lockie McKinnon to look after Hidden Valley.

We were most fortunate in having these wonderful people as our neighbours. Life in our remote pub would be impossible without their valued support.

Chapter 8. THROWN IN THE DEEP END

We arrived in Daly Waters a week early to learn the ropes, before taking over the pub. However, it quickly became evident Bill, Ruth and Stuart wanted to be out as soon as possible and teaching us was not high on their agenda. In addition to this problem, they each seemed nervous and in a constant high state of anxiety. I wondered what could be the matter.

Settlement date was set for the Thursday prior to the annual Daly Waters Rodeo Weekend and as Bill and Ruth were experienced in ordering for the rodeo weekend we assumed they would have done all the ordering for this event. But as the pub was being purchased "walk in walk out" they didn't want to pay for any extra stock and therefore ran the stock levels down to a minimum with no extra stock ordered for the rodeo. This left us in a very bad predicament, as it took a week from ordering to delivery and we had precious little time. I was not impressed.

We grew concerned with their behaviour and realised we needed to quickly order the rodeo stock, so it would arrive in time for the busy weekend ahead. I was very frustrated by now and one night I showed it, whilst the three of us were in the office. I questioned their nervous behaviour and asked what they were hiding from us. I pushed hard for answers but instead of providing them, they shut down completely and said they wouldn't let me into the hotel until after settlement. I was bloody seething by this time and so I did stock ordering from the camp-ground. It was very testing times for all of us.

Settlement day arrived but instead of being an exciting day, they wouldn't let any of us open the hotel until they received a phone call from their lawyers and bankers confirming the funds were cleared. Once again their behaviour was most unsettling and I kept wondering what the hell they were hiding from us. Bill and Ruth resolutely stood at the office door waiting for the phone to ring and would not allow us to start bar of kitchen preparations for the day.

The minute the call came telling them the funds were in their bank account they jumped in their fully loaded car and drove out of town without looking back and the bar finally opened that morning, with no help from the Henley's. Bloody good riddance I thought to myself but I continued to wonder what they were hiding from us.

As the Henley family drove out of town, the rodeo came into Daly Waters. With little or no idea of what to expect, we commenced trading ... AT BLOODY LAST.

Bill said it would be busy and there would be heaps of drunks and at the very last minute, the night before, he told us he "closed the bar early during rodeo so the customers would move to the Hi-Way Inn", several kilometres away. He added he "locked the gates into the campground to stop the rodeo goers camping in there. You don't want them freeloaders". These decisions made absolutely no sense to me. Why would you force the rodeo people, who drove all this way, to camp away from the pub? Many travelled hundreds of kilometres and would be looking for a place to rest, to have a good time and a drink with mates they may not have seen for a year.

As fortune would have it, Bob Knight from Dunmurra Wayside Inn paid us a visit that day and gave us some valuable information, just before the rodeo moved into full swing. Firstly, he told us the Henley family weren't liked by the rodeo people and then he reiterated, the previous year Bill closed the campground and closed the pub early. He said it really upset everyone and on top of this, their son Stuart upset a few of the station hands, who in turn, threatened to "come back and get him" this year. Now I started to understand why the pub went on the market and why the Henley's were so keen to be out of town before the rodeo.

When Bob first came into the bar, he walked up to me and said "you'd be Mark, not Phil" to which I replied "how did you know"? He responded "I was told you were the one in the new black hat". "Oh that. What do you think"? I said proudly. He thoughtfully came back with "Mark, when a man walks into a territory bar wearing a black hat, he is there for a fight. It's a signal and it goes back many years. I'd get rid of it son ... you're going to have enough on your plate this weekend". The hat disappeared before he could turn around and later that day I mounted it on the wall.

Bob also gave us a few hints on the expected troublemakers and gave us the names of who we could trust if it got out of hand. He informed us the police were already at the Hi-Way Inn with Val, well away from the rodeo. If we needed help he suggested we should ring her. "Why ring her' I thought. We'd met Val once so far and were yet to meet any of the police. I wondered why they were not here with us as we were 200 metres from the rodeo and Val was several kilometres.

It seemed pretty clear to me when the pub closed everyone would go to the Hi-Way Inn and was probably why the police were there. Why would we even consider closing early? We were in this hotel for our business and so why would we send business down the road to our opposition. We quickly made a decision we weren't going to close early and we felt the police should have at least some presence at the Pub.

Throughout our first day, rodeo people started arriving. We were lucky the day started quietly, as a semi-trailer full of alcohol and food arrived in the morning and it took us all day to put it away. The rodeo wasn't due to commence until the Saturday but we expected plenty to arrive on the Friday afternoon and evening.

The first thing we did after Bill drove out was unlock the gate to the campground and erected a sign reading "FREE CAMPING ON RODEO WEEKEND". As the rodeo goers arrived they were shocked the gates were open and many came into the pub to make sure they were allowed to camp on our grounds. We said yes and at no charge and through this we made plenty of friends. Many said they hadn't come into the pub last year because of the previous publican's attitude and they fully intended not coming in again this year … until they met us.

By late Friday afternoon, the pub was busy and it was all hands on deck. The girls were flat out making steak sandwiches whilst Phil and I were opening cans as quick as our fingers could keep up and the two staff, including

Leonie's brother, were helping out with whatever they could.

Late in the day, two police officers from Mataranka paid us a visit and when we informed them we were letting the rodeo people use our camping ground for free and were going stay open very late each night they tried to talk us out of it. I wondered what information we were missing and I said to them "surely it's better to keep them here than have them drinking and then driving out of town" and they replied "we don't think it is a good idea. Bill saw too much trouble last year, so he closed the bar early and we think you should do the same". I replied, "there is no way that is going to happen and if we need help we'd like you to be here". It is obvious they weren't happy, so they said they would come past a few times and we should consider closing early. I think they were looking after Val. I didn't know what power she had over them but there was obviously something going on.

The day turned into night, the Pub was getting full and so were the patrons. It was loud and it was fun. We met everyone who came into the pub, from station owners to truck drivers, jackaroos to jillaroos and camp cooks to campers and we met the ageing rough Territory legends like Ronnie Ogilvie, horseman Dave Mills and another chap who was recently gored so badly by a bull, he nearly died. He spent the entire night showing his wound to everyone whether they asked or not. And then there were the impressive rodeo champions like the Tapp family and the Underwood's. What a mixed bunch of people in one place at one time. Behind the bar, Phil and I were having the time of our lives whilst the girls tried to keep up with the meals. The cowboys shouted at each other and to each other across the room and they shouted each other drinks like there was no tomorrow. We were going through beers faster than we could grab them from the fridge but the Bundy rum was flying out and I secretly hoped I ordered enough.

Bob Knight warned us of a few potential probable troublemakers. The Groves, Darcy's and the MacFarlane's headed his list and unsurprisingly they caused the biggest problems the first night. These three families loved a stoush with each other or anyone else in reach. The night went so fast and we were so busy we hardly noticed how many people kept coming in the bar until it overflowed into the street. I remember one of the police officers Kim coming in the bar and telling me "you need to stop them drinking on the road". I replied, "you stop 'em, I'm not".

He looked most unhappy, then left and headed back to the Hi-Way Inn and safer ground.

We experienced our share of trouble but it never went out of control. At one stage I saw a coloured lad playing 8-ball against a mate of one of the Groves boys. "Boorie" Groves went up to the table and said it was his game. The young fella went to argue the point but was hit on the nose by the fastest right jab I'd ever seen and he flew across the pool table, just as you'd see in a movie. I couldn't believe how quick the punch was thrown and I vividly remember looking at Phil and saying "there is no way we are going out there tonight. They can sort it out themselves". Thankfully no-one in the crowd looked to us to sort it out. A few in the crowd dragged the two of them to the front door and out onto the street where they formed a circle and the fighters ripped into it. This seemed fine until one big station lad, Kurt Hammar, king hit the young coloured fella and the fight was over. At the bar, several others mumbled about the cowardly king hit but Kurt was huge and no-one took him to task on it. There were a few skirmishes through the night but generally they all got on well and drank plenty.

At about 3am on our first night we called last drinks. After midnight the drinkers started heading back to camp and some went to the Hi-Way Inn. Some said they felt guilty about not seeing Val and I said, "I don't". I simply didn't care about her or the police, we were fine. When we called last drinks, the last few drinkers said they were happy to go to their camp with a roadie on us and we closed up. As we closed up we said "all up at 6am to hose the bar out, restock the fridges and prepare for another long day".

I slept like I never slept before and less than three hours later we were back into it. We all appeared on time together and with smiles on faces. Leonie and Toni started to make bacon and egg sandwiches whilst Phil and I restocked the fridges. At 7am we opened the bar but after restocking, it was obvious we needed more refrigeration if we were going to be this busy again. More than a few patrons told us the Daly Waters Pub was known for the coldest beer on the track and we spent so much time rotating beer from the store to our small cold room and then into the bar fridge and all were struggling to keep up. On top of the vast amounts of beer cans consumed, we poured over twelve flagons of rum on the first day and I wondered if the forty-eight flagons I ordered was going to be enough.

Hangovers were evident as the drinkers from last night came in for breakfast. Our girls were kept flat out in the kitchen with the bacon and egg sandwich a big hit. Some washed breakfast down with a Bloody Mary's and many drank beer and at around 11am the bar emptied. The Rodeo Association served from drinks from their own bar at the rodeo ground and with plenty of sausages on the BBQ, the pressure was off for a few hours.

I even took the chance to walk the two hundred metres to the rodeo ground for an hour and I couldn't believe what I saw. The same young guys that were drinking heavily and beating each other up were competing against each other and helping each other up from the dirt after being bucked off by some very angry huge Brahman bulls and wild horses. A few of the lads suggested "the publican might like to try" but I gratefully rejected the offer on the premise I was required back at the bar.

That night we were flat out again and the next twenty-four hours reproduced it again. By the end of the weekend, we were all absolutely stuffed, as were the rodeo visitors. Many came in for breakfast on their way home to their cattle stations scattered all over the Northern Territory. It was an incredibly successful first weekend in our "new" pub. The ancient old office safe was bursting with dirt and booze-stained notes and "back of house" was a real mess. But we struggled through and, pleasing to us, we were thanked by the "locals" and quickly we felt were, almost, accepted into the fold by them.

The end "rum count" showed we poured all of the forty-eight flagons of rum and half a dozen "square bottles" (750ml) leaving very little rum left for the week and there were only a few cartons of beer left, no ice and very little coke. Importantly we survived and knew we would do it even better next time.

What an introduction to pub life ... talk about thrown in the deep end. Originally, I considered commencing trading, in our first hotel, a day before the busiest weekend of the year was foolhardy but looking back on it, I believe it was a good thing. We learned so much very early on, about each other, the pub and the locals. Our future at Daly Waters Pub looked exciting.

Chapter 9. A LITTLE BIT OF LUCK GOES A LONG WAY

In 1930, when Bill Pearce opened his store in Daly Waters it was three weeks before his first customer drove into town and unfortunately the Pearce's witnessed the car drive straight past the pub without stopping. A week later, a car stopped but it was already well provisioned for the drive to Newcastle Waters and only dropped in for a "cuppa" and a "hello". Three months after opening and having served only a few travellers and the telegraph station workers, a Tiger Moth started delivering the mail but the Pearce's knew a handful of travellers and locals plus an occasional mail plane was not enough to sustain their existence at Daly Waters.

The next three years were tough for the Pearce family but everything changed one day in 1934, when out of the blue to the Pearce's, Qantas announced regular flights to-and-from Singapore and Sydney with Daly Waters as the first and last Australian stop. To cap it off, Bill was granted the refuelling rights and Henrietta was in charge of refreshing the passengers. It was their lucky day, as quickly other connecting air-routes opened to Perth and Brisbane.

When I read the book "Two at Daly Waters" I said to Leonie "we will need the Pearce luck, if we are going to be successful".

My statement turned out to be prophetical, as within weeks of us moving to the pub, Aussie battler and comedian Paul Hogan released a movie, which broke all box-office records in Australia and in 1986 it became the highest grossing movie in the world. Crocodile Dundee was the story of a fictional Northern Territory character and many of the outback scenes were shot in the Territory. By the end of 1986, around one in four Australians had seen the movie and wanted to be like Mick Dundee and experience the outback.

It was our lucky day and Pearce moment.

Our major problem was the Territory lay thousands of kilometres from every Australian capital city and the roads were amongst the worst in the world. Until 1986, Darwin in the Northern Territory was connected to Adelaide in South Australia by what could best be described as a rugged track, perversely named the Stuart Highway. The highway has always been affectionately known by Territorians as "the Track" and that is how I referred to it also.

Over the years, the Territory end of the Track was upgraded to a single strip of bitumen with a wide shoulder to allow cars and road-trains to pass by without stopping. However, until the early 1980's, the South Australian section consisted of a good bitumen road in the south from Adelaide to about fifty kilometres past Port Augusta and then a dangerous dirt track with deep bull dust and corrugated sections for almost a thousand kilometres to the Northern Territory border.

In the early 1980's during our work in surveying, Phil and I heard extra funding was coming from the National Highway Project to ensure the Track would become fully sealed from Adelaide to Darwin in time for the bicentennial year of 1988. We were lucky to have that information, as the sealing of the Track would ensure the Daly Waters Pub would finally enjoy a bitumen road to Adelaide, enabling tourists to do interstate trips and loops and by loops I mean Adelaide - Perth - Darwin - Adelaide or reverse. For those from Brisbane or Sydney or even Melbourne, it gave similar loop possibilities, for example, Sydney-Brisbane-Darwin-Adelaide-Sydney. The possibilities for tourists were endless and by the end of 1986 we were seeing more and more cars and caravans but we also more tourist coaches. It was incredible and the number plates varied from all around Australia.

A map showing the highway routes (red) crossing Australia

When we purchased the pub, five to ten people camped with us per night and a few in the motel. We hosted a coach lunch every few days and a coach or two would drop in for a drink and photo opportunity each week. By the end of our first season, the number of coaches stopping at Daly Waters Pub had tripled. It was our "Bill and Henrietta Pearce" Qantas moment in our time at Daly Waters.

The major tourist coach lines of Australian Pacific Tours (APT), AAT Kings, Wollongong Coaches, Evergreen, Contiki and others starting phoning in late 1986 to book their visits and lunch itineraries for 1987. These coach tours came from all over Australia. The diary was getting full and very soon one coach luncheon per day was booked. On some days three coaches were booked in for lunch and we expected many others to drop in for a look. These tourist coaches held fifty people each and whilst their meal was paid for by the company we knew they would spend plenty on souvenirs. Phil and I knew there was plenty of work to do around the pub to make it ready.

On some days we would have four or more coaches at the pub.

The coaches would arrive and the first item on the
agenda was to take photos of the pub

Chapter 10. DALY LIFE

A "normal" Daly Waters Pub day commenced at 6am and finished when the last person left the bar … in all probability it would end early the next morning.

Leonie and I would wake at 5.45am and at 6am I would prepare the bar for the day, whilst Leonie performed office work. Our yardman's (yardie's) first job was to fire up the donkey hot water system, clean the toilets and ensure they were fully stocked with paper before "polishing the stones", our saying for the daily chore of raking the gravel, on the road verge from the front of the hotel from the corner of the pub to the caravan park. This not only removed all leaves and rubbish but when raked in the same direction, it presented the pub beautifully for the day ahead. The yardie then moved into the beer garden to repeat the exercise in there and then he would clean the outside areas, wipe down all the tables and chairs, reset ashtrays and clean the BBQ and table and place the tablecloths on it ready for the days coach luncheons. He'd also check all the gas bottles, load the Weber kettles with heat beads, fix anything needing fixing as he went and feed our pets and restock anything needing restocking including cold rooms and dry stores.

At the same time as our yardie was working outside, I would sweep, hose out and mop the bar, then restock the fridges before wiping the bar clean, replace yesterday's bar runners and clean the unique ashtrays, designed as a hubcap with a hole in it upside down over a hubcap up the right way. These unusual, highly photographed object, stopped the fast-spinning overhead fans from blowing the ash out of the bottom hubcap. Then I'd clear the money from the pool table and sweep the cloth and then clear the ever-popular jukebox of its takings. I'd take the money from these into the office and swap it for the till floats with Leonie after she counted the previous night takings and reorganised the floats from the safe. We ran an "open till" because it was busted and therefore Leonie didn't have to reconcile the previous day takings but simply counted it, retained a float and banked the excess. Even to our untrained mind this wasn't ideal business practise but we were left with no option.

The "open till" with a visiting thief

At about 6.45am, we would all take fifteen minutes break for a cooked breakfast of bacon and eggs and baked beans, or similar. We enjoyed breakfast with our staff as it would be the last time we could have time to sit together for the day.

By 7am I was ready for opening the bar for the breakfast customers and early travellers. Leonie and Toni would be in the kitchen preparing for lunch and cooking breakfasts for the next couple of hours and Phil would be outside performing building work and maintenance. The yardie would be into the caravan park by now to continually click the circuit breakers back in and to roll up extension leads as the overnight visitors left. Leonie's helper would be looking to get into the motel to clean rooms and make up the beds. The dirty linen needed to be washed and then hung out to dry and the rooms ready for new guests by lunchtime.

Patrons would commence entering the bar from 7am and I would be kept busy all day pouring drinks and fuel. If it became too hectic I would call Phil into the bar until the need for help passed. Leonie and Toni would start setting the beer garden for the coach lunches at about midday. A large table would be covered with a table-cloth and then platters of salads, bread, cold meats and the roast chickens would be put out as the coaches full of tourists arrived and desserts would be served later.

At around lunchtime the coaches would start arriving, having driven in the morning from Tennant Creek, Mataranka or Katherine. The coach hostesses were patient and well organised women who would bring the guests into the bar, instruct them to get a drink and then ask them to immediately go to the beer garden for lunch. The hostess would add "there will be plenty of time for looking around the bar after lunch" and would urge them to eat as quick as possible, knowing there was generally another coach arriving in an hour. It seemed an impossible task each day

but the Leonie and Toni rarely failed to please the
hostesses and their passengers.

In addition to the coaches, many driving tourists and
locals visited the pub every day. Therefore, Leonie and
Toni cooked and served over 100 coach visitors per day, as
well as a similar amount of drive-in visitors. Each non-
coach visitor would have the choice of food from our
"normal" menu of the standard dishes of steak sandwiches,
schnitzels, streaks, mixed grills and fish and all the food
came from a tiny little kitchen at the rear of the pub. How
the girls did it amazed me.

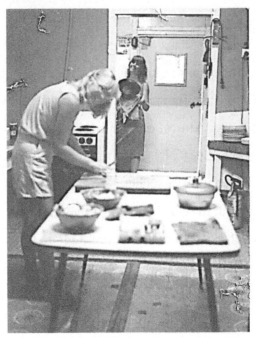

Toni preparing lunch and Leonie doing breakfast dishes
in the tiny kitchen

After lunch service, our yardie would repeat his
morning ritual of cleaning the beer garden and polishing
the stones in front of the pub and then he would again
restock the fridges. I would attempt to clean the bar around
the patrons and the girls would clear the tables around the
leftover patrons in the beer garden and then clean the
kitchen, all in preparation for the dinner rush. The minor
lull in trade was welcome and each of us would try to grab
a quick lunch of leftovers from the coach lunches usually
including roast chicken, ham, salad and bread.

However, most days threw up a curve ball. A plane or
helicopter may need refuelling, a car might need a tyre
changed or a travelling salesman might drop in, wanting to
sell their wares. Almost daily a local cattle-station hand or
owner, or possibly Kalala Station boss Roy Beebe, would
pay us a visit and want a chat. Government workers may
call in wanting to relate some information about the water
tank or electricity generator or wanting me to accompany
them on an inspection of the facility or to check we were
fulfilling our contract. Sometimes the police would drop in
and want to talk about an incident and other times it would
be a journalist or photographer wanting to do a story on the

pub or an artist wishing to paint it and there was rarely a normal day without a machinery breakdown or an incident. We never knew who was coming in the door next.

Most afternoons I was kept busy booking tourists into the caravan park and motel as soon they came into the bar. I would greet caravan tourists with "gidday mate, it looks like you want a caravan site. Before we take you there you'd better get your order in for the beef and barra BBQ tonight". Then one of us would take them into the caravan park, guide the caravan into their site, show them where to connect to the power and point to the showers and toilets they should use. We had some fun with many of these vanners, who were always excited to finally be at the Daly Waters Pub. Sometimes, I would entertain them in the bar while Grant took their keys and parked their van in the park. On one occasion I "stole" a young couple's keys from the bar. Grant parked their van and even set up their annexe as they sat back and had a few too many drinks. After Grant returned, I replaced their keys without their knowledge. Much later, they walked outside to move their car and caravan and to their surprise it wasn't where they left it. We showed them to the caravan park and they were delighted.

At around 5pm the bar would start to fill up with locals and tourists. By this time there would normally be at least two of us, flat out in the bar. All diners were previously informed what time they'd be eating, so in this way we were able to control the situation and not have the entire 150 persons in the bar buying drinks.

At about 5.30pm I would go into the beer garden to cook the BBQ dinner. Leonie and Toni and their staff would have set up the salads and have the rump steak and barra cut-up for cooking. Most afternoons Leonie would spend at least two hours cutting the barra fillets into half and full serves as well as doing the same with the rump steaks. Cooking a BBQ for over one hundred people every night was hard work and the continuous smell of the BBQ took my hunger away. Instead of finishing the cooking and having a meal myself, I would generally head back into the bar and serve until closing.

Most of the guests would head off to bed at around 10pm but as you would expect, there would always be the stayers who would hang around the bar and beer garden swapping information and telling stories or playing music on the jukebox and 8-ball on the pool table. I met new people every night and therefore the bar work was never boring. By about midnight most would have gone to bed but if they hadn't I would try to convince them it was time to go. Sometimes the crowd refused to leave and therefore, on occasions, I would stay open very late into the next morning or all night. Fortunately, or unfortunately, our license allowed this, which made the next day a very long day and so, whoever closed the bar would generally try to sneak a sleep in mid-morning or mid-afternoon the next day.

Our daily pub life was repetitive and long but I loved it all and thanks to the great hardworking staff to back us up, it was a great life. The busier we became, the more staff we required and tragically after a few short months we would be without Phil and Toni, making the employment of good staff even more important.

Chapter 11. LET'S GO SHOPPING

Ordering and receiving deliveries, due to our distance from major cities and distribution hubs, was one of the biggest problems of living at Daly Waters.

Approximately 90% of all food and drinks consumed in the Territory arrives from overseas or other Australian states on semi-trailers, ship or aircraft and most of the freight goes directly to Darwin. At Daly Waters, we watched our beer, spirits, wine, meat, vegetables and groceries go straight past our pub on its way Darwin. The entire truck would be unloaded in Darwin and then our goods were reloaded onto the truck and came back down to us a few days later. Thankfully we inherited a very good freight deal with Gilbert's Transport, based in Strathalbyn in country South Australia about 2,500 kilometres away. Gilbert's delivered freight of all varieties to Darwin from Adelaide. They would completely unload the semi-trailer and "backload" with our weekly order. When I say weekly order, I need to stress this was our only chance to order most items. If we forgot to order something, we wouldn't receive it for another week. Suffice to say, the pressure was on when ordering and as this was pre-computers, our old adding machine, pen and paper would have to suffice.

A Gilberts Truck coming up the Stuart Highway

Weekly ordering went something like this. Leonie and Toni made-up the food and groceries order and Phil and I made-up the drinks order. It was all written down by hand and when we were satisfied it was correct, we would phone the suppliers and quote the product, the product code, the number of inners, litres, cases or singles as we required. It would have been much easier if it all came from one place but it didn't. Fruit and veg came from one supplier, meat from another, groceries from another, beer from one brewer and different beer from another brewer, spirits from one wholesaler and soft drinks from another. We also ordered ice, cigarettes, fuel, tyres and oil plus stationery, toilet paper, cleaning products, plastic plates and cutlery and more and more. Take a look in your pantry and the chances are we ordered it weekly for the pub. It was a huge logistical exercise and it simply needed to be done very well, every single week, as one mistake would be costly. Imagine forgetting the beer. We would run out within a couple of days. It didn't bear thinking about and so we took our time to make sure it was correct.

Generally, at about the middle of the next week and always during the day, the Gilbert's Transport semi-trailer would drive into town and park next to the pub. One of two drivers would deliver to us each week. Banga one week and then Claude the next. Both drivers were wonderful blokes and they regularly gave us tips on how we may do things better. These guys worked the incredibly difficult job of driving these massive rigs for days on end and then come off the highway on a skinny little road to deliver to our little pub. We were incredibly lucky to have such patient men doing the job and I should mention, we didn't have a forklift, a trolley or even a slide. Everything was hand unloaded onto the ground, or into a ute and then manhandled again inside to the store or cold room. Banga and Claude didn't sit in the driver's seat and watch this happen. They jumped into it with us and together we "got the job done". To put it into perspective too, we are talking fresh food, frozen food, perishables, cans, bottles, fragile goods and ice. We are talking a large quantity that increased every week, for the entire time we were there.

It was Banga who suggested we form a "Conga line" during one memorable delivery. He was running late after suffering two punctures on the track and he was losing his patience as we unloaded. To make matters worse we were busy in the bar, so he jumped out of the truck and said "bugger this Mark, there's ten blokes inside doing nothing. Why don't you make their day and you offer free beers, to help unload this stuff". I immediately went inside and said, "c'mon you guys, who wants a free beer". They all looked around and said "bloody oath" and I added, "okay, there's a truck out there to unload, then you get your beer". Outside they came and we formed a Conga-line from the door of the truck parked directly out front, through the front door and into the storeroom behind the bar. Banga would drop a box to the first guy who would revolve and half toss it to the next guy and so on. I was last in line and knew exactly where the product was needed. The girls took their food into the kitchen stores or Grant took the booze to the liquor store. We unloaded the truck in record time, Banga was back on schedule and it worked so well we repeated the same exercise many times during the next couple of years.

A small Conga line unloading the rodeo beer order from
truck to trailer to ground.

Most deliveries went without mishap but our second
rodeo delivery went horribly wrong. By this time our pub
was very busy and the weekly delivery was stretching our
increased storage to the limit. Our order for the Daly
Waters Rodeo weekend broke the storage "camels" back.
Banga arrived on the Wednesday with a full semi-trailer
load of goods for us and it was all hands on deck. There
was so much stock on the truck, we decided to fill the two
pub utes with cartons of beer and get them out of the way.
So we reversed the old grey Toyota up to the truck trailer
and started loading it up and up. The ute appeared to be
handling it easily and so we kept piling it higher and higher
until at about six feet high (ten foot above the ground) we

said enough. One of the pub workers jumped into the driver's seat to slowly move away and then came the loudest BANG. The rear left spring of the ute snapped and turned upside down, causing the ute to immediately drop on its side. The load of beer tilted and hung for a second or two before collapsing and crashing to the dirt road below. I reckon about forty cartons of beer cans fell the ten feet to the ground and next minute there were sprays of beer shooting into the air as the beer frothed and sprayed out of all the damaged cans until the cartons softened and then the spray went everywhere. It looked like a huge fountain. We were all in shock and all we could do was wait for it to stop. Time was short, so we kept unloading the truck onto the second ute and then onto the ground near the truck to let Banga get on his way. And then it was all hands on deck to retrieve any undamaged cans, give them all a good wash and get them into the store or cold room. This took nearly all day and was a most unpleasant job in the hot Territory sun and dust.

Unloading was a tough job but it was also a highlight for the tourists. It gave me a chance to explain to everyone present how we received our deliveries. At every delivery, offers for help came from the bar. We never knocked help back.

One beer stack for rodeo weekend... a lazy 300 cartons

Lindsay Carmichael, our Coca Cola distributor, lived three hundred kilometres to the south of the pub, in the isolated mining town of Tennant Creek. Lindsay owned the Coca Cola distribution business for this area and, at the time, drove the longest Coca Cola delivery run in the world. His delivery run went from Tennant Creek, in the centre of the Territory, east 250km on the Barkly Highway to the Queensland border and 350km north to Borroloola, on the Gulf of Carpentaria and then 250km west to our Daly Waters Pub, before heading 300km south to home.

Lindsay's truck would leave home fully laden and returned home empty a few days later. Sometimes, if Lindsay felt like a drink, it took longer. He unloaded the truck himself and hand trucked the coke cartons into our store himself. We always tried to help but for the most part, he preferred to do it.

We purchased our barramundi from Ken Oliver, a professional fisherman, 300km east at Borroloola. Ken and his boat, the MV Julia, were well known in these parts and Ken was held in high regard for his fishing and as a good man. We were fortunate to have him provide us with his fish but as Ken was always fishing, the art of arranging deliveries for the barramundi was causing us quite a few headaches.

We were most fortunate when Lindsay heard me say we were having barramundi delivery problems. Without hesitation Lindsay offered to bring it to us on his regular fortnightly Coke run. This sounded like a great idea but it became greater when he said, "and all I want is a square bottle of rum for each delivery". From then on our barramundi, all seven tonnes of it per year, came to us on the Coke truck thanks to Lindsay.

For the next couple of years, Lindsay would ring from the Loo and ask "how many this time". Leonie would already have the kilograms we needed worked out and would instruct Lindsay, who would drive to Ken's cold-room in Borroloola, remove the correct amount of fish, normally around 200 kilograms, cover it in ice and deliver it to us the next day. Lindsay never missed a delivery, we were so lucky to have him and Ken supplying our pub.

Fruit and vegetables came on the bus from Katherine, with Leonie placing orders and deliveries occurring twice weekly. We were very fortunate Katherine Fruit and Veg operated out of Katherine. The owners were wonderful people and they rarely let Leonie down with supplying good quality produce in the ordered amounts.

Our fuel was delivered from Tenant Creek. We used a small independent supplier, who also supplied oil and parts but using a small independent also meant they only delivered when we ordered and he would not deliver an order of less than 10,000 litres per time. The price was higher than the "big" operators were paying on the highway but we didn't have their overheads and therefore we were able to compete on the bowser price.

Our tyres came also came from Tenant Creek and believe it or not we purchased a lot of tyres. It is hard to imagine, in the little outback town of Daly Waters but for much of the dry season, we repaired or replaced at least five tyres per week. Many tourists, particularly the young ones, only wanted second hand tyres and whilst we had trouble buying enough of them, we generally were able to satisfy.

Provisioning the pub was challenging and stressful, particularly as we grew but it is part of most businesses and over time it became easier to manage.

Chapter 12. ITS ONLY MONEY

In the 1980's ATM's and EFTPOS didn't exist. Everything was done by cash or cheque making travel in the outback tough for tourists and daily life interesting for the locals. Banks were important in the outback and at Daly Waters Pub there were three of them.

YOU CAN BANK ON IT

One of the first pieces of advice we received came from Bob and Raylene Knight, owners of Dunmurra Roadhouse sixty kilometres to the south. On our first day they drove to the pub to introduce themselves and welcome us to the area. During the conversation Bob asked how we intended banking the takings. We looked at each other and said, "ummm, the same way it's done now we think". He replied, "and how is it done now?" We weren't sure how to respond. The previous owners showed us how to bank the takings and at the same time told us not to disclose to anyone how it was done. It is so long ago I suppose I can tell the world now.

The problem in the 1980's, in the Northern Territory, was how do you safely bank a pile of cash every week when you live 300 kilometres from your bank and you haven't the time to drive there yourself as there isn't a cash pick up or delivery service.

The businesses on the Stuart Highway all did their banking by different and secretive means so we were surprised by the directness of Bob's query. To ease the tension Bob said "okay here's my advice. If you use the Greyhound Coach, as you probably already do and will continue to do, then make sure you swap your banking days around. Don't bank the same day every week. Sometimes bank fortnightly. Sometimes twice in the one week. We all do it that way and it works because no-one knows when anyone is banking. No-one. You know the money isn't insured right"? "It's not"? I said. We didn't consider the banking would be an issue but it was now. "Bob, are you sure this is the only way"? I nervously asked. He responded "you can bank on it mate" with a smile.

So what happened was interesting ... and without cash in transit insurance, scary.

Banking went like this. Leonie would count the cash each week on a different day and fill out a deposit slip for the ANZ Bank in Katherine. The cash and the deposit slip would be stuffed into an empty Jim Beam or Bundy bottle box. The box would be wrapped in white paper, stamps

127

stuck on the box and the ANZ Bank address in the Main Street of Katherine written on the front. This box would be added to our mailbag for collection by the Greyhound Coach heading north every two days on the way to Darwin from Adelaide. When the coach arrived at the pub we would load our mail bag and the local cattle station mailbags into the trailer on the back of the coach and off it would go.

It needs to be pointed out this little box of cash could hold anywhere between $1,000 and $40,000 depending on the trade the previous week and the regularity of the deposit. That is heaps of cash, even now. In 1986 it was enough to buy a house in a city.

So each week our Bundy box of cash left the pub in a trailer on the back of a coach and ended up in our bank account. This happened every week and every week it we banked successfully. After a few weeks, we didn't give it a second thought. It was never mentioned again ... until. Until Leonie and I drove to Katherine, in May 1987, to pay a visit to the bank to meet with our bank manager, at his request.

We parked in the Main Street and walked a few hundred metres north to the bank. Along the way I noticed the posties push bike leaning against a hairdressing shop window with the postie inside casually talking to the shop owner. What I also noticed made me instantly feel sick. Sitting at the top of his open postie handlebar bag lay our box of cash on its way to the bank!! And we both knew it contained over $30,000, sitting there for anyone to grab and run off.

Even though we knew someone delivered the box from the post office to the bank it never occurred to us it would happen that way and would be so obvious. We were both in shock as we stumbled into the bank manager, Ian's, office looking like we'd seen a ghost. When we explained what we'd seen, Ian said something like "everyone does it that way. It's so simple we don't think any would-be thief would consider it was happening".

Ian then explained why he requested our visit and asked "I have a question which may seem strange but … are you paying yourselves a wage"? We replied, "ummm, no. Should we"? "Okay, are you aware of your current financial position"? he asked next. "No" I replied and innocently, naively said, "are we in some sort of trouble"? "No", he said "in fact, it's the opposite. You're banking large amounts of cash each week and your loan is quickly being repaid. However, I'm concerned you will have a tax problem at the end of the financial year. Do you have an accountant"? It was my turn again, "No, well we did but we haven't heard from him. I think he's in jail. Do we need one"? He then added something like, "for reasons of edict, I cannot recommend a particular accountant, as there are a few in Katherine … but there's a very good one just around the corner" whereby he shook our hand and bade us goodbye and good luck.

Without going into detail, Brad Gooding, the accountant around the corner, instantly became our accountant and for the next few years his sound advice saved us paying much unnecessary taxation.

We continued to bank "on the bus" during our time at the Daly Waters Pub and true to Bob Knight's word, nothing ever went missing. However, one Greyhound coach trailer burnt to the ground somewhere south of Tenant Creek a few years later. I'm glad it wasn't ours.

You may wonder "how does it happen whereby we wouldn't be aware of our financial position". I can tell you with honesty, it was easy. We worked eighteen hour days, seven days a week, and as we lived in and therefore lived off the pub, we didn't spend a cent. We didn't take a wage because we didn't need one and because we were new to the world of business, we didn't know it mattered. Our cash-register was an open drawer behind the bar and we employed no accountancy system at all. We simply paid bills when they arrived and banked the excess cash each week. We paid our staff in cash, correctly and by the book and we paid the staff income tax by cheque to the ATO. We didn't look at our bank or loan statements because we didn't have time to read them.

WHICH BANK

The Daly Waters Pub operated a Commonwealth Bank of Australia agency. The bank appointed Leonie as the bank manager and warned her someone would call in to do unannounced audits. Leonie's job was to take passbook deposits. Other than for locals, deposits were rare, whereas withdrawals were frequent. She would need to write the correct amounts in the customer's passbook, check the balance and previous transactions were correct, and then stamp the book with the Daly Waters Pub CBA stamp. At the end of each day, the transactions would need to be balanced and a daily sheet filled in. Each week required a similar sheet to be posted to the bank in Katherine. It took time. Leonie didn't have time to spare and the commission for the pub was minimal but it was a service someone needed to provide and it brought people into the pub.

During 1987 the first audit occurred. On a particularly busy day, and in the middle of lunch service, a short man came up to the bar and flashed me a CBA business card and then asked me to take him to Leonie. As soon as I saw the card I knew he was there to do a bank audit, I responded we were way too busy right at the time but if he'd care to wait until after lunch I'm sure she could see him then. But our little pesky rotund short pink skinned balding man wasn't having any of this and demanded to see Leonie immediately. Once again, with more force this time, I said "now you listen here mate, I don't care who you are but my wife is flat out looking after fifty paying guests and as soon as she's finished serving them lunch she will be only too happy to show you what you need to see. Now, you want a beer or do you want to make this more difficult than it already is"? He refused the beer but took a seat outside and waited.

After lunch, he did his audit of Leonie's branch banking records. Leonie kept the records as best she could, but she was always frantically busy and so the odd closing off date or signature was missing and this "all by the rules" bank jockey teed off on her by threatening to remove the branch authority if she didn't scrub up better next time and for her to expect a warning letter after he returned to his branch office. Leonie came to me, in quite an upset state but there was nothing to do about it now, so we continued serving our customers. Later in the day the bank jockey returned to Daly Waters and surprisingly booked a room in the motel for the night. I thought he was here to give Leonie more grief and was about to tell him to stay somewhere else when he said, "and I'll have a beer now and book in for the Beef and Barra BBQ everyone is talking about".

After checking into his room and doing his end of day paperwork (what else would the wanker do in his room) he came into the bar and drank a couple more beers. A bit later and whilst slightly drunk he fed up on our Beef and Barra BBQ and afterwards, consumed several more beers. At 10pm he was drinking double rums and not the singles he thought he was drinking. By now he was getting rowdy and at 11pm I asked him to leave the bar and he staggered to his room.

The next morning, soon after opening the bar, the bank man came in and paid his bill. As he was leaving he casually said to me "oh, by the way, slight accident last night. I farted and followed through" and he was gone. It took me a minute to digest what he just said, but when it sunk in I immediately went to tell Leonie. The little banker was bloody lucky he left, because if Leonie discovered the runny poo IN the motel bed prior to him leaving town he would have been in big trouble.

We never saw him or any other auditor from the bank again nor did we receive the warning letter he promised to send. This was just as well for him as Leonie already was penning her own letter to his branch manager, exposing his terrible behaviour before, during and most importantly after the audit.

BUSH BANK

The definition of a bush bank could read "a place where a business allows a local or itinerant person to leave money, with complete faith that it will be there when he returns. No interest is paid and the only identifier for the owner of the note is their name in their own handwriting on the note".

A small section of the "bush bank" deposits.

There are several bush banks in the outback and the Daly Waters Pub "Bush Bank" was as famous as the Barrow Creek Hotel bank to the south of us. The Daly Waters Bush Bank not only displayed Australian notes but also many overseas bank notes. In our time at Daly Waters Pub only a few visitors or locals came back in to claim their money from the bush bank but their money was safely held. When we sold the pub the bush bank funds were treated as part of the pub and not the "cash on hand" to ensure they remain forever.

WALL STREET

Most of the local station hands and a few of our pub workers preferred to bank on "Wall Street". We invented Wall Street as a way to help our staff and local jackeroos cope with cash-flow problems. Wall Street was the wall connecting the bar to the office and on it, we pinned the "banking records" of the participants.

It worked like this. Billy from Kalala comes in with his pay cheque and opts to join Wall Street. We take his cheque and write on a piece of paper the amount, for example $200. If he wants a beer we give him the beer and write - $5 balance $195. It was simple but it did require trust. We didn't get them to sign the sheet and so they needed to trust we did it honestly. If I was asked about this I'd respond by saying "now mate, do you really think I'd risk getting caught for five measly dollars. I wouldn't have a local customer for the rest of my life, it's simply not worth it for me".

The reason the station workers liked this bank was really obvious. Firstly they were only paid monthly and secondly, they never carried cash around when riding horses, mustering cattle, fixing fencing or clearing out turkey nests (dams) or water tanks and troughs. So after they'd done a hard day's work and if their route came back to the station past the pub and they felt like a beer they, therefore, needed money and under normal circumstances they wouldn't have any. By depositing all or a portion of their pay with us they knew they'd have a balance available on Wall Street to withdraw from.

This system worked incredibly well for all parties as long as the workers didn't overdraw too much or leave the area owing money. Both happened but only on the odd occasion. Roy Beebe appreciated us adapting Wall Street for his workers and before sacking them he generally attempted to find out if they owed us money so he could ensure they paid us. It didn't work every time but at least he tried. With the workers depositing their pay on Wall Street it not only created loyalty to the Daly Waters Pub but it ensured the local station hands could get some spending money, if they needed it.

Around Australia horse rider Steve Nott, who worked for us whilst waiting for the wet season to pass, used Wall Street from the day he arrived and six months later when he left he actually owed Wall Street money. A rare and fine achievement by a great man.

Chapter 13. THE CAVALRY ARRIVES

I was so preoccupied in the pub, at times I forgot there was anything else of importance. However, I never forgot my family. I rang home whenever I could and I attempted to make a call at least weekly. We are a close loving family and I loved hearing mum, dad and my sister's voice but I found it incredibly difficult to explain what we were experiencing in our busy lives, how hard we were working and how exciting and stressful it was. Therefore I couldn't wait for my parent's first visit.

We were incredibly busy during our first months at the pub and immediately needed help. Leonie's brother Warren helped during our first week and the rodeo but we needed more permanent assistance. Phil mentioned a family friend was enquiring about working in the pub and we jumped at the opportunity. A young fresh faced lad, Grant Wood, arrived from Adelaide and immediately commenced work as our yardman, barman and general helper.

Grant quickly became our most valuable asset. He arose early without fail and completed his tasks with enthusiasm and care. His ever-present smile and happy blue eyes were a blessing and welcomed by everyone.

The cavalry in the form of my mum and dad, finally came to Daly Waters in late 1986 and oh boy, we needed their help. It was my father's first time back since he stayed overnight on his working trip in a Bonds Tours bus in 1949. After looking around he said "nothing has changed much really, except the walls in the motel now go to the ceiling. When I was here there was no ceiling at all. The pub has hardly changed though, there's more on the walls but in essence it's the same layout and it is how it should stay forever". It was so good to see them, I couldn't wipe the smile from my face. That night we enjoyed dinner together for the first time in many months. Later, Dad and I sipped on a few beers and eagerly discussed the many chores we needed done.

The next day, I put mum and dad to work, not that they needed to be pushed. Mum helped Leonie clean and scrub and put many things away we hadn't time to get to. Dad, who was originally a sign-writer, did exactly that. He skilfully re-painted our two huge signs on the main road, the same signs Phil and I poorly painted a few months before. Dad also made new signs for the donkey hot water service, toilet signs (Mares and Fillies and Colts and Stallions), Pub Customer Parking and many more.

Some of my dad's signwriting

When we purchased the pub there were little timber stick signs in trees for many miles each way out from the pub declaring "DALY WATERS PUB 20mi" and then "Cold beer 25km" and then "GOOD MEALS 10mi" and so on. Dad decided to repaint them with kilometres on them all and add a few more. I reckoned we became the most signposted pub in the world. Whilst dad was out on the highway, a girl with a blue heeler dog and a pack over her shoulder walked past. She surprised dad and then she shocked him by asking "how far to the pub mate". An incredulous dad, perched high on his ladder, looked at the sign he was nailing to the tree, clearly reading "HISTORIC PUB 5km" and said, "about five kilometres, I'd reckon. I'll be heading back there soon if you need a lift" to which she said "nah mate, its sweet, my bike broke down, I'll walk, I've scored a job there. See ya for a beer later". The girl turned out to be motorcycle riding Annie, a terrific worker and a rough diamond, who became a great friend and valued member of staff.

Annie arrives for work with motorbike, blue heeler and swag

The two large signs dad painted for the highway turned out to be a great investment. Our nearest opposition was the Daly Waters HI-WAY INN, a truck-stop fuel station with a bar and small camping area about ten kilometres away out on the Stuart Highway. It was dubiously named Daly Waters, which I didn't consider it fair as it wasn't in Daly Waters and therefore was trading off our history and name. It became evident quite early the owner Val would do anything to intercept our customers and make them her own. On many occasions tourists drove into the pub saying "so this is the Daly Waters Pub. The lady at the truck-stop convinced us we were at Daly Waters and so we stayed there last night. When we left and saw the little signs in the trees we discovered this incredible Pub. We wish we stayed here". Some others would say "she told us we were at Daly Waters and even told us it was her famous beef and barra BBQ". This happened often enough to cause me to fight against it, so I modified our large signs. Our sign now displayed an additional section below it, reading "CHEAPEST FUEL ON THE TRACK" and showing our price. Val hated this and let it be known this was war but it didn't worry me.

Leonie's parents Jack and Shirley visited us soon after my parents and Jack kindly offered to man the fuel station. Unfortunately for Jack, he arrived at the same time I took the fight to Val and discounted my fuel. If Val lowered her price then I changed our sign and lowered our price and I didn't care if I didn't make anything from fuel. We were a historic Pub and we wanted the tourists to visit and buy drinks, souvenirs and meals. Val selfishly decided fuel wasn't enough for her and tried to take as much of my business as she could ... it was time to fight.

Poor old Jack suddenly went from enjoying a lazy day, reclining in a deck chair in the shade waiting for a car to refill, to being inundated with a line-up of cars and caravans and trucks. He would fill them up and send them into the Pub to pay and to ensure we didn't miss any payments, he'd run across the road and shout to me at the bar "Forty dollars for the guy in the green shirt driving the blue Valiant". I'd write it down and then eventually catch up with the guy in the green shirt and collect the fuel money. It thought it was great fun and business was booming but poor old Jack became so stuffed by the end of the day he rarely stayed up much past dinner.

Leonie's dad Jack, pumping discounted fuel

If the cars stopped arriving for fuel in great numbers, he knew something was amiss, so he'd take a drive to the Hi-Way Inn to check their price. If it was lower than ours he'd let me know and I'd then send Grant to change the price on our signs. We were kept so busy, I was forced to order fuel twice weekly and I considered this was a great problem. The fuel came 300km from Tennant Creek and during one delivery the driver said "Val isn't happy Mark. Be careful of her, she can cause trouble". I didn't care. I ran a good pub and wasn't going to let a selfish woman, at a truck stop, ruin my pub business.

Val's next attempt to thwart me occurred when a Main Roads manager, who was based in Katherine, came into the

Pub and said I needed to remove all of the signs on the highway. I knew this guy well and I liked him. He'd already given us a gift of a traffic light, which was eventually installed in front of the pub as a joke and so when I asked him why I needed to remove my signs, he embarrassingly said, "because they're not approved and I have received a complaint about them. Please don't make this any harder for me than it already is". I knew who the complaint came from and I was furious and so I said the signs were simply repaints of the original signs. They had been on the Highway for decades and were installed well before the Hi-Way Inn existed and I wouldn't remove any of them until I saw it in writing … and he'd better be able to show me where it says my signs are not legal. I was fuming.

A week or so later I received a phone call from the Main Roads manager pleading with me to "keep the peace and remove the two large signs". He said I could keep the little tree signs but went on to say I wasn't allowed to display the price of my fuel. I almost leapt down the phone to strangle him, and once again said "show me where it says my signs are not legal and I will comply, but only after every other illegal sign on the Stuart Highway is removed first. Including the two signs owned by the Hi-Way bloody Inn"! And I hung up on him.

That was the last I heard about my signs, as they stayed up but now I created an enemy down the road and stretched my friendship with a government employee I really liked. However, I stood my ground. The historic Pub is what the tourists came to see, not a roadside truck stop with no history, pretending it was the real thing. My feud with Val never ended.

It was wonderful when family visited and so when Grants parents Les and Betty visited the pub in 1987, Les being a gifted artist, drew an amazingly detailed sketch which we had etched onto a copper plate and sold as a quality souvenir table placemat or wall hanging. It can be seen on the preface page.

Grant was always up for a good time or a new adventure and as he worked at the pub for most of the time we were there, he is mentioned many times throughout the book. Grant eventually left to backpack around the world and ended up in Copenhagen where he ran a recording studio, which came as a surprise to me as I didn't know he was into music.

Chapter 14. PROFICIENT IN BEING DIFFERENT

When we purchased the pub, behind the bar was a very large sign reading Daly Waters Pub "ME-AN-YOU" displaying a series of corny but amusing meal names including Steak Samige, Am Buggers, Trane Smash and Bum Nuts on Toast and more. It also read "Credit given to women over 80 accompanied by their mother" and on the left side "We don't serve women, bring your own". For some reason, the tourists found this all extremely amusing and they'd line up to take photos of it. I can't take credit for inventing this ME-AN-YOU idea or for featuring the ME-AN-YOU on our souvenir tea towel, of which we sold many thousand, but very soon after moving in, I wished I could have. The previous publican who came up with the idea read the tourist market spot on, as the souvenirs offered were all very popular.

The pub sold four main souvenirs. The tea towel, a teaspoon, a t-shirt and a postcard. The level of sales of these items amazed me and by the end of 1986 stocks of all of them were getting low. The lead in time from ordering to receiving the tea towels and spoons was so long, three months, we negotiated pricing and quantities for the 1987 season late in 1986. The order numbers sounded mind boggling to us then, and it still does today. Our first order was for 10,000 tea towels, 2,000 teaspoons and 10,000 postcards. We also ordered 1,000 t-shirts and 1,000 singlets per order to be made locally in Darwin. Incredible numbers for a little outback pub and it didn't take long for us to realise the order wasn't big enough.

Daly Waters Pub postcard circa 1986

We sold the shirts for $15 each, the spoons for $5 and tea towels were $5 each or 3 for $10 and they all walked out the door. The postcards were 50c each and the Daly Waters post-box was full of them every day. The number of multi tea towel sales to individuals was amazing but none more so than the lady who hopped off a tourist coach one day, immediately marched into the bar and asked for our best price for thirty-six tea towels. I asked her if she was ordering for the entire coach to which she replied, "them, no way, they can get their own." So I asked if she was buying them for friends at home and she replied, "no way, they can get their own too!" My next, obvious, question was "then what do you want thirty-six tea towels for"? She immediately responded with "last year a friend gave me one of them as a present and I love it so much I'm going to make curtains for my kitchen out of them. The only reason I came all this way on that rotten coach was to get my curtain tea towels".

Late in 1987, our souvenir supplier told me we were the highest seller of souvenir tea towels in Australia and one of the biggest seller of teaspoons. I never wanted THAT honour. I hoped it would be for selling the most beer or rum, not a bloody tea towel and therefore it wasn't a record I was proud of ... at the time.

The incredibly popular Daly Waters Pub souvenir tea-towel.

In the Territory, you could find most eastern Australian beers but if you asked for it by name the chances are the bar staff wouldn't know what you were talking about. You didn't order a beer in the NT, you ordered a white can (Carlton Draught), a yellow can (XXXX), a red can (Melbourne Bitter), a black can (Swan Lager), a green can (Victoria Bitter) or a blue can (Fosters) and for takeaways, more correctly travellers, you didn't purchase a carton, it was a box.

If your tastes were a bit fancier you could try ordering a Crown Lager but the chances of any pub having it would have been very slim in the 1980's. A common tourist misconception in the Territory was all Territorians drank NT Draught beer from the famous 2 litre Darwin Stubbies but in my time I never ever saw a local drink a Darwin stubby. However, I did witness many tourists purchase a Darwin stubby in the bar and attempt to scull it. In 1988 a Brahman bull named Norman won the Humpty Doo Hotel Darwin Stubby Sculling Championship in a world record 47 seconds. Norman's win was widely publicised on TV and caused huge interest around the world. After he won, we were selling a pallet of Darwin Stubbies every couple of weeks but none to locals. The best time I saw a human scull a Darwin Stubby was a couple of minutes. It seemed to me the biggest problem was the huge size of the beer and the relatively small size of a human stomach ... the stomach is simply too small. The story goes Norman polished off a few pies and a six pack after he set his world record. I suppose it's the advantage of having four stomachs.

At one stage the story went around suggesting Darwin Stubbies made people sick and the beer was inferior. Word quickly spread around the Territory caravan parks as we heard the same story almost daily and our Darwin Stubby sales fell considerably. It was my belief the reason some people became sick was, in most cases, they were taken home and put on a bar or mantelpiece for many years and then if they were opened, years after they were purchased, the beer would be off and it was no wonder the drinker may become sick. Very early on I decided to discount Darwin Stubbies with the aim to lead the Track in sales. Most pubs were selling them for $12 to $15 each and so we sold them for $9.95. We were paying about $7.50 for them so we still earned a bit of profit, but more importantly, I saw it as a talking point and attraction for the caravan and coach tourists. This strategy worked a treat as the coach drivers and hostesses told their guests "don't buy your Darwin Stubby until you get to Daly Waters Pub, they're the cheapest". From then, we started ordering Darwin Stubbies by the pallet load.

At Daly Waters Pub we also sold a canned beer named Red Centre Lager. It was introduced into the NT to capture some of the tourist market and it featured a red Ayers Rock on the front. Some visitors started asking for it and so when

I placed my next order with the brewery in Darwin the brewery representative said, "you know it's made in Adelaide don't you". I said, "no, why would it bother me". The guy on the other end of the line responded, "no-one drinks beer from South Australia up here mate". I wanted to argue with his comment but pushed on and ordered twenty boxes to which he responded, "errrr, must be a bad line, did you say twenty cartons"? "Sure did mate and next week I hope it'll be more" I replied.

After the stock arrived I put one can behind the bar next to the other cans displaying what we sold and waited. It didn't take long before someone asked about the can and added, "hey mate, where's it brewed"? I thought quickly, so I responded "just south of Alice Springs mate" and he was happy. He didn't hear me add, under my breath, "in Adelaide". Red Centre Lager cans soon became a tourist hit and we struggled to keep up with sales. I reckon most eventually sat on mantelpieces and would never have been opened, just like most Darwin Stubbies but I had the last word with our rep when I rang with my order about a month later and finished the order with "oh, I almost forgot, you'd better send a pallet of the Red Centre Lager. Yeh, a pallet". I was greeted with stunned silence at the other end before he finally said "I need to tell you, Mark, you sell more Red Centre Lager than anyone else in the Northern Territory. I don't know how you do it"? Finally I was famous for selling more of something, than tea-towels.

We sold wine. In fact, we sold plenty of wine. And just like beer, it came in a box. Well, most of it.

Out of respect for our location, the only casks we sold were Coolabah Casks to honour the Eucalyptus Coolabah tree, very common in our area. Well, it's not really the reason but it made a good story to tell our patrons and we sold heaps of Coolabah wine. It was the only red wine and white (sweet and dry) wine we poured by the glass and the tourists loved it.

The aboriginal manager of Wave Hill cattle station would come in regularly and load up his ute with Coolabah Casks, sometimes leaving me with only just enough to get through until the next order. I liked the Wave Hill manager. He was always well-dressed and talked nicely to me. As I helped him load his ute one day I asked him "mate, you have to drive past three pubs to get here, why not buy it from them"? He responded "ahhh, good question young fella. I like THIS pub mate" and then, as he jumped into his ute, he gave a wink and added, "plus at ten bucks, it's cheaper here". Later on, I found out the manager of the Top Springs Hotel, the closest pub to Wave Hill Station, sold the wine casks to tourists for $15 but to the aborigines off Wave Hill Station for $25 and more. I hated hearing that, as everyone was an equal to me. We sold casks for ten bucks to everyone, so no wonder he drove to our pub to fill the ute.

We also sold bottled wine but the only wine we sold by the bottle was Wolf Blass Red Label white wine or red. There wasn't much demand for bottled wine in the bush and to be honest, the staff Leonie and I probably ... no definitely ... drank more of this wine than we sold. However, whenever a patron came up to the bar and asked "can I see the wine list" I'd turn around, grab the display bottle of Wolf Blass and say "here's the wine mate" and then I'd put the bottle on a slight lean to the left and add "and now it's listing". It always received a laugh and we sold a fair share of wine through that bit of fun. The wine list enquirer would sometimes buy a bottle and then go outside and tell their friends to "go and check out the wine list". A second or third sale could be generated from another bit of Daly Waters Pub humour.

Being a territory pub we sold heaps of Bundaberg (Bundy) Rum. Bundy is generally mixed with ice and Coke but is also consumed as a chaser with a beer and sometimes in a shot glass to be sculled. At our first rodeo, we poured forty-eight flagons of rum into plastic cups for the jackaroos in four days. Lifting a two litre flagon of rum sixty-six times to pour sixty-six measures of rum was bloody hard work. Midway through 1987 a young station hand from Renner Springs cattle station, about two hundred and fifty kilometres south of Daly Waters, occasionally frequented the pub on his day off. His name was Darryl Price and he was a good lad. Darryl eventually asked me for a job and as I liked him, I agreed to take him on. Darryl worked well and loved the old pub. Darryl wasn't a very good morning person and loved working late nights, so whenever I could grab an early night and I would let him close up. One morning I came into the bar and it was a big mess, it must have been a big night. I went about cleaning it and getting ready for the day's trade when I heard snoring coming from under the bar. I pulled back the bar curtain to find Darryl asleep on the bar-runners on a shelf under the bar with a half full VB can next to him. I poured him a glass of Berocca and took a photo.

A week later a story appeared in the Northern Territory Times "Darryl to keep off the grog – or else". I wonder how they got hold of that little bit of Daly Waters Pub news?

Darryl slowly coming to his senses after a long night behind the bar

One day Darryl and I were talking about the upcoming Daly Waters Rodeo and I mentioned the huge amount of rum we sold and how hard it was to pour from the flagons and he said "I reckon I've have the solution. We use it at B&S Balls in NSW. Leave it to me." I possessed no idea of what he was on about. I didn't even know what a B&S Ball was until he told me it was a Batchelor and Spinsters Ball. In reality a B&S was a huge party held by farmers where all the girls and lads dressed in their finest suits and dresses and danced and drank all night. A couple of weeks later I was working in the bar and in came Darryl wearing a

157

plastic looking backpack and holding a handgun of sorts. I said "what the hell is that thing mate"? He replied, "THIS is the answer to our rodeo Bundy problems". I was still none the wiser and said "I need more info Darryl". So he said "okay, it's a sheep drench gun. It's used to squirt a precise measure of medicine down the throat of sheep. In our case, we simply fill the tank on my back with Bundy and set the handgun to pour a full nip, squeeze the trigger with the gun in a glass and Bob's your uncle" and then he demonstrated it. I couldn't believe my eyes. It was sensational and it not only worked but we became the talk of the territory 1987 rodeo weekend. Jackaroos loved the fun and theatre of it and many would drop a five dollar note onto the bar and ask for the shot to be directly squirted into their gaping mouth. We sold a record amount of Bundy at the 1987 rodeo weekend, mainly due to Darryl's brilliant idea.

Darryl serving Territory legend Ronnie Ogilvie at the
rodeo

Footnote: In 1987 a young Dutch girl Andrea started
working at the Pub. Andrea was a wonderful help to
Leonie and became a great friend to all of us. Darryl and
Andrea fell in love, eventually married and now live in
Queensland with their two children.

Before we purchased the pub, Bill and Ruth regularly
cooked a weekend BBQ. They cooked BBQ steak and
baked barramundi in an oven in the kitchen. The customers
served themselves with salad and a potato bake in a dining
room out the back of the hotel. It was a good meal and
attracted a few of the local station people plus some
tourists but in the Territory the word "weekend" means
nothing. Tourists don't travel with days in mind and bush
Territorians don't work a Monday to Friday week. It

seemed obvious, to be successful, we needed to create a signature meal, to attract the widespread attention of locals and tourists and it needed to be available every night during the dry season.

So as we became busier, the need for a signature meal became more urgent. I came up with our signature dish the "famous BEEF and BARRA BBQ". Patrons could order a steak, a barra or a half steak with a half barra. Every steak was cooked to order (i.e. well done, medium etc.) and every piece of fish cooked on the BBQ as it was ordered. No ovens, no microwave, no pre-cooked and no fatty chips. We were sourcing excellent King Island rump steak from our good supplier Sourey's in Darwin and our barra from Ken Oliver in Borroloola.

Phil and Grant's constructed the wonderful "bough shed beer garden" and we installed a long half grill, half plate BBQ with a big side table for displaying the salads. We designed this area for coach lunch use during the day and BBQ use at night. The outdoor area could comfortably seat about 100 people and regularly held heaps more.

The steak arrived as whole rumps and the fish as whole fillets, so Leonie would spend a couple of hours each day preparing sufficient portions for the BBQ. She also spent time with the girls preparing the beautiful dinner salads.

This was in addition to serving the coach lunches when the girls fed fifty to one hundred people every day as well as bar meals. Those girls worked so hard in very cramped conditions. They were amazing.

Throughout each day the tourists would arrive at the hotel and we'd tell them about our Beef and Barra BBQ and encourage them to stay and book in for dinner. As they booked we would tell them what time they would be eating. I could cook about 25 meals at a time so the first 25 orders came out at 6pm. The next 25 at 6.30, the next 25 at 7pm and so on until everyone was fed. By the middle of 1987, I was cooking until 9.30pm and we were doing about 120 to 150 meals per night. Leonie would hand out the plastic plates as I called out the names. I'd then put their Beef and Barra on their plate and they would help themselves to salads. It went like clockwork ... but it was damn hard work. I cooked pretty much every night and Leonie prepared the dinners and helped me every night. By the end of 1987, we were very tired. We should have employed someone else to do it ... but we knew part of the success was because we were both out there with the customers. It took years for us to understand you can't do everything.

It became an incredible success story for us and the pub. What made it all the more incredible was we served the meals on plastic plates with plastic knives and forks. Some diners would exclaim "I'll never cut my steak with that knife" but it was rare anyone came back to complain. The steak was so tender the knife fell through it.

I am seen here hard at work cooking the Beef and Barra BBQ.

(Maybe Leonie should have washed my apron)

The BBQ became so famous, through word of mouth from the thousands of caravan tourists, it spread like wildfire. Each night our diners would be camped somewhere around Australia telling anyone who would listen about the historic Daly Waters Pub and its famous

Beef and Barra BBQ. Business boomed and even a UK journalist dropped in and wrote an article about the pub, for The Times of London.

Pub with plenty of cheer

Drawing: BRIOD COLE-ADAMS

THERE is nothing more Australian than a bush pub and the one at Daly Waters is a beauty. Apart from cold beer in a hot spot, it offers original outback architecture, a crowded history and a unique opportunity to conduct official banking business across a bar.

Daly Waters, 600 kilometres south of Darwin and 400 kilometres north of Tennant Creek, just off the Stuart Highway, has six houses and 17 permanent residents (there were only 12 until recently when a family of five moved in, creating a population explosion). The pub is the heart of the place. When Mark and Leonie Venables took it over a couple of years ago, they found they had also acquired the motel, the caravan park, the bush store and the petrol station. Mark is responsible for running the local power station and is the agent for Telecom, the Commonwealth Bank, Australia Post and the Bureau of Meteorology.

Fate has brought remarkable people to Daly Waters. Long before the bitumen came this way explorers and cattlemen, pioneers of the overland telegraph and pioneers of aviation, Lady Louis Mountbatten and pianist Arthur Rubenstein, Australian nurses and American bomber pilots had all passed through this unlikely outpost in the remote heart of a dry continent.

The first white man known to have set eyes on the place was John McDouall Stuart in 1862, who named it after the then Governor of South Australia, Sir Dominic Daly. There is still a true trunk with an "S" cut into it not far from the pub. Bushmen say it was probably done by one of Stuart's party, but not by the great explorer himself: the axework is too sloppy. Either way, Stuart was a happy man when he camped here — not just because he found water (there is a creek and, a little further north, a large waterhole called Stuart Swamp) — but because he had at last broken through the dense bend of lancewood scrub that had frustrated his earlier efforts to cross Australia from south to north.

WITHIN a few years, telegraph linesmen were following in Stuart's footsteps. An overland telegraph station was built at Daly Waters in 1872. For a time, the line from the south reached only as far as Tennant Creek so a pony express was organised: messages from the outside world were tapped out to Daly Waters and horsemen raced south to Tennant Creek where they were relayed on to Adelaide.

A Western Australian expedition seeking traces of the lost explorer Ludwig Leichardt might have perished in the desert had it not been for the telegraph line and Daly Waters. The party was harassed by hostile Aborigines and desperately short of water 300 kilometres west of the newly established line. One of its members, Alexander Forrest, set out to seek help, came upon the line and followed it to Daly Waters where a rescue party was organised.

It was during this period that overlanders from Queensland began moving vast herds of cattle into the Northern Territory and, later, the Kimberley. Daly

Waters was a crossroads when the roads were the roughest of tracks. Just when someone first set up a tavern of sorts is uncertain, but Mark Venable believes a licence to sell booze to drovers was issued in 1893. The present Daly Waters pub was constructed by Mr and Mrs Bill Pearce, who arrived here in about 1930. Their story is told in Elizabeth George's book, 'Two at Daly Waters', a minor bush classic which is now, alas, out of print.

Bill Pearce had worked for years in the territory at a mine in a place called Marranboy, further north. When he decided to make a new start at Daly Waters he brought with him Marranboy Cyprus pine that he had cut and dressed, for he knew it was the one timber that the voracious white ants would not touch. The Cyprus and corrugated-iron building is still much as it was in the Pearce's day: no glass in the windows, just flywire, which is all that is needed in these parts.

The Pearces had a hard time of it for a few years. He earned what he could as a bush contractor; she provided meals and refreshment for the occasional passing stranger. Then Daly Waters became the distribution point for a weekly airmail service and Mr Pearce won the contract for refuelling the little plane. The pilot took to spending the night at the Pearce's homecum-store. It was a small beginning to events which were to put them on the world's maps.

When Qantas launched its first Brisbane to Singapore international service in 1934, Daly Waters became a refuelling point (Lady Mountbatten was the first passenger). Soon the little public house in the scrub was part of a rapidly expanding air network of internal and overseas services. Almost everyone who visited Australia by air during the 1930s came via Daly Waters. Years later, Mrs Pearce recalled the day when Arthur Rubenstein flew in from London at the same time that the violinist Jig-berman arrived on a plane from Perth. The two men, who had last met in Vienna 15 years earlier, were briefly and improbably reunited on a bush airstrip in the middle of the Never Never.

DURING World War II, Daly Waters became an important base for Australian and American warplanes. An RAAF hospital was stationed here after the bombing of Darwin. Most of the evidence of those hectic days has disappeared, but the deserted airfield along which airliners and bombers once rumbled can still be seen, big enough to take a jumbo jet though its tarmac is breaking up. Not far away is the old flying fox which was used during wet season floods to transport Mrs Pearce's formidable scones and pies across the creek that lies between the pub and the airstrip.

With tourism all the go in the territory, the old pub is enjoying a second heyday. Weary of the ersatz "traditional" bush bars that they find in every other roadhouse, travellers with an amazing variety of accents are turning off the highway to find one of the few examples of the real thing. Mark Venable swears he has no intention of tarting the place up, and I can report that the mighty beef and barramundi barbecue over which he presides is of a standard that even Mrs Pearce would approve.

Mind you, I am not sure what the bar which offers credit to any woman over 60 who is accompanied by her mother — or what Bill Pearce would think of the golf course; there is one fairway which you play 18 times.

In Saturday Extra tomorrow Peter Cole-Adams ends his journey at Ayers Rock.

The Daly Waters hotel.

Journey into Australia

PETER COLE-ADAMS

Article by Peter Cole-Adams as it appeared in The Times of London

Unfortunately, the supply of tender steaks didn't last forever. In 1988 our supplier Sourey's was taken over by a large company from Victoria River, who sent us cheaper meat sourced from poorly bred NT cattle. We told them we didn't care what we paid and to send only the best beef they could buy but they kept sending inferior product and so I kept sending the worst cuts back and refused to pay for it … but it kept happening. It caused us stress and sometimes embarrassment. One day, I was so sick of receiving the lower quality meat, I woke before dawn, grabbed the entire order, jumped in the car and drove the six hours to Darwin. On arriving at the butcher, I marched in on the manager, dumped the meat on his table and said "if you reckon this meat is acceptable then you eat it, you prick. I'm finished with you". I then went to a few other meat suppliers until I found the meat we wanted. It came from Beef City Toowoomba and it was great for the rest of the time we were there.

Word of mouth advertising was our friend and the tourists travelling the "track" in their caravans were our best friends. They would move, in all directions, from Daly Waters praising our pub and the Beef and Barra BBQ and telling everyone to "not miss it". We were so lucky to have stumbled across this winning combination.

I still meet people who have just returned from the Daly Waters Pub and almost all of them say "you really need to have the BEEF and BARRA BBQ".

As more coaches brought more tourists to the Territory, even more of them stopped into Daly Waters Pub for a look and a comfort stop and one in two of these coaches stopped for lunch. On some days, two or three coachloads would visit but as we catered for other tourists, as well as the locals, we could only handle two at a time. One day, nine coaches dropped in, plus one hundred visitors in caravans in the campground and twelve guests in the motel. Busy ... you bet we were.

As if Leonie and her girls didn't have enough on their plate with breakfasts, daily counter lunches and motel cleaning, these almost daily coach lunches became quite a burden. The lunch we offered was salads with sliced meats and freshly roasted chicken and dessert for fifty hungry tourists. This entailed the girls preparing all of the salads into serving bowls, cutting the bread, slicing the cold meats and cooking, then dividing up the chickens and preparing a dessert of fresh fruit and cream. It soon became interesting.

Prior to leaving Adelaide, I approached the guy who owned the chicken shop near where we lived and asked him if he would sell his recipe for his chicken skin baste. I asked this because it was hands down the best roast chicken in the world, due primarily to the tasty outside skin. He responded by giving me a small sample and said, "here, take some home and try to work it out". We tasted it at home but there was no chance of working it out, so I returned a week later and said "please sell me the recipe. I'm going to the Territory, it's miles away, and I won't be in competition with you." He still wouldn't sell it to me but he offered to sell me a twenty-litre bucket of the powder and said, "there you go, it should last you forever". Little did he, or I, know how busy we were going to be roasting hundreds of bloody chickens.

I should also explain here, both Phil and I owned newish Weber kettles in Adelaide. We knew there was already one at the pub but we took the punt to take both of ours with us, just in case. In time we found out what a great move we made. We also purchased quite a few of those individual chicken roasting stands with the little meat juice tray built-in. In time we were so glad we did.

Leonie worked out she needed to cook eight chickens to feed a coach load of fifty people and we could only fit four chooks per Weber kettle. If one coach booked for lunch, one of us boys would put the heat beads into two Webers, with the firelighters and get them going at around 10.30am. Leonie would then add the beautifully basted chickens at about 11am to be ready for serving, nice and hot and cut into pieces, at midday or thereabouts. If two coach loads booked for lunch, we needed to get three Webers going and do a second cook ... and so on. The Weber kettle is a magnificent sturdy piece of cooking equipment and our Weber's carried a ten-year warranty but I don't think anyone at Weber expected them to be used every day of the year and sometimes for a few hours each day in the searing Northern Territory heat.

The first signs of a problem with our Webers were the enamel hoods and bases started to blister and the next, most noticeable problem, was the angular legs started to sag near the top where it joined the base of the enamel bowl. We put it down to overuse and heat but we needed those Webers every day, so running repairs to the legs were carried out as needed and the fencer figure-eight knot came in handy again.

One day a big guy came into the pub. We started talking and he said his name was Ross and then he casually mentioned he was from Weber in South Australia. So I took him out the back and showed him our crippled Weber's and asked what he thought. He couldn't believe the state of the Webers he saw and when we told him how much cooking was done, he was amazed. Unfortunately, he didn't agree to replace them under warranty. Those struggling Weber kettles, complete with their wire bandages, managed to survive the next two years of everyday cooking. They were truly amazing to the end and Leonie always received compliments for her roast chooks. Ross should have put his marketing hat on and offered regular replacement Webers. He could then use our old Webers for advertising the durability of a Weber.

As a footnote, when we sold the pub there was only a tiny amount of the chicken baste left, and so it wasn't a lifetime amount but a lifetime at Daly Waters Pub amount.

The fear of a fire was constantly on my mind during our time at Daly Waters and fire arrived in several forms.

THREE STOOGES

In time, we decided we needed to create a larger beer garden to expand the amount of area for patrons. During construction of the bough shed beer-garden, Phil decided he needed some angle iron to use as braces.

Phil came into the bar a day later and asked for a hand next door to hold a ladder. I had no idea what he was doing but off I went with him. Across the side-road from the pub was a decrepit old half demolished building which apparently was a shop many years ago. Phil discovered some angle iron in its roof which he reckoned was perfect for the bracing he required in our beer garden.

He placed a ladder under the roof as well as the oxy-acetylene torch cutter and was ready to go. I stood at the base of the ladder whilst he climbed to the top and perched himself in amongst the rafters. With a click of a lighter, the oxy-cutter started flaming and Phil proceeded to slice through the first angle iron rafter. Anyone who has seen an oxy-cutter in action will appreciate it sends sparks flying in all directions. It's not the place to be if you are below one of these, exactly where I found myself. In a shower of sparks holding a ladder while Phil kept cutting through steel angle iron rafters.

After a few minutes, I thought I heard a strange noise, and so I said, "hey Phil, stop, what's the strange noise". Phil stopped and we heard nothing. So he continued. A few minutes more and again I heard a noise. A louder crackling noise this time and then I smelled something. It took a minute but it dawned on me I could smell burning. "Stop Phil, something's burning". He stopped and we looked around. I wasn't on fire, Phil wasn't on fire and nothing inside the shop was on fire. But the crackling was there and the burning smell became worse. "Shit, its outside" Phil said and out the door, we ran, to be confronted by a wall of flame in the meter high grass heading towards the pub.

This didn't look good. Phil ran for the rear shed and I ran for a garden hose at the pub rear door. I grabbed the hose, turned on the tap and headed for the fire. By now it was about forty metres away from me and about twenty metres from the side of the pub. I ran as fast as I could but just like you'd see in a Three Stooges movie, the hose reached its limit well short of the fire, became taught and as I kept running it flung me on my back.

This really didn't look good now. Phil came running out of the rear shed with two spades and threw one to me. We raced to the fire front and proceeded to keep it away from the hotel by swatting the fire out with the back of the spade. I don't know how we did it but somehow we managed to keep it away from the wall of the pub.

The fire well underway

Fortunately for us, the wind blew the fire sideways along the side of the pub and out to the rear. It then struck me we were burning Roy Beebe's grazing country and there was nothing to stop it. So with Grant helping now, we headed into the scrub and patted out as much fire as we could. Fortunately again for us, the land to the rear of the pub was salty and poor and didn't support grasses very well and therefore the fire burnt itself out within an hour or so.

We all wandered back into the hotel very relieved, dirty and thirsty after the ordeal and within an hour, Phil was back into the roof removing angle iron.

Roy Beebe wandered into the bar a day or two later and said to me "I hear you caused a bit of a scare Mark. You know it could have burnt the whole way to Katherine, don't you". "Yes Roy, I'm really sorry ..." I replied but he shook his head and said "shit happens ... but it would be best if you didn't let THAT SHIT happen again" and he was off. I reckoned it was a light let off, for such as stupid mistake and I know any of his lads would have been instantly dismissed, if it was them who started the fire.

FIRE ENGINE

It was late on afternoon in the pub, when the lights flickered on and off several times, before settling down. From experience, I knew there was a problem at the power station and so I jumped in the Ute and drove down there, at speed.

When I arrived, to the power station yard, everything appeared in order. However, when I opened the large steel door and entered the big generator shed, I was confronted by a huge fire and smoke billowing from the first generator motor. I immediately knew it could only have just started, as the room wasn't filled with smoke and the engines weren't flooded, as yet.

The generator on fire was revving high and was out of control. It was revving so high, I thought it was going to blow up. I also noticed the second generator switched on automatically and was taking the load of the town supply. Therefore the revving motor was not under load and this, along with the fire heating the turbo charger and injectors, was causing it to go into "over-speed". This was potentially a dangerous situation, unless bought under control.

I went to the control board and turned off the problem motor but it continued to run and over-rev. I then grabbed a huge fire extinguisher, housed on a nearby trolley and pointed it toward the motor. Within about ten seconds the fire was out and I was able to see the cause. The motor kept over-revving as a spout of diesel fuel spurted high into the air, from a broken fuel line and then came back down, directly onto the blue-hot turbo-charger. Within a minute it caught fire again. Again, I sprayed the fire extinguisher over the fire and again it went out. But I wasn't getting anywhere as I couldn't work out how to turn the revving motor off and it caught fire again.

I should point out, the noise in the shed, at this stage, was unbelievable. Each of these huge diesel motors was the size of a car and individually, each made a racket but with one of them spinning way above normal revs, it was horrendously loud.

I then remembered each motor was fitted with a diesel shut-off valve. I used it when I regularly serviced the motors and changed the diesel filters. So I put the fire out for the third time and reached to the tap on the end of the motor and turned it off ... but the bloody motor took forever to run out of fuel. I couldn't believe how long it took and at one stage wondered if I turned the tap the right way ... it's a strange thing but in stressful times, many negatives race through your mind, as you process all angles and look for solutions.

Finally the motor stopped and some semblance of peace was restored. Parts of the motor were blue-hot and it groaned and creaked as it slowly cooled down. It was so hot, I could hear the oil in the motor boiling. Fortunately, the whole shed didn't burn down, as its two generators were the only source of electricity for the town. And as fortunate, the back-up generator was of similar power and could easily handle the load until the Northern Territory

Electrical Commission mechanics could get to Daly Waters and fix the broken motor.

We experienced many problems, with the generators and the power system, over the years. Problems from fruit bats welding themselves to the overhead electricity wires and arcing the system out, to lightning hitting the wires and motors stopping for "no reason". But the payment from NTEC to maintain the system and read the meters was a welcome "wage" and as we were always in town, we were always available to attend to the problems.

WHEN A FIRE ISN'T A FIRE

It was a seemingly normal busy late afternoon in the Daly Waters Pub before a Britz Hire campervan raced into town and a hippy looking couple ran into the bar shouting in a broad English Midlands accent "there's a fire ... a fire out on the highway. It started like magic right in front of our eyes! We've tried putting it out with our blankets but it's taken off. You have to call the fire brigade"! Now whilst this wasn't a common occurrence we witnessed this behaviour before and we certainly saw it at again. As I tried to calm the Pommies down I explained "the Government sets fire to the Northern Territory each year. Oh yes, they do it on purpose. Oh yes, sometimes right

175

next to the road and well yes, it might appear dangerous to you but aborigines have been setting the outback alight for thousands of years and we have continued the role. Why … mmm, well, if we didn't then one lightning fire could burn the entire Northern Territory. Yes, it does go out. How, well the fires are set in the afternoon and the coolness of the night and early morning generally puts them out. No, the fires are set by government men in aircraft not by wild aborigines anymore. In fact, the team that set your fire are staying here in our caravan park and in about an hour they'll be back and you can meet them. They may even buy you a beer."

That evening the four NT Bushfire Council employees drove into town, having left their aircraft at the airstrip and after getting it ready for the next day's flying. These guys stayed with us each year. They'd put up a big tarpaulin between trees at the far end of the caravan park and set out their swags and equipment. During the day they drove to the previous day's burning line to ensure the fire was out and to ensure it covered the area they'd planned. From the ground, they would reset fire to any areas it missed and they'd extinguish any smouldering areas and spot fires. In the afternoon they'd prepare the incendiaries and take to the air in the late afternoon.

The incendiaries were small, bulb-shaped objects containing, from memory, phosphorus and water in separate sections. The idea was the plane flew along a predesignated straight line and at regular timed intervals, an incendiary was dropped in a pipe penetrating the floor of the aircraft. When the incendiary hit the ground the phosphorous would mix with the water and a chemical reaction would cause it to instantly ignite, thereby causing a small grass fire. This fire would slowly spread and a combination of timing and wind would hopefully cause the small fires to join together before the dew of the night put them out. This line of burnt fire-breaks, crisscrossing the Northern Territory in a large grid, was designed to stop a wild fire from spreading too far. Sounded good in theory and generally worked in practice, however sometimes the Stuart Highway cut through the firing line and some hapless tourist, unaware of the cause or aim of the fire, would attempt to put it out. In the process endangering their lives and generally burning their belongings without extinguishing the fire. Normally a local would come across the frenzied activity and set them right. And sometimes they did their best to put it out. It appeared obvious to me the fire that started "like magic" in front of these tourists' eyes was caused by an incendiary dropped by our bushfire team.

That evening the NT bushfire team met the Pommy tourists in the bar and shouted them as many beers as they could drink. The next day those two Pommies left with a great story to tell their mates back in the UK as well as a monumental Daly Waters Pub hangover ... all at no charge, if you don't include the two burned blankets.

Chapter 16. PULLING YOUR LEG

When you walked into the bar you stopped to take it all in. It was unavoidable as hardly a section of the walls or bar front was without some form of interesting article glued, pinned, nailed, screwed, drawn or hung from them.

One day in the middle of a ferociously hot spell, when the temperature reached 50 degree Celsius according to the welders from the NT Gas pipeline, who knocked off early and came in for a cooling beer, I decided we might be able to relieve some of the heat in the bar by removing the ceiling access panel above the bar.

These welders were an interesting group. Some would arrive from Darwin in a chauffeured car. They were always well dressed and sometimes one of them would be in a suit. They'd wait at the pub to be picked up by someone from the workers camp thirty kilometres away and then we wouldn't see them until the end of their work stint in a week or two when they'd be dropped at the pub and get collected to be taken back to Darwin. I was told these guys were the best welders in the world and they flew first class around the world being paid a huge wage for their skills. Apparently, they were so skilful they could weld a fully gassed pipeline. I suppose you'd only ever make one mistake.

So back to the ceiling panel, I clambered up on top of the fridge and stood on top of the inoperable till and pushed the panel up and into the roof. As soon as I did this, a blow of hot air came up from the bar and into the roof space. The roof space was cross ventilated with louvres and the relief was immediate. It was like turning an exhaust fan on. While I was up there I hoisted myself up and into the roof space to see if there was anything interesting to find. And so there I was looking around whilst sitting on the opening with my legs dangling through the hole when a customer came into the bar. He couldn't see anyone behind the bar and the welders didn't say anything to him. He suddenly saw something move above the bar. All I heard was "JESUS CHRIST what's that" whereby one of the welders quickly responded with "oh it's just the publican, he's been up there for days. We send him up a Bundy every now and then".

I climbed down to serve the tourist and everyone had a huge laugh when the chap said "mate, I saw the legs move and it scared the living daylights out of me. I thought you were a ghost or something".

It gave me an idea. So a bit later I grabbed an old pair of my jeans, some socks and a pair of my shoes. I stuffed them with paper and rags and made them look like a real pair of legs. I then climbed up to the opening and moulded them to look like someone was lying in the ceiling with their legs dangling through the opening. Someone suggested I put a rum flagon up there and so with an old empty flagon half full of tea the job was complete. Almost.

I remembered he said, "when the legs moved it scared the shit out of him". I needed to be able to move the legs. So I found some light fishing line and climbed back up. I tied one end around the ankle of one of the legs and fed the other end across to a beam and then down to the wall next to the till. A slight pull on the line and the leg swayed forward and backward in a lifelike motion.

The drunken electrician's legs with a flagon of Bundy and Fosters

So from then on if we thought to do it when one of us went to the till we would give the line a tug without the customers knowing. The results were hilarious. Someone would generally see a leg move and gasp. They'd tell others but the leg would be still. We'd let them think they were dreaming and then we'd give it another tug. In the end, the whole bar would be laughing and in stitches. Photos would be taken and we would tell the story of a drunken electrician who went up there on a job and has never come down. And I'm not pulling your leg.

Chapter 17. PUB PETS

When we arrived at Daly Waters we doubled the animal population overnight and in time it would increase even more. Leonie and I bought with us from Adelaide in the car, "Max" the cat, our two Bourke parrots "Burke and Wills" plus two cockatiels. It made for an interesting 2,400km drive in our VW Combi van. Max initially thought his luck changed, with parrot dinner sitting next to him on the back seat but the parrots took a nip at his nose, very early on and any potential problems ceased. Phil and Toni also bought their dog to keep everyone in line.

MAD MAX

Initially, we wanted Max as a companion for Leonie, whilst I was constantly surveying in the bush. Maybe Max was our substitute child, as we "forgot" to have our own children. Max was a beautiful Chinchilla kitten and grew up to be an intelligent and loving companion for both of us. Max readily accepted being on a lead and would follow like a well-trained dog. He travelled well and would sit on top of the back seat taking it all in. Max rarely complained about anything and was the most adaptable pet I've ever seen. In his sixteen years, he lived with us in six houses, three pubs, an oyster farm, a prawn farm, two bush dongas, a caravan and two apartments.

Max stayed inside the house for the first month at Daly Waters but, whilst he was inside, he sat at the front window looking at the action in and around the pub. When we eventually started bringing him over the road to the pub he was already quite accustomed to seeing plenty of cars, coaches, animals and people. We started him on a lead in the beer garden and then took the lead off. He never wandered away and most days he'd follow Leonie around from the kitchen to the motel and then he'd take a break on a table in the beer garden, or his stool in the bar under a fan, where he enjoyed the constant attention and petting by locals, tourists and staff.

Max on his stool in the bar on Christmas Day 1987

Dogs would come into the beer garden on a daily basis and, as Max rarely spent time with dogs, we were very surprised to see Max stand his ground by arching his back and hissing at the dog until it backed away. It was only on rare occasions the bluff didn't work and when it happened Max would leap vertically and scamper up the lancewood posts to a position of strength above the invading dog.

Max did have a compulsion to chase any large insect or reptile and it concerned us. He'd regularly come to the kitchen door with a lizard to show off to Leonie and we were very worried one day it would be a snake. Fortunately, we never saw him grab a snake but on one occasion we dragged him away from the tail of a huge Territory centipede as it slithered through the beer garden with Max in close pursuit.

DALY and NUTWOOD

One day a loud and dirty old Holden station wagon with no exhaust pulled up in front of the pub and in came an aboriginal couple. They found a female kangaroo out on the highway, hit by a car and she was carrying a little joey in her pouch. The girl opened her cardigan and there was the tiniest little kangaroo I'd ever seen. I called Leonie into the bar and she immediately fell in love with it. They asked if we could care for it and did we want it. Without hesitation, we said yes and they handed it over. To put the size of the joey into perspective I stood it on the bar and it was exactly the height of a green (VB) can.

With no idea how to raise a baby kangaroo, we asked ourselves "should we put it in a box and feed it calf formula and does it need anything special"? We needed help. Quickly.

And then a minor miracle occurred when in the door walked a bloke in a khaki uniform. He saw the little kangaroo on the bar and immediately wandered over and introduced himself as Jeff Angel (absolutely true) and he was a Northern Territory Wildlife Officer. Jeff really was an angel as you will read.

Jeff was full of advice and said we needed to act immediately to keep the little joey alive or he wouldn't make it through the night. He asked if we could find a small pillow case or something similar, so Leonie ran into the office and came out with a calico bank bag. Imagine a white calico bag about the size of a small ladies handbag. Jeff held it in front of the joey who was still standing in the bar. The joey immediately stuck its head inside the bags opening and in one movement dived inside, did a shuffle and roll and turned itself over. We peered in the bag and the joey was already comfortable and closing its eyes.

Jeff told Leonie to hold the bag with the opening at the top and said "I don't suppose you have any calf formula or evaporated milk" and was stunned when we said we have both. "Okay you'll need to use them in a day or so but for now the little fella, yes it's a boy, is in shock and needs a little bit of tepid water. Boil some water and then cool it down to tepid and feed him through an eye-dropper. Do you have an eye-dropper? Okay great, then let's not stuff around, get the water and dropper". Jeff held Daly close and said to keep him warm at all times and the best way is to wrap the bag in a woollen blanket. And keep him dark and quiet after a little feed of the water.

We put all the requirements together, wrapped him up and then Jeff showed us how to drop feed him with the eye dropper. We opened the bag and put the dropper to his mouth. His tiny little mouth could hardly open enough for the tiny plastic teat but it worked and he took a little water before falling asleep during the feed. We then wrapped him up and Leonie said "Daly". "What", I said. "His name is going to be Daly". We took Daly into our office and hung the bag from the back of the office chair in a blanket.

Jeff needed to leave, so he left us with instructions and added "I'm sorry to tell you this but he probably won't make it. He has no hair, and those ones rarely survive the shock. I'm heading to Borroloola and will be back in a few days. If he's still alive I'll talk you through the next months of Daly's life. Good luck. You won't be getting much sleep".

That night after we closed the pub we took Daly to our bedroom and we shared a night with Daly the kangaroo and Max the cat. Daly needed feeding every four hours, entailing boiling water then adding formula and evaporated milk and then letting it cool to body temperature then dripping it into his tiny mouth. Max was intrigued and maybe a little jealous of this new competitor but in typical Max style he put up with it.

When we woke the next day Daly was still alive and in fact, he was quite energetic. He downed his formula quickly and immediately fell back to sleep. This happened every four hours and exactly the same each time. Eagerly accept the dropper and then fall asleep. For three days we were on alert he might go backwards. But he didn't, he thrived. His eyes grew wider and brighter and on the third or fourth day Leonie raced into the bar and said, "you need to come and see this". We hurried into the office and there was the bag hanging from the chair and there was Daly's head peering from his "pouch" in anticipation of a feed. It was incredible and we were both in tears of joy.

Jeff came back into town on about the fifth or sixth day and he couldn't believe what he saw when Leonie carried the bag into the bar with Daly's head protruding out the top, just like you'd see a Joey with his head poking out of mums pouch. Jeff thought little Daly was going to survive. There was every chance of Daly getting diarrhoea or a cold and either could kill him but the worst was over. Jeff needed to leave us once again, so he gave more feeding advice including feed him about 10% of his body weight each feed if he wants it and said he'd be back again in a month or so.

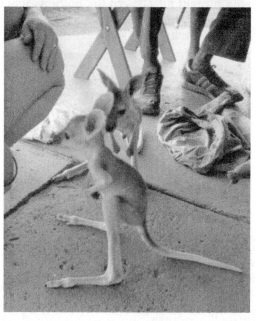

190

Daly in the top photo and Daly with tiny little Nutwood in the foreground in the bottom photo.

The next few weeks went really well for little Daly. He grew in height and weight and quickly grew a covering of soft hair. His daily schedule of drink and sleep didn't alter much but his eagerness grew and his anticipation for each feed meant he woke earlier and earlier. He shared the office with Leonie and would sit for hours waiting for her and then watch her every move. Leonie was Daly's new mum and he loved her feeding and cuddling him. Poor Max was moved down the attention order, as was I.

During this time we received another gift of a joey. This joey was bought in by Kalala worker Dallas. He found it near the Nutwood Downs Station turnoff and it was in very poor shape. We named it Nutwood and we tried to keep it alive by following exactly the same procedure as Daly but unfortunately, the poor little fella didn't survive. It was a sad time for all of us.

Jeff came back though a couple of months later and couldn't believe how well Daly was. Daly only experienced one episode of diarrhoea but he was over it quickly. We were accustomed to the four hourly feeds but were relieved when Jeff said we could eliminate the 4am wake-up feed but keep up the rest of the four hourly schedule. When we asked for how long he said, "months, Daly won't go on solids until about six months or nine months of age". We gasped "how many months"?

We gratefully eliminated the 4am feed but at 7am when Leonie opened the office door the next morning she was greeted by a cold shivering Daly standing on the concrete floor in the middle of the office and giving out a little yap, he repeated until Leonie found the bank bag, which he immediately dived in. A quick feed and he was fast asleep. This would be repeated almost daily until Daly became accustomed to not getting his 4am feed.

Pretty soon Daly outgrew the little calico bank bag and we progressed him to a pillow case. Joeys go to the toilet in the bag and this meant Leonie needed to swap the sleeper, with a freshly washed one every couple of days. The pouch swap was a funny event to witness. Leonie would remove the pillow case from the chair and put it on the floor. Daly would clamber out and do a quick hop around the office before diving into his new case, Leonie held with the opening about 30cm above the ground. Daly would put his head in as if inspecting his new house and then leap in, do a somersault and poke his head out to make sure Leonie was impressed. She'd give him a cuddle and then she'd go back to work.

Daly grew more confident and so we decided to let him out every now and then for a hop around the pub. But his confidence was limited to following Leonie everywhere. If she went outside Daly would follow. Into the bar and in he'd come. Other people didn't bother Daly as long as Leonie was around. Sometimes he'd hop off and forget where she was. You could detect the panic and he'd raise himself up and peer around yapping until he found her or she found him. It was hilarious and the tourists loved it. We found ourselves another tourist attraction.

Daly at about three months of age with me in the bar

At about six months old Daly was a lively excitable bouncy boy kangaroo. He grew to more than 90cm tall and was much steadier on his legs than before. He'd come bounding out the office each day to explore his home until panic would set in and he'd race back to the office and leap into his pouch or he'd find Leonie and nuzzle up to her and get under her feet. By this time the tourist coaches knew about Daly and so each day he would be paraded out into the bar or beer garden by Leonie for everyone to take photos of. He experienced no fear of the tourists and was very well behaved ... until one day a three-year-old boy walked up to Daly near the pub door. Daly and the boy were of similar height and as Daly has never seen a human creature the same height as himself it scared him. So Daly did what nature intended a young kangaroo to do, he lightly bit him on the arm and put his arms around the boy's neck to play whilst playfully thrusting his long legs out in a kicking motion. Young male kangaroos do it in the wild and he was doing it now. Daly didn't know why he did it, nor did he understand why the boy started screaming out so loud and crying. So Daly did the natural thing for an animal, he bit the boy again and took flight. He hopped out the door and into the beer garden and then in panic he raced around looking for Leonie. Daly was eventually found near the pub back door trying to get inside to the sanctuary of the office. Daly was so relieved when Leonie found him and let him in the office he jumped into his pouch and we didn't see him for the rest of the day.

As Daly grew in stature his confidence in outside adventures took him further and further away from the office. His favourite early morning exercise was to do fast laps of the pub. Max the cat would watch Daly with amused fascination and although they never bonded closely each had a healthy respect, touched with fear, of the other. Leonie would let Daly out of the office and feed him with cereal and formula in the beer garden and then Daly would leap into the air, shaking and excited before taking off around the perimeter of the pub building to do his laps. Daly would hop so fast he would forget where he was, so he would have to stop and get his bearings before continuing. When he wandered far enough and was exhausted, he would hop into the bar and come up to the little batwing door at the bar, where he would stop and yap, demanding someone let him in so he could find Leonie and be taken to the office and into his pouch for a sleep.

Daly's exercise routine was viewed by hundreds of tourists and soon became legendary. Tourists would arrive and ask if Daly was awake. We would tell them to be patient and if they were lucky enough they may get to see him. At some stage each morning Daly would come out from the office and into the beer garden to be fed by Leonie. The tourists would stand in a semi-circle and watch and take endless photos. Daly was oblivious to this as he was more interested in his meal. Then he'd take off for his laps and the tourists would come back to the bar for more photos.

Daly taking a "comfort" break when doing a lap of the pub.

One day an American man asked in typical drawl "Goddam, what are you feeding that critter"? Leonie replied "Kellogg's Cornflakes and baby formula". Well, the American was so gob-smacked he excitedly told his wife to "get a photo of me with the little critter" and as he posed next to Daly he said to Leonie "young lady, I am a Senior Vice President of Kellogg's in Michigan, U.S. of A. and when I get home a photo is going to feature in our company newsletter. This kangaroo is gonna be famous". Daly already was.

On many occasions the bar would be full of tourists and Daly would come into view out the front of the pub. Everyone out the front would be taking photos and thinking they were witnessing an amazing and rare event. And they were. I'd ask everyone inside the pub to be quiet and calm and tell them if they were quiet then a kangaroo might come into the bar. This would normally result in "yeh sure mate, who are you trying to kid". What would normally happen next never failed to get oohs and ahhhs and the immediate clicking and flashing of cameras as Daly would hop up to the front door and stop. Then he'd give a yap or two announcing he was "home" and then bound between the legs of the tourists and find his way to the bar's batwing doors. This happened at least once a day for many months and even I never ceased to be amazed at Daly's behaviour.

Daly loved Leonie and even when fully grown he would leap up and into her arms for a cuddle and kiss. But Daly had a distinct dislike for two people he never overcame. One was a cook who helped Leonie in the kitchen. When she applied and was successful in getting the job, over the phone from Darwin, she finished by telling Leonie "I'm a big girl but I do my job". Well, she did her job okay but she didn't endear herself to Daly as on the first day she stood on his tail. Daly took a big bite into her ample calf and bounded outside yapping and very annoyed. She treated the wound with a large bandage and continued with her work but a few hours later Daly came back into the kitchen looking for Leonie, spotted the cook, hopped over, yapped angrily and bit her again. Every day after she would arm herself with a wooden spoon and every time Daly came into the kitchen she held the spoon aloft and declared war. One evening I walked past her caravan, where I found her sitting on the caravan step drinking from a huge jug of Bundy and Coke. I asked how she was going and all she said was "I hate Daly" and very soon after, she left.

Leonie with Daly at about one year old

(He was always preening himself to impress her)

The only other person Daly didn't get on well with was our "Ned Kelly" looking barman and round Australia horseman Steve Nott. We were never sure why Daly disliked Steve, who was a very calm and likeable guy but every time Daly came into the bar when Steve was there Daly would hop over to Steve and attempt to nip him on the leg or bum. We employed another barman Taffy, who looked very much like an outlaw, with his long beard and

Akubra hat. Taffy never suffered to constant attacks Daly inflicted on poor Steve.

During our second Daly Waters rodeo, Leonie spied an aboriginal girl carrying Daly on her shoulder through the beer garden and towards the road. All I heard was Leonie screaming "STOP ... what are you doing ... put my kangaroo down". I ran into the beer garden to hear the girl say "what ya mean your kangaroo. This one mine. Just caught him out the back. Bloody good tucker". This wasn't going to be easy. Here was Leonie screaming at the girl whilst trying to take Daly off the girls shoulder and the girl steadfastly resisting her attempts. Daly wasn't happy and was kicking and yapping and eventually he forced the girl to drop him. As soon as Daly hit the ground he reared up and tried to bite the girl before turning to Leonie and leaping into her arms for protection. There was no denying this was Leonie's kangaroo and both women went their separate ways. The aboriginal girl left in one direction and Leonie went the other ... straight to our house behind the pub where she placed Daly safely inside.

This story has a very funny ending. After we eventually closed the pub we went to our house (we moved from across the road to behind the pub into an Atco donga). When we returned, we discovered Daly standing in the centre of our queen size waterbed. He loudly yapped when he saw Leonie and tried to hop off the bed to go to her. But the waterbed would sink each time he tried to hop and he'd fall on his face, then stand up with a confused look and try again. It was so funny, as tired as we were, we were in hysterics. Leonie picked him up, cuddled him and then grabbed his pillow cover, so he could dive inside. That night there were four in the bedroom. Leonie, me, Max and Daly. Our family.

As Daly grew and grew older he became more adventurous. It was always our intention for Daly to go where he wanted to go. If he left for the wild we would be sad for our loss but happy for him. Daly started venturing further away from the pub and staying away for longer periods. It started with an hour then two or three and then one day he didn't come home. Leonie and I were very sad and thought we may never see him again but the next morning I was serving behind the bar when in the distance I saw Daly hopping down the road towards the pub. As usual, I told everyone to be quiet and they would possibly witness something special. And as usual, Daly hopped to the door, saw me and yapped and came to the batwing doors. Leonie heard the commotion and came running into the bar in tears. Daly came through the doors, made an attempt to bite Steve and leapt into her arms. Daly slept the entire day and next night and didn't come out of his pillow case until the following morning. We're not sure what happened but Daly must have become scared in his first night away from home and the next few days he spent close to the pub and Leonie. But after a few days, he started wandering again and in a few weeks, he enjoyed another night away. This habit grew into two or three nights but he always returned home at some stage. One day our neighbour George came into the pub and told us he saw Daly with some other kangaroos up the road. So now we knew what he was up to. He finally realised he was a kangaroo and not a human.

When we sold, Daly was spending all of his time away from the pub and whilst we missed him, we appreciated he was always meant to be with his mates.

BOOF

Kalala cattle station owner Roy Beebe knew we were animal lovers and so one day he pulled up out the front of the pub and walked in with a baby Brahman calf in his arms for Leonie.

Being a man of few words he explained the mother left the calf after the first feed and therefore the calf should survive but needed calf formula straight away … and off he went. He didn't even ask if we wanted it. Fortunately, we were able to obtain extra formula from the stock inspector and the calf took to it immediately. The little calf took to it so quickly it kept pestering anyone and anyone for a bottle. We named him Boof because his head was too big for his skinny body ... hence "boofhead".

Daly at three months old with his mate Boof in the background at about one month old

We temporarily fenced a small area behind the pub for Boof but much of the time, as he grew, he was free to roam the backyards of the pub and through to the camping ground. Gradually Boof started eating grass but after three months he still had an insatiable desire for formula. We went thru bags of it and he constantly mooed for more. So at this stage, we were caring for a joey and a calf and trying to run a busy hotel. Both Boof and Daly required four hour round the clock feeds and so sleep for us was minimal.

One day Leonie came out the back of the pub to find Boof swallowing a motel bed-sheet that was hanging on the long clothes line minutes before. All I heard was Leonie screaming and cursing as she chased Boof around the yard. Eventually, we caught him and somehow with much effort, we managed to pull the sheet out of his mouth and stomach. Yuk, what a mess. Boof spent the afternoon in his holding yard whilst Grant and Phil built a fence around the clothes line.

The new clothes line kept Boof at bay for a week or so until Leonie went out the back to find Boof fully stretched over the fence with a sheet, blowing in the wind towards him, in his mouth. Once again we retrieved another slobbery sheet. We decided we needed to put Boof off the lure of bed-sheets so we found a couple of old tea towels and soaked them in Tabasco Sauce and draped them over the fence next to the clothes line. We all stood back and watched as Boof came up to the fence, smelled the tea towel and started licking it. He pulled back immediately and shook his head so hard I thought he'd fall over and all the time his long pink tongue was working overtime around his mouth. He backed off and we thought we'd put him off linen for life. But we hadn't as the next day Boof ate both Tabasco infused tea towels. He hated the taste but we think he must have been hooked on linen.

So poor Boof was locked in his small yard whilst we worked out what to do. Unfortunately one day he escaped his yard and when he was being chased away from the inevitable lure of the clothes line he ran past a sharp star dropper and sliced his belly wide open. It was a terribly deep cut and I could see his intestines. Phil ran over to get the local stock inspector Pat Barry who was also an experienced vet. Pat came back with his stitching needle and strong cord and instructed us to grab Boof and lay him on his side with the injury up. After catching Boof and getting him on his side Pat wandered into the yard and proceeded to "sew him up". So you need to picture two men with cowboy hats holding him down and another hatted one pulling a large needle and thick cord through his hide. Boof wasn't at all happy as he stared at Pat with one big sad brown eye wondering what the hell was going on. After Pat finished the sewing, he washed Boof down with some Dettol and salty water and said, "he'll be fine but he won't be friendly with anyone for some time". Pat was

205

completely correct on both counts. Boof recovered almost immediately from the injury but the mental scar lasted longer. Boof would have nothing to do with anyone wearing a cowboy hat for a couple of months. If anyone without a hat walked up to Boof, he would happily run over to them for a pat but if the person put a hat on he would run to the furthest corner of his yard.

Boof at about one month of age, just before the injury

In the following weeks, Boof grew stronger and we knew the clothes line fence wouldn't hold him back any longer. So we moved him to a new larger yard, we constructed just for him, next to the campground. Here the campers could pat him and he could roam. Each day we would let him into the campground for a while to mow the grass and get some exercise amongst the campers. He loved people provided they wore no hat.

One day a young female German camper came running into the bar screaming "your cow is eating our tent". Grant and I went running into the camping area and sure enough, Boof was standing next to a small two man tent with the "fly cover" half way down this throat. It took three of us to remove it with much pulling. I apologised profusely and washed the fly cover as best I could and suggested at least they'd have a great story to tell their friends back in Germany.

Another time and another camper came running into the bar shouting "your calf is eating a power lead and it's still plugged in". Again I raced into the camping ground to find Boof walking along slowly "inhaling" an electrical extension lead and indeed the other end was still plugged in. The first thing I did was turn the power off and then grabbed the lead. At this stage, there were about 3 metres of lead left on the ground. After five minutes of pulling there was a fifteen-metre slobbery power lead laying in front of me. It's amazing he wasn't shocked during his feast.

When we sold the pub Boof was still living in the large yard and thrilling the campers. He still ate the occasional tent and did develop a liking for bread and beer, we allowed the campers to feed him. He loved it and thrived on it and it seemed almost every camper loved him. The children loved feeding him bread and the dads liked giving him a beer and Pat Barry assured us both of them were good for him.

THE BIRDS

We quickly put an aviary up in the beer garden entrance for our birds and they seemed to really enjoy the setting under the Bougainvillea trees. The visitors to the pub enjoyed seeing a bit of "local" wildlife and it added to the whole atmosphere of the pub.

Our little, well-travelled Bourke parrots were named after explorers Burke and Wills. These intrepid explorers were the first white man to cross the country from south to north. Unfortunately the "real" Burke and Wills perished near Innamincka.

Our Bourke parrots, Burke (right) and Wills

It wasn't long before our birds received a new housemate when road train driver Dave pulled up in his truck in front of the pub and discovered an injured owl wedged in the bull-bar, and so he came into the bar with a beautiful barn owl for us to care for. Al, as he was quickly named, settled in quite well and thrived on rump steak leftovers as well as the many insects and lizards running around. Al gave the most incredibly intense stare. He would outstare anyone and everyone and he seemed to know when he won because he'd fluff up his feather and turn away from the loser in disgust. We couldn't put Al in with the other birds though because the main prey for owls is mammals ... and other birds. So Al had his own cage, next to our pets. In the beginning he would stare at them in anticipation of one day getting a feed. It didn't take long however for them all to become mates. One day I caught Al and Burke sitting next to each other at the wire preening each other. Wonders never cease.

Everything went well for a while until we noticed Wills, our pretty little female Bourke parrot, was missing. On closer inspection, we located a "children's" python with a prominent belly bulge in a corner of the cage. It was unable to escape through the wire due to the recently swallowed bird inside it. The snake was easy prey for yardie Grant and I don't know what Grant did with it but fortunately, the snake didn't bother us again. It was a very sad day for Leonie and I. Wills was a lovely little bird and we would miss her. Burke survived his time at Daly Waters and returned to Adelaide with us, giving him the honour of travelling further than his namesake, the explorer Burke.

TWO LITTLE PIGS

Paddy Heatley was a big burly fencing contractor and a regular at the pub who did fencing and yard building for Roy Beebe.

One night Paddy asked us if we'd like a couple of piglets from his property at Larrimah to fatten up. He suggested if we fed them pub leftovers and the outer salad leaves they'd be ready in about four months to eat for Christmas. It sounded like a wonderful idea, who doesn't like roast pork, so we gratefully agreed.

A week later Paddy dropped off two tiny pink piglets. They were about the size of puppies. Phil constructed a small yard out the back with a sleeping hut, water trough and plenty of shade. The piglets were so small I initially thought we'd made the yard far too large but they would change quickly. We decided not to name the piglets to ensure we wouldn't get too attached.

Initially, the piglets were fed on formula and it was fun to do. As soon as we walked towards the pig pen they'd come running as fast as they could to the fence to eagerly suck on the bottle teat, whilst their little tails wagged, and they oinked loudly. The routine of four hourly feeds could have been a chore but, as everyone wanted to have a go, the feeds were rotated amongst ourselves and many times were shared by patrons and tourists. So now we needed to feed a calf, a joey and two piglets.

The piglets grew so quickly it seemed they changed overnight. They progressed from formula to formula mixed with cereal and then cereal with water and then to anything they could get into their mouths.

When we purchased the pub we inherited a store room full of Kellogg's cereals. I found it incredible, there were so many boxes in there. Apparently, a truck rolled on the highway and a section of it was full of Kellogg's cereal boxes. The Henley's drove to the scene and loaded about one hundred boxes into their car, to be used for guest breakfasts. They could have fed a small city with the amount in the store and it was all out of date. So it became pig food and they loved and thrived on it. It wasn't long before they progressed to salad leaves, food waste and pretty much anything we would throw over the fence. In early December we decided it would be a great idea to invite all the locals from town and the nearby stations to the pub for a Christmas Eve Roast Pork dinner.

Phil being a great welder and fabricator made two pit-roasters out of 44 gallon drums cut in half. The legs were made from salvaged steel, stainless earthing rods were used for the spikes and bicycle wheels on the end were added as the pulleys. We scavenged two windscreen wiper motors from old cars left at the dump as the rotisserie motors and by using Telecom rope Phil was able to fabricate two excellent spits. So everything was now in readiness for a magnificent Christmas feast in the Daly Waters Pub, except we needed to butcher the pigs.

We asked local tour operator Andy Hind, who was already invited to the lunch, if he knew how to butcher a pig and he said "bloody oath, done a hundred of 'em out bush. Three days before the lunch I'll come down here to do the job. You need to get a big bath filled with water and a roaring fire underneath it. Get it to boiling and let me know when it's done. Also, you'll need to get the pigs in the garden shed over there the morning before. Put some paper or grass on the ground and make sure they have water but don't feed 'em and let them sleep in there overnight. Okay, understood, see you next week".

So with everything in readiness, the time came to get the pigs in the small tin garden shed. Now, these pigs never been out of their yard and when Phil and I went into the yard the pigs instinctively knew something was wrong. They backed away and then as we ran after them they careered around their yard oinking like never before. We needed a better plan. These pigs were always hungry and so we laid a trail of cereal from the yard to inside the shed and we hid. It didn't take long before they came to the food trail and slowly, cautiously ate and followed it across the dirt and finally into the shed, whereby we raced from our hiding place and slammed the door closed. Now, there were two unhappy pigs who, in their life, never experienced this sort of stress and it was most upsetting to them. For the next hour or more they oinked and oinked and tried smashing their way out of the shed. Fortunately they settled down and by nightfall they almost seemed comfortable. But they were starving and Andy told us not to feed them. So we ignored their pleas for dinner. Our job was done and now it was up to Andy.

The next day Phil and I filled the bath with water and lit a roaring fire underneath. In an hour or so it was ready to boil, so I shouted across the road to Andy, who grabbed his rifle and a big knife, and with "okay let's get it done", we headed for the shed. On the way he grabbed a rope off his fence and threw it over his shoulder. He looked like Wyatt Earp on his way to a hanging.

Andy said he was very happy with the setup as he professionally threw the rope over a branch of the tree near the bath and tied a noose in each end at ground level. He leant the gun against the tree and skilfully threw the knife into the tree like a circus act. I was easily impressed. He then wandered over to the shed and asked Phil to quickly open the door then close it behind him. He then instructed Phil to re-open the door on his command, whilst I peered through a hole in the shed wall.

Andy went in and then started the loudest squealing I've ever heard. The shed started shaking and banging before Andy yelled "NOW"! Phil opened the door and out backwards came Andy dragging a 30kg screaming and kicking pig. As soon as Andy was out he shouted "Shut it quick" as he dragged the squealing pig over to the bath. He then put his leg across its belly, grabbed the rifle, put it to the pigs head then "BLAM" and silence as Andy sliced its neck to bleed the now dead pig.

It was around about then the other pig decided he wasn't hanging around for it to happen to him. Pigs are intelligent animals. It took the pig about one minute to sum it all up and think "I'm out of here" as he started thrashing around in the garden shed. We could clearly hear him crashing into the flimsy tin walls and then "CRASH" and a metal sheet flew off the wall and the pig went racing out the opening and across the dirt at the back of the pub.

As quick as it happened Andy was almost as fast. In a flash, he grabbed the rifle and took off in pursuit. Andy managed to get one shot off as the pig turned left and headed towards the beer garden. I knew this wasn't going well as Andy followed at full speed, and Phil and I followed Andy. The pig went racing thru the beer garden, past a group of about ten tourists sitting having a beer, with Andy rifle raised in pursuit and then us in pursuit of Andy.

At the entry to the camping area, Andy managed to get off another quick shot as the pig decided what way to go. It missed the pig and then the pig was off into the empty camping ground. This was getting out of hand and we screamed at Andy to stop shooting but he was on a mission. We ended up out near the scrub at the back of the camping area and finally, Andy managed to get his gun up against a tree to steady his aim and from a distance of about 100 metres, he dropped the pig with one magnificent head shot. It died instantly.

Then whilst Andy headed back to the first pig, Phil and I carried the dead bleeding pig back from where it fell. It involved coming back through the beer garden where we saw Andy receive a standing ovation and remarks like "hey it's Crocodile Dundee" and "it's the best thing that's happened to us on the holiday". In typical Andy style, he ripped a couple of his tour brochures out of his back pocket, rolled a ciggie and told them all about killing a pig.

When Phil and I returned, we slit the throat of the second pig and waited for the hero. As soon as Andy arrived he picked up the first pig and put the nooses around each foot and hauled the pig up the tree to his shoulder height. He then swiftly opened and emptied the gut onto the ground before cleaning out the rest of the internals and generally tidying up. In minutes both pigs were "dressed" and ready to drop into boiling water. Andy, obviously performed this job many times before but when asked about it said, "the wild boar I normally kill, need a vehicle with a winch and a block and tackle to lift 'em into the tree". Andy and I lowered each pig into the boiling water and left them there for a few minutes. Andy kept checking if the bristles were loose with the back of his knife and making sure they weren't cooking and then he said "out now … quick" from where he easily removed the bristles with clean swipes of his knife. "Job done", he said "now you need to hang them in your cold-room until Christmas Eve. Let's have a beer".

Andy and I lifting a scalded pig from the bath of boiling water

Very early on the morning of Christmas Eve Phil dragged the two spits into the beer garden and filled the barrels with some well-seasoned local hardwood. He then fired it up and we waited for the coals to form. In the meantime the girls were putting together a heap of wonderful salads.

By about 7am the coals were glowing and we put the pigs on. Phil and Grant carefully wired the pigs to the long spike so they wouldn't sag during the cooking and at it was all systems ready to go. We were told they would need about six to eight hours to be perfectly cooked and so on they went.

The pigs slowly rotated above the coals and gradually took on colour. Phil and Grant basted them regularly and after about four hours they were looking and smelling great UNTIL the rope, driven by the wiper motor pulley that turned the bicycle wheel and spit and thereby turned the pigs, melted. Unfortunately, no one was manning the spit at the time and I was in the bar serving a few customers when I noticed huge flames out in the beer garden. I shouted out to Phil and we raced across to the fire. It was clearly evident what went gone wrong. The pulley rope was lying on the ground and the pig wasn't turning, this caused the fat from under the outer skin to melt and drip onto the coals, instantly igniting them into high flames. The flames, in turn caused more fat to melt and, well, in essence, we started a huge uncontrollable fire. It was an emergency.

We couldn't get close enough to lift the spit off and we knew not to put the water hose onto it, so Phil did the next best thing and grabbed a huge woollen blanket from the clothesline and threw it over the pig. Incredibly it stopped burning just long enough for us to lift the spit and two pigs off the coals. Catastrophe averted but now what. The pig wasn't fully cooked yet, but the crackly was crispy and perfect and so we cut and yanked the crackly off the pigs and then wrapped the pigs in alfoil then put them back on the spit with its new rope. Fingers were crossed.

A couple of hours later and in front of twenty eager locals and our pub team we took the pigs off the spit and carved them up. I have to say it was the best spit-roasted pig I'd ever eaten. The crispy crackling was magnificent and the pork was moist and tender. The girls put together a great salad buffet and everyone loved it. We enjoyed a wonderful Christmas Eve and an incredible roast with all our locals and friends. The first spit was a huge success despite the mishaps along the way.

Spit-roasted pig for Christmas Eve dinner in 1986 prior to the fire

Footnote - year two and everything went to plan without any mishaps. Pat Barry did the butchering, the pigs behaved and the spit went without a hitch. Boring really but another great day with friends and family.

THE HORSE SHOUTER

Our yardie Grant loved horses and therefore it didn't take him long to purchase a lovely ginger coloured station mare he named Bella (beautiful girl). Grant would get up early and do his yard work as well as restocking the bars and fridges. When completed, he would saddle up Bella and go for a ride. One day when he returned I asked if I could take her for a ride. Having never ridden a horse, as I didn't trust such big animals to behave, I was nervous. I once witnessed a couple of racehorses we part-owned in Adelaide buck our jockeys off and I considered if an experienced race jockey could be bucked off, then I must end up in the dirt.

Grant was happy to let me have a try but he said "Bella has a mind of her own when she's too fresh. Let me take her for a gallop to tire her out and then you'll be fine". So Grant headed off for a long gallop. Ten minutes later he returned and declared her ready for me. So I climbed aboard in my standard attire of jeans, Akubra hat and my Japanese riding boots, my thongs.

Grant suggested I walk her up the side of the pub and when I get to the scrub out the black I turn her around and walk her back. He also said, "don't let her trot until you are settled on her and don't gallop under any circumstances". So we started walking from the front corner of the pub and down the side. Bella was a large comfortable horse and it felt great ... until she decided to trot. Hence why I hate horses. They do things a car doesn't. If I wanted my car to go faster I'd put my foot down on the accelerator and to stop I'd push the brake pedal. I didn't put my foot down but this horse decided to trot and then I was scared. I bounced up and down and as I came down Bella was going up and next minute I was out of control. Belle sensed this and she took off at a full gallop. Bella and I went past the end of the pub, past the clothes-line Boof kept eating, past our "donga" house behind the pub and past the back fence. I pulled on the reins but Bella was at a full uncontrolled gallop and then I heard Grant shout "GET OFF NOW ... JUMP".

I remember this as if it was today. I pushed down on Bella's shoulders with both hands and pushed myself into the air and off to one side and I flew through the air. I hit the ground hard and rolled several times in the dirt before coming to a violent halt up against a termite mound. I looked up to see Bella disappearing into the scrub in one direction and Grant coming towards me in the opposite direction. I tried to stand up and was waiting to grab Grant's arm for support ... but he ran straight past me and into the scrub looking for Bella. Oops. I somehow recovered to my feet and found my thongs. One was blown out (this means it pulled a strap out through the base of the thong) and so I carried both back towards the pub. As I hobbled past the clothes line I heard hysterical laughter and from underneath the motel bedsheets, I saw Leonie doubled over in laughter at my misfortune. I said "did you see what just happened to me" and she said, "why do you think I'm laughing so much". I could see I wasn't getting any sympathy there so I kept hobbling back into the empty bar. I sat down and fixed my thong, cleaned myself up, bandaged the areas of broken skin and put on a fresh set of clothes and went back to work with a pronounced limp. Grant and Bella returned half an hour later but he didn't talk to me for the rest of the day. Leonie simply laughed at me each time I limped past and the tourists all asked how I received my injuries, to which I replied, "breaking in a wild horse". It wasn't so big a lie.

Chapter 18. DEAD SET LEGENDS

The Northern Territory has seen its fair share of legends and at the Daly Waters Pub, I was fortunate to meet a few. Unfortunately, my book came too late to share with any of them.

TOM "THE BREAKER" COLE

Just before we purchased Daly Waters Pub I read a book of true bush tales named "Spears and Smoke Signals" by a legendary Territorian horse breaker, buffalo shooter and crocodile hunter Tom "the Breaker" Cole. It was a spellbinding book about one of the toughest men to ever work in the Territory. The book and Tom's style of writing made me dream of one day experiencing the exciting life and pioneering spirit only the Territory could offer.

In 1987, a giant man in typical Territory attire of big Akubra hat and RM Williams shirt, pants and boots walked up to the bar. I instantly recognised him as big Tom Cole. Tom must have been eighty years old at the time but he still stood tall and looked strong. His driver introduced Tom to me and said they were revisiting some of Tom's favourite places before releasing his autobiography the next year, to be named "Hell West and Crooked".

When he shook my hand, Tom squeezed it was like it had been placed in a vice. His hand, by comparison to mine, was the size of a boxer's glove. He took a stool at the bar and immediately ordered a Bundy rum ... straight, no ice, and no mixer. I poured it and he sculled it down and ordered another. I grabbed the bottle from the back bar and poured again. He grabbed my wrist and said "best you leave it here son and save your energy. You like rum?" I replied, "yeah, I love rum and coke". He then said "you'd better pour yourself one too ... but if you're gonna drink with me, you drink it the same as me. Straight".

So I downed a few quiet rums with possibly the Australia's most famous living outback legend and there was no-one to bother us. We chatted and I asked him some questions about his times at the Daly Waters Pub. He told me his times at the pub were infrequent but each was an enjoyable, long lasting drinking session. He asked how a city slicker ended up owning a piece of history in the outback of the Northern Territory and I told him of my surveying experiences and how ended up here.

After about half an hour, his driver suggested it was time to leave. Tom said, "well, we'd better have one more and then I'd better go". Whilst we enjoyed the last rum together he said "so thank you, Mark. As you love the bush so much, I'd like to give you some valuable advice". "Yes please, anything" I replied. So Tom started "It's simple, when travelling in the outback make sure you carry some rum as pain relief from a snake bite". He sculled his rum and stood to his full six feet six inches and said with a wink as he left "and always carry a small snake".

Tom's next book, Hell West and Crooked, was released in 1988 and went on to sell over 100,000 copies making him one of Australia's best-selling author.

GEORGE P ETTENHEIM JNR

In April of 1987 a Holden Commodore pulled up in front of the pub but this was no ordinary Holden Commodore. The car was covered in solar panels, polystyrene foam, aerials and a fifth "bicycle" wheel hanging from the back. Three or four guys jumped out and wandered into the pub. One of them carried a large video camera and filmed the walls and bar whilst the others wandered around and checked it all out. Eventually one of them said he loved the pub and would kill for a beer but they still have many miles to do. I asked what they were they doing in a car with all the stuff hanging all over it. He told me they were testing equipment and road conditions for the Solar Challenge car race, to be held later in the year that went from Darwin to Adelaide. He then introduced me to an American, the guy with the large camera, and said he was George P Ettenheim Jnr and he was developing the solar vehicle with General Motors and it was to be named the GM Sunracer.

We only talked for about twenty minutes but it was long enough for me to realise George was a most interesting person and a high achiever.

George described he was going to win the inaugural Solar Challenge because of superior solar-panels, a stronger battery and a special electric motor, all designed specifically for this vehicle, for this race and for these conditions. I left in no doubt who would win the race that year. His attention to detail was mind boggling. And then he really blew me away when I asked what he did in his previous life.

He reeled off his inventions and feats one after the other. They included founding Popular Mechanics Magazine as well as designing and making the Gossamer Albatross (first man pedal powered flight across the English Channel) and the Gossamer Condor plus the amazing the Flying Pterosaur (flying dinosaur) proving dinosaurs could actually fly.

When George left he said "I look forward to seeing you in a few months as we go past the pub on our way south" and I couldn't wait for that to happen.

A few months later the race started in Darwin on a brilliantly sunny day. The expectation was for the Sunracer to finish the day somewhere around Daly Waters 600km from the start. At about 4pm a police van came into Daly Waters and one of the officers, Bill Tuckey, came into the bar. He said, "who's Mark". I said it was me. He said "I have a message from George P. He apologises for not coming in but the car is going so fast we are struggling to keep up in our police car and he thinks they may reach Tenant Creek tonight. They went past here at 100kph". As he left I asked him if he was going the whole way to Adelaide and he said he was. So I grabbed a beautiful copper lithograph of the pub and I wrote on the back, "Congratulations on winning the inaugural World Solar Challenge 1987 from Mark and Leonie Venable" and asked the policeman to give it to George as they crossed the finish line. Naturally, George went on to win the race.

Checking out Dennis Bartell's solar car, well behind the
leader, GM Sunracer

I didn't hear anything for a couple of months and then in
December 1987 a letter from George arrived and he said;

Dear Mark

No time to stop but Bill Tuckey gave me the print and
your note, <u>many</u> thanks. Sorry, we didn't stop but there
were certain pressing matters!

George (Included in the envelope was a photo of George
and his son on a tandem racing bike)

Soon after, I received a parcel containing a t-shirt sent by George from AeroVironment Inc of Monrovia California.

George on the back of his tandem racer, with his son Terry steering

ROY BEEBE

As mentioned previously, the town of Daly Waters lay in the middle of the one million acres of Kalala Station, owned by the Beebe brothers Roy and Mick. The brothers also owned a couple of other huge cattle stations. Mick lived at Uckaronidge, south of Daly Waters, whilst Roy lived at Kalala.

Roy wasn't a daily pub patron but he would drop into the pub to meet a stock agent, or a contractor, or to celebrate the completion of a muster, by shouting his workers a few beers, or just to say hello. Roy was a giant man, much in the mould of Tom Cole. Incredibly, they were both soft spoken and gentle for such tough outback men, who you would have expected to be brash, demonstrative, loud or even rude. Not in their cases.

Roy Beebe with a roped steer ... a big gentle man

Roy completely controlled his workers, in a good way. Some told me Roy was bad tempered and you didn't want to be around him when he went off. So they feared Roy and at the same time they respected Roy. But three station hands in particular, Dallas and Dave and Brett, idolised the man. From my experiences with Roy it was obvious, if Roy liked you he would cut you some slack and even show some affection but if he didn't, then life wouldn't be great.

During our time in the pub, I cashed the severance pay cheques of quite a few station hands, after they were sacked on the spot for doing something, in their opinion, was a minor mistake. Typically, a station ute would pull up in front of the pub and a dirty angry young man, who wasn't permitted to travel in the front seat any longer, would leap off the back and quickly grab his swag and kitbag before the ute sped off in a dusty hurry back out to somewhere on the station. The young fella would then storm into the bar with a crumpled cheque in his hand and chest the bar. Then it would normally go something like this. "Bloody Roy just sacked me and I didn't do a damn thing wrong. He's a rotten bastard. Can you cash this cheque? How much is my pub bill? Shit, that much! What time is the next coach? Tomorrow ... shit! Can I get a beer?

Generally, I would discover they had "left a gate open and a few bloody cattle were let out." And they wondered why they were sacked ...

I felt lucky when these boys called in and paid their pub bill. Roy knew most of the lads owed me money, so he'd always have someone drop them at the pub or he would warn those, with their own vehicle, to pay their pub bill. On several occasions, Roy dropped past the pub a day or so after sacking a worker. He'd wander into the bar and ask in his deep slow voice "hey Mark, did the young fella fix you up yesterday" and almost always my answer would be "yes he did. Thanks Roy". He once said "he was a useless prick, left a gate open and I lost 1,000 head. It'll take us a week to find em " ... and the sacked worker said it was "a minor error" ... I don't think so.

One morning Roy pulled up in front of the pub in his green Toyota utility, wandered in and said "hey Mark, I have a yard full of cattle that have been living in the scrub for years. I thought you and Leonie might want to see them." I said "we'd love to. Thanks Roy" to which he said, "well you better get Leonie and let's go". So I grabbed Leonie from the kitchen and raced out the front and jumped in with Roy. Leonie and I shared one seat for many kilometres as he sped into the bush on tracks I didn't know existed.

Whilst Roy sped to the muster he described what was happening. He told us these cattle were never mustered and possibly never seen a man. He explained, the properties were so vast, very few were fully fenced and these scrub cattle wandered the unfenced bush areas of Kalala and surrounding stations for decades. As part of the NT Government Brucellosis Eradication Program, the cattle stations were being forced to catch or shoot these scrub cattle to then leave them stock free until this grass borne disease was eradicated. These areas could then be declared disease free, fenced and eventually restocked. After Roy captured and removed all the cattle the government would bring in helicopter snipers who would shoot any remaining cattle until there were none left? Whilst this wasn't popular with the station owners, in particular, a neighbour Pat Dunbar at Nutwood Downs, it did help develop and fence the NT and the sale of any suitable mustered cattle provided good cash flow. Roy also explained the two methods of how cattle were mustered into a yard. The cattle, where we were heading, were mustered by helicopter the day before.

Roy explained how they would erect a large yard in an open area and place two very long fenced wings leading away from the yard to form a "shute into the yard". The chopper pilots would go a long way out from the yard and with sirens blaring and death-defying low altitude flying they would scare the cattle together and then in combination with horses, vehicles and motorbikes the cattle would be forced as a large group toward the yard. When the cattle reached the "fenced road" they would be funnelled a kilometre or so into the "temporary" holding yard whereupon the gates would be closed and the cattle effectively captured. This is what confronted us when we arrived, a tired, confused, scared mob of cattle who'd never seen a human let alone a chopper, a car or a fence.

Roy explained his preferred method of mustering was to catch the cattle whilst they were watering. But this couldn't be done with scrub cattle. In previous years Roy erected fencing around all the natural water points on his property. He then built "Turkey nest" dams near man-made bores in suitable open flat areas. At the suitable open watered areas, he placed "spear" gates in the fence-lines to enable cattle to move in to drink and then leave whenever they wished. These spear gates were unique as they forced the cattle to push the gate open on the way in and again on the way out.

The cattle would become accustomed to this and it became their downfall. When Roy needed to muster the cattle he would simply close off all the gates around the natural water holes and then "lock" the outward going spear gate at the turkey nest where he wanted to catch the cattle. In this way, the cattle could move in to drink but couldn't escape. Within a few days, Roy would catch every beast without the need for expensive choppers or manpower.

Eventually, we arrived at a big open area with a huge temporary cattle yard in the centre holding hundreds of cattle. There was dust in the air from the beasts nervously pacing around and at one end was three incredibly long triple road trains next to a fifty metre long fenced race and ramp up to the first road train. Roy's workers were milling around smoking and talking but as soon as we pulled up next to the race they ran off to their nominated stations. Some of them looked in surprise and amusement at the publican and publican's wife being in Roy's car. We jumped out of the car and Roy casually hopped up onto his bulbar. We joined him. Roy shouted to the lads "okay get em moving".

The procedure became obvious as Roy explained what we were about to witness. The cattle were in a big yard and on the far side of the yard were a few station hands on horseback. The shute went from the yard and then up to the trucks and was built with several slide gates in its length. The first gate let the cattle into the race in single file, the second gate directed suitably fit cows and calves to a separate holding yard and the third slide gate directed young, not ready for market, cattle into another yard and the rest, the mature cattle, would be sent up the ramp to be trucked to the meat works.

So the boys in the large yard whistled, prodded and shouted the cattle into the shute. As a beast entered the race Roy would shout WORKS or BREEDER or KEEPER. The second gate was manned by a young lad who, on Roy's instruction of BREEDER, would slide the gate closed and in turn open another gate to the cow and calf yard. The third gate was directly in front of us. Roy's instruction for this gate to be closed and a side gate opened was "KEEPER". This was for the not yet mature cattle. The WORKS were mature and old cattle ready for the meat works. All the gates were opened for these cattle to enable them to run the full distance of the race then up the ramp into the truck.

The whole operation ran smoothly. In most cases, Roy didn't have to say much, as the lads knew what to do and generally they could pre-empt what gate needed to be opened or closed, thereby negating the need for Roy to say anything. After about half an hour Roy asked Leonie if she would like to "man a gate". It wasn't really a question, so Leonie hopped off the bull-bar as Roy shouted to the lads "STOP boys, Leonie is going to operate that gate lad". He then winked at me and whispered, "this is gonna get interesting now Mark". The young lad stepped away and Leonie, dressed in cut-off jean shorts and a vibrant hot-pink top, stepped up to the gate. Roy shouted "get em going boys" and the first gate was opened.

Leonie "manning' a gate with some station hands looking on in amusement

The first cows entering the race were directed to the first gate and they were followed by a young bull. Roy called to Leonie "KEEPER". Leonie closed her gate and the young

238

bull went into the yard as planned. Leonie turned around and looked scared but also very pleased with herself. Unfortunately, in her excitement, Leonie didn't hear Roy call "WORKS" and therefore didn't open her gate. Down the race came a huge angry horned Brahman bull. It was thrashing his head from side to side trying to attack every fence panel and get out of the race. The bull's horns were too wide for the race and kept hooking into the fence panels. The first two lads jumped back as it came through their gates, Roy calmly said "you might want to get back Leonie" but Leonie was frozen in fear and still hadn't opened the gate. Roy again said "get back Leonie" but she resolutely stood at the gate. The huge bull arrived at her gate and crashed into it. He was too large to get out of the race into the side opening that went into the KEEPER yard and with one huge horn locked into a fence panel he was effectively stuck in place. Roy jumped off the bull-bar and the two of us hurried to the race. Roy gently moved Leonie back from the gate and told one of the lads to close the KEEPER opening. He then slowly approached the bull, which due to its tight fit in the race, stopped thrashing and was now motionless but snorting heavily through huge flared nostrils. Roy calmly placed his hand on the rear flank of the beast and brushed its hair in the opposite direction to what it naturally laid and in doing so he revealed a faint cattle brand.

By now most of the station hands gathered around this huge beast stuck in the race and we were all watching Roy calmly stroke the bull from its rump to his huge neck and head. Roy then returned to the rump and exposed the brand again. He thought for a minute and declared to us all "this bullock must be over twenty years old and has wandered over 150 kilometres from its original home. I know this because this is the famous wineglass brand of Newcastle Waters and this design was in use up to about 1966 when they made new branding irons and it changed slightly." I reckon I saw a bit of emotion in Roy as he said "WORKS" but then he returned to normal and said "that beast will dress at over 1,000 kilos and possibly set an abattoir record. What a beauty".

Dave and Brett attempting to control the Newcastle Waters bullock.

"Let's go boys, get em moving" said Roy, and with that, we jumped in the Toyota and Roy took us back to the pub.

As time passed I came to understand what really happened on the day. I believe Roy saw the bullock in the yard earlier and drove to the pub especially to take us out there to be a part of Territory history. I know Roy liked seeing us lovingly raise his gift of the Brahman calf Boof and he appreciated our invites for the station people to attend the pub for Christmas Eve dinner and to a few other events. I believe Roy wanted to show us his appreciation in the best way he could and it was definitely appreciated. A wonderful memory.

A few months after the Brahman experience Roy called in the pub and asked me if I wanted to witness the delivery of his new Robinson R22 mustering chopper. Naturally, I said yes and he replied "well you won't have to go far because it will drop in here tomorrow to refuel. Be ready with a drum at about 11am".

Until now Roy hired choppers and pilots every time he wanted to muster. They were expensive and needed booking well in advance. The Territory was well serviced by some highly experienced pilots but they came at a cost and you couldn't wake up in the morning and decide to "get the chopper out". So Roy decided to purchase his chopper from Queensland and hired a young inexperienced pilot to fly it to Kalala and then work for him mustering cattle and taking Roy on aerial visual surveys of his stations. I could see Roy was excited at the potential of this modern workhorse.

The next day at around 11am Roy drove into the pub and we waited for the chopper to arrive. We refuelled helicopters on the block next door to the pub by wheeling a 44 gallon drum of Avgas with a rotor hand pump to the chopper and filling it up. I could fill two to three Robbo R22 choppers from one drum of fuel.

About an hour later the chopper arrived with young Andrew the pilot. Roy asked him why he was so late and Andrew then said he'd experienced severe headwinds and it slowed him down. Not a good start. So I filled the chopper up with Avgas and Andrew took off to Kalala. Before he left Roy said he was taking his first flight with Andrew the next day to go to Tanumbirini Station, another station he owned 250 kilometres to the east of Daly Waters.

I was working behind the bar the next day when Roy drove through town in his green Mercedes saloon at very high speed, screeching around the corner in front of the pub. I ran out the front in time to see him disappear into the distance heading east.

Later, one of Roy's road train drivers, our good mate Dave, came into the pub for a drink. He was on his way back from Tanumbirini Station. I asked him why Roy drove there today, instead of flying in his new chopper. With the question, Dave burst out laughing and said "you'd better ask Roy, Mark. He'll be here shortly."

A few minutes later Roy made one of his rare appearances in the pub and he didn't look happy. He bought himself a drink and stood with Dave at the bar. I didn't know whether to ask Roy but it didn't matter as Dave said with a cheeky grin "Mark was just asking me why you didn't fly in the chopper with Andy today Roy". Roy's face went a little red and he said "you wanna know why I drove my ten thousand dollar Mercedes and didn't fly in my brand new, couple of hundred grand chopper. I'll tell you why. I find out this morning the chopper can't fly with Andrew and me because we weigh too much. He tells me today, just when I'm ready to leave. Why didn't they tell me it can't take a hundred kilo pilot and a hundred plus kilo me when I bought the damn thing? Bastards."

Then Dave says "tell him the other bit of news Roy". Roy, who is fuming now, says "so the chopper takes off and I jump in the Merc and head to Tanumbirini. I'm furious and so I get there in a couple of hours and no bloody chopper. I'm thinking is the bugger lost or what. Or has he crashed? I don't know what to think and then about ten minutes later I hear the noise of a damn chopper coming and finally, he lands. So he gets out and I say where the bloody hell have you been? And he says he's been trying to keep up with me. I say, you what? And he tells me the chopper is flat out at ninety miles per hour but in the headwind, he could only do about seventy. He saw me pulling away from him and couldn't do anything about it. I was doing bloody ninety in my Merc thinking he'd beat me easily. So now I own a chopper I can't fly in and a chopper, so slow, I can drive faster than it. Bloody hell".

Dave and I laugh and Dave then says "and the rest Roy". And Roy starts again "and if that ain't e-bloody-nough. I say to Andrew, ok fire her up and let's start mustering. Simple enough, right? Wrong! Andrew says he's almost out of fuel and needs to fill up. I say you've only just left bloody home you can't be empty. And Andrew says he can only do a maximum of three hours cruising but as he's been flat out trying to keep up with me he's nearly empty after two. Bloody hell the Merc is still half full and I've been all the bloody way there and back. Shit."

Roy finished his drink, gave us a wink and left. Dave and I burst out laughing. It was one of the funniest moments, I would ever witness at Daly Waters and I bet Roy enjoyed a good laugh on the way home too. A very special man.

LOCKIE McKINNON

When I first met Lockie McKinnon he was working as a station hand for Steve Atwell, the manager of Hidden Valley Station. Steve started coming into the hotel every week to collect his mail and enjoy a cold beer. They previously went to Dunmurra Wayside Inn but for some reason changed to Daly Waters Pub. We all liked Steve and Lockie as they were a fun couple of blokes. Steve was about thirty and many years younger than Lockie, who must have been about sixty at the time. Both loved a big drink and they'd often sit at the bar for many hours at a time. Steve drank about four to Lockie's one and Steve paid for every drink consumed, to Lockie's constant amusement.

Great mates Lockie and Steve at the Daly Waters Pub

Lockie called everyone "thing", because he couldn't remember names very well. He displayed a wicked sense of humour and was always smoking his thin self-rolled cigarettes. Steve drank white cans and straight rum chasers whilst Lockie generally drank white cans with the occasional rum chaser.

We loved Lockie. He was a very interesting man who loved telling stories of his past. Lockie told us he left Adelaide (Norwood) when he was only twelve or thirteen years of age. He walked and hitched lifts to the Territory where he learned to ride a horse and work with cattle eventually to become a "stockman and self-styled packhorse bagman". He would move from station to station living out of his saddlebag and taking any jobs available. Incredibly, for a man who couldn't remember our names from one day to the next, he could remember the name of almost every station owner he worked on, throughout Australia.

One of Lockie's favourite stories was about our own cattleman Roy Beebe. As Lockie told the story it went like this and it never varied no matter who he told it to.

In the sixties, Lockie earned a contract to move a couple of hundred head of cattle from Uckaronidge Station, for the Beebe family, to a buyer in Queensland. Lockie collected

247

the cattle and started the drove. Slowly but surely he moved them across the Barkly towards Queensland. According to Lockie, with a cheeky smile, he managed to pick up a few extra clean skins along the way. So Lockie's herd kept growing with unbranded cattle and the extras made his progress even slower. Lockie said he was camped one night about three quarters the way to the destination and running a couple of weeks late when he saw vehicle headlights approaching. Lockie immediately doused his camp fire and sat in the darkness. He swears he would have been almost invisible in the dark and considered himself safe when right next to him a voice says "do you have a cuppa for a tired traveller". Lockie was shocked someone snuck up, without him even knowing he was there and replied "I don't feed the travelling public. Piss off". So this bloke stands up and walked off. It was ten minutes before a car started and drove off.

Anyway, Lockie woke the next day and kept moving his cattle. A few days later he delivered the cattle and took receipt of a letter from the buyer noting the number of cattle delivered, exactly matching the cattle he left with. Now you're probably wondering what happened to the extra cattle he picked up along the way. In those days no one trusted anyone. So Lockie returned to Uckaronidge to get paid and the reason for him needing the note. But no one would pay anyone to move cattle they didn't own so on the way back he would drop into each station he went past and try to sell them the unbranded cattle. By the time he returned to Uckaronidge, he'd already earned a healthy wage but with still quite a few cleanskins to sell there was work to do. He camped not far from the station and rode in the next day to get paid and hopefully sell some cleanskins.

Lockie in a serious moment, with his favourite filly, "Thing"

Lockie described how he tied his horse to a fence a wandered over to the shed where a few station workers are having a tea break. Lockie asked if they would share a cuppa for a tired drover when one of them, a big man, stood up and said "we don't feed the travelling public. Why don't you piss off"? Lockie instantly recognised the voice and remembered the dark night a few months ago on the stock route to Queensland. According to Lockie, he responded by saying "fair call" and asking where he could find one of the Beebe brothers. Whereupon the big man said with a smile "I'd say you're talking to one of them right now Lockie McKinnon. I'm Roy Beebe and I feel we've met before".

Lockie said he received his pay, left his cleanskins in the bush, where he could find them later to hopefully sell to the Beebe's and went to the nearest pub where he booked a room and drank for a week or two until the money ran out. Then it was back to work again. So he returned to locate the cleanskins he left them but according to Lockie, they were gone and he still blamed Roy Beebe for stealing them.

Roy verified almost every part of Lockie's story except the final part where he was accused of stealing Lockie's cleanskins from the bush. According to Roy, Lockie was so lazy, he "stored" his cleanskins in a Beebe holding yard not far from the station. Roy said he fed and watered them for a couple of weeks but when Lockie didn't return, he considered them his property and branded them with his own brand, as he earned every right to do.

Lockie always finished the story with a cheeky smile and said "you wouldn't believe Roy Beebe. A year later I moved more cattle for Roy to the market in Katherine, and I bloody well knew most of them were mine".

Lockie moved to Daly Waters in 1987 for a few months rest. He lived across the road under Steve and Bronwyn's house and slept on a stretcher bed. Lockie was a true bagman and continued to live out of his bag. I gave Lockie a job at the pub lighting the donkey fire each morning and doing odd jobs. Lockie rarely slept well so he would arise early and wander across the road to the pub to light the fire under the donkey and boil his billy for a cuppa and a smoke. One morning Lockie told me we were getting short of timber and offered to take the ute and get a ute full. I asked him where he proposed getting the timber from. He replied "Roy's place" and added "Roy didn't have a problem" … so I said go for it.

So Lockie and I went to this huge pile of timber cross members. Each was about 3 foot long and 4 x 4 inches, there were thousands of them and they were perfect. He loaded the ute until it looked like an Egyptian pyramid and unloaded them at the rear of the pub. Lockie had the privilege of access to enough timber to last us a few years.

Each morning Lockie would arise on schedule at about 5am, grab a heap of timbers, light the fire under the donkey and sit close to it whilst smoking and drinking his morning cuppa. After about a week using the new timbers, Lockie started complaining of severe headaches and nausea. We were very concerned one day when he came into the bar after lighting the fire and enjoying his cuppa and he was very vague and seemed drugged or something. Lockie was always a bit vague but this wasn't normal. So we put him on the coach to Katherine Hospital. We rang the hospital and described his symptoms and how long he was like this. In the afternoon we received a call from the hospital. Lockie was suffering from arsenic poisoning and they were concerned he was being poisoned by someone. As soon as the doctor mentioned arsenic I knew the cause. The timber cross members were treated with arsenic, for termite proofing. It was common in the Territory and this was obviously coming out of the timber in the smoke, Lockie sat in every morning.

Lockie returned the next day but before he returned home, we'd already removed all the arsenic-laced timbers and replaced them with freshly sawn snappy gum and lancewood. Both timbers smelled much better anyway.

Lockie found out Phil and I were ex-surveying people who worked extensively in the bush and shared a passion for feats of old explorers. One day, out of the blue, he said "I know where Leichhardt went". When quizzed by us he told us some stories of his days as a stockman around Victoria River Downs. He said some of the aboriginal elders told stories, handed down from generation to generation, of a white man, with a tall hat, on a horse. Bearing in mind Leichhardt died in around 1848 and Lockie was in the area almost 100 years later the stories must have been handed down through at least four generations. It is quite feasible because a tribe inhabiting the inland Victoria River area coming across a white man must have been an extraordinarily memorable occasion. Lockie said he was shown a rock wall painting on Victoria River Downs of a bearded white man with a tall hat on a horse and the aboriginals told him the white man lived with them for some time before moving west. Lockie told us he could show us the rock wall but unfortunately it opportunity never eventuated. What a pity.

Famous Territory musician and politician Ted Egan wrote a beautiful and haunting song about Lockie

McKinnon's life. He named it "The Last of the Packhorse Bagmen" and it went on to become a country classic. Ted also told a story of when he met Lockie in 1973 in the Maree Pub, when he went there to write a few songs. According to Ted, "a standoff between himself and the taciturn McKinnon lasted for three days, Ted watching from his corner over a beer, McKinnon at the bar, smoking, drinking rum and beer chasers". Ted then went on to describe a verbal stoush between a couple of young Afghan Aborigines and an older Aborigine male. Lockie stepped in and said to the young lads "he'd buy and sell you couple of bastards any day of the week". Ted then went over to Lockie and asked him who the old aborigine was? Lockie said "How's it going Ted" and told him it was Tommy Russell, the famous brumby rider and shooter. Ted and Lockie became daily companions for the next couple of weeks and three decades later the memories inspired the song.

Lockie was a true outback legend who brightened our days. I will never forget his cheeky smile and his use of the name "thing" for all of us.

ROSSIE ROBINSON

A month or two after starting at Daly Waters Pub, I noticed a particular bloke would call in occasionally for breakfast or sometimes for a beer and rum later in the day. He would sit by himself at the same corner table and face the bar. He never said much but I noticed he observed everything and would always say "thanks" on his way out. I had introduced myself and tried to make conversation but he seemed to want to be alone. His name was Ross and he drove a brown Ford station wagon, completely full of boxes and stuff. Even the front seat was used as was the roof.

One day I sat next to him after he finished breakfast and said "this one is on me but only if you tell me something about yourself". So he told me his "Ross Robinson story" and left.

Ross Robinson lived at Borroloola, 300 kilometres due east of Daly Waters on the MacArthur River near the Gulf of Carpentaria. He once owned the pub but now owned the local store and a freight company. He travelled each week to Katherine to do banking and buy some necessary items. He travelled by car rather than his truck, because the truck was too slow. He seemed a nice bloke and when he left he said something I'll always remember. He said "I've sat here and watched you work. You will do very well here".

From then on when Ross called in he would sit at the bar and we'd have a good chat. From others, I learned he was a local legend and they showed me a photo of him riding a bronco on the wall of the pub. He took on the run down Borroloola Pub when no-one else would. He then revamped the local store and supplied the locals with what they were after and didn't rip them off. He also owned a truck and delivered fuel and freight to stations and settlements all the way to Queensland. Ross's sense of humour and self-depreciation allowed him to name his trucking company "Forgetful Freight Lines".

The Pub photo of Rossie riding the bucking bronco

Ross was in the pub one day and heard me mention, to no-one in particular, we were struggling with cold room and freezer space. He immediately interjected and said he thought he owned the answer for us. It was sitting out of Borroloola. Apparently, a crab fisherman owed Ross a few thousand dollars so Ross took his truck to the crabber camp and removed the container sized blast freezer. The crab fisherman couldn't raise the cash so Ross was happy to sell it to me for the $4,000 he was owed. It seemed too much money but I knew a cold room that big would cost double or triple. So I said it was a deal but it needed to be delivered and dropped exactly where I needed it. The deal was done and a week later Ross arrived with a huge cold room for us. With no idea how he planned getting it off the truck I left him with the problem. Phil spent a couple of hours helping whilst I manned the bar. Then I heard some banging and crashing so I wandered out the back to find two sheets of iron missing from the side of the pub and the door of a huge cold room was in their place. It was almost perfect. Our only problem was we didn't need a blast freezer, we needed a cold room and a normal freezer. So Ross called his fridge mechanic mate Andy in Katherine, who promised to come down in a few days and fix it up. Andy arrived a few days later as promised and not only adjusted the container to operate as a cold room at one end and freezer at the other but he serviced all our other equipment. Andy turned out to be a very handy bloke to know. He was always travelling the Stuart Highway and he loved the pub. So we received great service from this terrific little guy.

In late 1988 Ross invited us to Borroloola to stay with him and attend the annual Borroloola Game Fishing Championship. So we organised two days off and headed to the "Loo". When we arrived Ross informed us "there was some work to do".

Firstly we needed to take some other fisherman out to Centre Island and leave them there for the night. So Ross, Leonie and I along with three guys we'd never met launched Ross's boat and sped the forty kilometres out on the MacArthur River into the ocean. Along the way we entered a fog bank and visibility dropped to less than ten metres. Ross knew the river well and kept his foot down but it was very scary. At one point we rounded a sharp bend at speed and were confronted with something in the middle of our path. Ross pulled the throttle back immediately and we slowly came up next to the bow of a boat with a red buoy attached. Holy crap, what's doing here I thought. Ross nudged past it and said it sunk yesterday when the driver took a turn too fast and hit a rock. He then added "it occurred ten kilometres upstream from here. I wondered where we'd find it today". He didn't say what happened to the skipper or crew! We powered away and soon we were heading out from the mouth towards an island in the distance. Things were going well until we hit a mud bank in the middle of the ocean. The propeller dug in and the boat slid to a halt. Ross tilted the outboard motor up and said "everyone out and push, except you Leonie. You keep an eye out for crocs."

I certainly didn't forget, we were in crocodile-infested waters, as we motored past several on our way to the mud bank. I wasn't keen on getting out of the boat but didn't want to embarrass myself, so out I jumped and the five of us pushed the boat through the mud until we found ourselves in deeper water. I couldn't get back in the boat fast enough. We were all covered in mud but we didn't care. We weren't eaten and that was a relief.

Finally, we arrived at the barren Centre Island and pulled up on a beach where a fisherman's shack was prominent. We left the three others on the island and Ross said we'd be back tomorrow to pick them up. On the way back Ross stopped for a fish. We didn't catch much but Leonie did haul in a really good size Snapper. We eventually returned back to the 'Loo' at dusk where we enjoyed a BBQ with Ross and his wife and it was early to bed.

The next morning Ross informed me he needed to do an urgent freight delivery and asked if I could take his boat out to Centre Island and pick up the three fisherman, we left there. My God, I thought. I don't know these waters and what if we hit a mud bank and it's only Leonie and me. "Yes, I'll do it. No worries" I said. Leonie was horrified and mouthed "what the hell are you thinking". But it was too late. Ross helped us launch the boat and said "follow the river, straight line to the Island and watch out for the mud bank. I should have marked it on the plan. Don't worry you'll be right. See you tonight". And with that, he left. I started the motor and off we went. It was about forty kilometres of river navigation and then a similar distance out to the Centre Island fishing hut. With the boat cruising on the plane, we kept our eyes peeled for anything object in our way. We saw the bow of the submerged boat early and slowly slid past it and then we were out into the river mouth. We sped across the water toward the island and then "zzzzzzzzzrrrrrrr" as the propeller started skimming on the mud bank. I put the throttle down and we hoped for the best. The boat slowed several times and once I thought we were a goner but finally the water colour changed and we were into deeper water. It wasn't long before we reached the beach and loaded our cargo of three fishermen, their gear and a chiller box of fresh fish. They had a good night but were covered in bites from midgees and mosquitoes. I thought they'd want to stop for a fish on the way back in but fortunately, they were so tired and itchy all they wanted was to get back to town and have a shower. On the way back, I again took the mud bank section flat out and told everyone to keep as far forward in the boat as possible. In doing so, the propeller was raised a few inches and we were able to skim across the bank at high speed without incident.

When I look at a chart now of what Leonie and I did it sends shivers down my spine. We were very lucky because if the boat stopped I don't know what would have happened. When we returned back to the ramp, Ross was waiting for us. He immediately came up to me and apologised. He took time to think on his delivery run about what he asked me to do and he realised how stupid he was. But everything was fine and we sat down and enjoyed a few cold beers whilst the real fisherman saw their fish weighed. Leonie was sitting with us talking to Ross's wife when her name was called out "and second place in the snapper section of the championship goes to Leonie Venable from Daly Waters Pub with a lovely snapper weighing 3lb 4oz ... well done Leonie". I can't remember what she won but I do know we celebrated well.

The next day Ross said he was required to deliver a load of fuel to Hells Gate Roadhouse 350km away on the Queensland border and would I like to come with him. So we headed off early and bumped and ground our way for five hours until we reached this tiny outpost with a petrol station and roadhouse in the middle of nowhere. After the very long drive over a terrible bush track we dropped the fuel off and turned around for the same horrible journey back.

On the way back Ross spotted a couple of bush cattle near the track and said, "I need a killer for the cold room and they are perfect". In those days in the Northern Territory, any cattle in unfenced, bush areas and bearing no obvious brand could be shot and taken by anyone. Very few abused this privilege and therefore it wasn't frowned upon or monitored. The common saying between station owners was "I eat yours, because your cattle taste better than mine". The reasoning was "if everyone ate the next door neighbour's cattle then, at the end of the day, everyone would be even".

Rossie pulled a rifle from behind the truck seat and asked me if I'd like to take the first shot. I said, "well okay

Rossie, but you may regret asking me". He said I couldn't miss it" and I could see the gun was fitted a long telescopic sight. So I leant against the tray of the truck, lined up the beast about 150 metres away and pulled the trigger. The gun was incredibly powerful and the shot sent the telescopic sight careering back into my eye. The eye I naively put too close to the scope. I immediately knew something was wrong as blood dropped onto my eyeball and all I saw was a red blur. Ross wasn't looking at me and instead said "you missed. How did you miss"? I already held my hanky to my bleeding eyelid when he finally turned to me and took the rifle. He took aim and fired at the other beast. It too, didn't die and it too, ran away. He couldn't believe it. So he took aim at a tree about two hundred metres away. He said he was aiming at a point about six feet up the trunk from the ground. He fired again and a branch three feet higher and to the right dropped to the ground. He threw the gun to the ground in disgust. No wonder we missed, the sight is out, I thought. The gun was bouncing around the truck without a cover and over the roughest tracks in the Territory... it was never going to be accurate. We both laughed, grabbed a beer from the Engel fridge and headed for the Loo.

When we arrived I went to the mirror to see a perfect circle cut around my eye socket and the beginnings of a black eye already starting. We thoroughly enjoyed an exciting three days but it was time to get back to work.

We saw Ross a few more times before we sold the pub but unfortunately, Ross died in a tragic aircraft crash in New Guinea in a plane he was test flying prior to buying it. A legend of the territory gone far too early.

Chapter 19. LOCAL TALES

In our time at Daly Waters, we became close friends with many of the locals. Some were colourful characters who came to the Territory before I was born. We had many fun times at the bar with these identities and they were never shy of telling a few tales. What follows are some classics.

RONNIE OGILVIE

Ron (Ronnie) Ogilvie was what they termed in the Territory a "death adder". A death adder roughly translated as someone who worked in the bush with cattle and horses, drank vast amounts of rum, and lived rough.

Ronnie was employed by Roy Beebe for several years and progressed from a bagman and droving on horseback in his younger years to dozer operator for Roy at Kalala. Ronnie skilfully operated heavy machinery including a huge D9 Caterpillar bulldozer and that feat would surprise many a person as Ronnie was old and battered, always drinking heavily and smoked like a chimney. Roy once told me Ronnie was one of the best machinery operators going around and despite his heavy drinking he could follow a contour to within an inch without needing a laser level like the "young whipper-snappers".

One day Roy came into the bar with Dave and both wore cheeky looks on their faces. Roy said "tell him Dave" and Dave replied, "nah, show him the photo, Roy". Roy said "whatever I said about Ronnie's skill with a dozer, I take it all back" as he showed me a photo of the huge dozer laying on its side. "This morning he was so hungover he couldn't even put it on the truck" as they burst out laughing and showed me the photo taken by one of "those fancy instant thingo cameras".

Ronnie, in the hat, leaning against the dozer in embarrassment.

TONY JOHNSON

Indigenous couple Tony Johnson and his wife Top End lived out on Daly Creek in a ramshackle hut made from scrap iron, timber and canvas. My best guess is they were about forty years of age back then, but I could have been out by ten years either way. Tony made didgeridoos from local timbers we sold to tourists. We paid Tony $15 for each didgeridoo and sold them for $25 but we also supplied Tony with other items including paint, food, fuel and tools. Some of what he paid for and others we gave to him. Tony and Top End also received a fortnightly cheque from the government.

Tony Johnson playing one of his didgeridoos

Tony told me they lived in Daly Waters because he married a lass from another tribe and neither tribe would accept the other person. Tony was from the Elliott area 150km south of Daly Waters and Top End was from Kakadu 500km North East of Daly Waters. I never found out why they chose Daly Waters but Tony's old car with its blown motor at their creek camp gave me a hint. Tony didn't believe in the aboriginal executioner spirit, the Kurdaitcha Man, who apparently inhabited the area, but I think Top End did as she would sometimes come into the pub saying she wasn't able sleep, due to someone making terrible screaming noises near her camp.

Tony and Top End always called me "Boss" and Leonie "Missus". We always called Tony Johnson by his full name and Top End we nicknamed Toppy. Toppy became very reliant on Leonie for her feminine needs and because she was too embarrassed in the early days to buy those items from me in our shop she would skulk around outside for an hour or so waiting for Leonie to appear in the bar. After a couple of months, she learned to wait outside and I would get Leonie for her.

Unfortunately Tony Johnson and Toppy drank too much and although we tried to restrict the amount they purchased Tony would always find a way around it. Tony played the didgeridoo extremely well and was a natural showman, and when he was cut-off from the booze he would sit out front of the pub busking with his favourite "didge" for the tourists who were eager to reward him with beer. This worked well for him as he'd get free beers and we would sell more didgeridoos and it meant more money for him.

As the tourist numbers increased so did the didgeridoo sales and this forced Tony to go further into the bush to make more didgeridoo. Making one didgeridoo is a difficult job even for an expert like Tony but we started selling up to ten per week and this required Tony spending several days per week in the bush cutting timber and making the didgeridoos.

To make a didgeridoo Tony and Toppy would walk miles into the scrub in search for hollow branches of local gum trees. Years of experience enabled Tony to spot a hollow branch and this was confirmed by Tony climbing the tree and tapping on the branch with a solid stick. If it "drummed" correctly he would then chop the whole branch from the tree. Then he would tap the length of the branch to hear where the hollow section started and finished. Then he would chop the long branch into didgeridoo length sections and the longer the hollow branch the more didgeridoos he could make. Tony and Toppy would then carry the cut didgeridoos back to their camp where they'd light a fire and season the didgeridoo for a few days by sitting it close enough to dry the bark off and heat the timber through but not burn it. Tony would then enlarge the hollow by pushing and pulling a long straight hardwood stick through the hollow branch many times. He would then use a big knife to round the ends and to remove any remaining bark to create a smooth outer skin. During this time Toppy would be in the creek making paint from different clays and black from the charcoal produced in the fire. The only colour she struggled to make was white.

White was usually made from a light coloured clay not found in the area, so Tony used Berger White jet dry paint. We didn't realise the problem, until one day he came in with white paint all over his hands and wet white paint on the didgeridoos. He didn't know enamel paint took days to dry and he couldn't get the paint off his hands no matter how hard he scrubbed with sand and water. I found him some Turps and told him to clean up and never use enamel paint again. God knows where it came from.

Toppy came in one day and told me Tony Johnson was across the road and he really needed to see me. Whenever Tony needed anything he was too embarrassed to ask me, so he'd skulk around for days until finally, Toppy would have to come and tell me he needed something. Tony was sitting under a gum tree next door to the pub. I asked "what's the matter" and he said, "Boss, Tony Johnson can't make didgeridoo no more". When I asked "why not", he said "no more tree Boss. Tony Johnson walks all day and no more tree Boss". Mmmm I thought. We have a problem. And then it came to me "Tony Johnson you need a car". "I can't buy a car Boss. Tony Johnson got no money". So I said, "you leave it to me Tony Johnson".

I knew one of the station hands wanted to sell his old Holden panel van because he couldn't afford to register it.

So I sent word to Kalala and the next morning I paid $400 cash for a green unregistered EH panel van. That morning Tony Johnson and Toppy walked into town and I presented him with the keys to his new car. Tony was so taken by the gesture he started to cry and so Toppy laughed at him, which upset Tony Johnson terribly. They really were a strange couple. I showed Toppy a photo of Tony Johnson and her once and she refused to believe it was her. She took one quick glance and said "that not me" and walked away. Tony begged her to come back but she said it was evil and refused to come back.

So off went Tony Johnson and Toppy in their new car and a full tank of fuel. Tony was a terrible driver and it took him the length of the road to find second gear. I should have told him not to go out to the highway and I hoped he knew to not go too far. Soon he was out of sight and I crossed my fingers.

Two days later Tony drove into the pub and unloaded ten beautiful didgeridoos and said "thanks Boss, this car number one". I told him to stay away from the highway as he disappeared into the dust. That night he stopped at the pub for a drink but I told him "you drink, you don't drive" and put my hand out for the keys. He thought about it for one second and threw them to me, so I said, "park it across the road first". And it became the normal park for the car.

I reckon it was about a week after he received the car he walked into town with Toppy from the opposite direction to where they lived. They both stopped across the road and sat in the shade where they'd normally park the car. I could see them and clearly here them arguing so I went across the road and asked them "what's going on. Where's the car". "Her fault" yelled Tony Johnson as she tried to belt him yelling, "I told you, Tony Johnson, I told you". When they settled down I finally discovered they ran out of fuel about ten kilometres into the scrub behind the pub. When I asked Tony why he didn't look at the fuel gauge he said, "doesn't work Boss". I said "it did a week ago Tony Johnson, I saw it" to which Tony replied, "but Boss it's been on E for two days, so I thought it didn't work". So I gave Tony a full jerry can from the servo and he and Toppy walked back to the car. I could have driven them but from a previous experience when I took them to their camp I knew they would expect it every time if I did it.

A week or so later and I saw Tony Johnson drive up to the bowser across the road and I thought great he's learned to look at the fuel gauge. I continued serving a bar full of customers from the two coaches in town and took no notice of the time the car was there. It must have been an hour at least before Toppy came into the shop end of the bar. I went to the kitchen and told Leonie Toppy must need some woman things but when Leonie went to serve her she said, "I need to talk to Boss, not Missus". So into the shop, I went. Toppy said "Tony Johnson can't pump up tyre Boss. It no work. He need help". I told her I was too busy to help Tony and he has to keep trying. I said, "it ain't bloody hard Toppy, tell him to push the hose on the valve". I think it must have been another hour before Toppy came back into the shop and said "Boss, you gotta help Tony Johnson, he no good. Very tired Boss. Pump no work". So I jumped the counter and ran over the road to the petrol station to find Tony sitting on the ground pushing the air lead onto a flat tyre whilst completely wet from sweat and looking like he was about to pass out from the heat. I said "quickly now, turn the compressor on and show me what's the matter. I'm flat out over there". Tony Johnson slowly looked up and said, "do what, Boss"? I repeated, "turn the bloody compressor on so I can what's the matter here". Tony looked to the little red tyre compressor sitting next to him and said, "turn what on Boss". So I bent over and flicked the very obvious black on /off switch from the clearly marked OFF position to the similarly clearly marked ON

position. The compressor leapt into life with a loud
BLLLLRRRR noise and the tyre immediately started
inflating. Tony looked at the compressor and to the tyre
and then turned to Toppy and yelled "I bloody told you to
turn the thing on woman. It's your bloody fault. I told her
Boss, I told her". She flew back with "you did bloody not
you useless ... obscenity after obscenity" as I walked back
to the bar. So after almost two hours, of Tony pushing an
airless pump hose nozzle onto a tyre valve with all his
might, Tony and Top End slowly drove to their camp
whilst still screaming at each other. It would not be a fun
night on the creek that night. Even the evil spirited
Kurdaitcha Man would have avoided their camp that
evening.

The next morning Tony and Toppy drove into town
from their camp on another flat tyre. The spare in the back
was also flat and so I repaired the tyres. I told Tony to be
careful when driving off road because we couldn't keep
repairing and replacing tyres. "No worries Boss", he said as
they drove away.

Two days later Tony Johnson rolled into town in front
of two coach loads of tourists on four flat tyres. The car
was weaving all over the road as the flat tyres rolled over
the rims. On the roof were about ten long gum tree

branches piled up high and tied through the front windows. It was an incredible sight and the tourists thought it was fantastic. Tony thought he was a hero and posed for photos for at least an hour. Rewarded with beers obviously encouraged him to stay longer than normal.

The next morning we fixed and changed five tyres and I said "Tony, enough of this". I told Tony we wouldn't fix his tyres anymore and he needed to learn to do it himself. We gave him some spare tyres and tubes and the tools for the job. Tony Johnson knew how to do it but he was a lazy man by nature and he always took a shortcut rather than doing anything properly. I knew this would end badly but we couldn't spend an hour every day repairing tyres for Tony because he refused to drive carefully through the bush. I told Tony Johnson to "never drive into town on flat tyres again. If you do I will take your car away".

Everything seemed to be going smoothly for the next couple of weeks. Tony was making good didgeridoos and he seemed happy. He managed the tyres well and I only needed to supply him with more patches but no more tyres or tubes. Then Tony Johnson and Top End left their camp. We hadn't seen them for a few days so we went to their camp. It wasn't obvious when we arrived there but a closer look showed they took their main possessions of clothes, food, tools and tyres and drove away. This concerned me because not only the car wasn't registered but it was unsafe on the open road at speed. But there was nothing we could do except wait.

A month later we received a phone call from a taxi company in Katherine asking if there was any money for Tony Johnson, waiting for him at the pub. We told the caller there were two cheques waiting for Tony and we could cash them for Tony if required. That afternoon a taxi arrived at Daly Waters Pub. It was the first taxi we ever saw in Daly Waters. Out hopped a beaming healthy looking Tony Johnson and Top End. They came in the bar smiling and in great spirits and asked for their cash. They then paid the taxi driver $270 in cash and, after he emptied their belongings out of the boot, the taxi left. I was gobsmacked and said, "where have you been Tony Johnson". Tony said he and Toppy were called away to a relative of Toppy's funeral at Kakadu. They spent two weeks in Kakadu and then drove to Pine Creek where the car blew the motor. So they hitched a lift to Katherine where they stayed with friends before deciding it was time to come home.

But it wasn't the same Tony Johnson. Something had changed. Tony wasn't interested in making didgeridoos but instead, he wanted to spend all day at the pub drinking. Top End hated Tony drinking all day and they continually argued. One morning Toppy came into the pub with multiple cuts and burns inflicted during a bad night at the camp and we decided enough was enough. We asked the Mataranka police to intervene and they decided it best to move Tony Johnson and Top End to Katherine where they could stay with friends and receive support.

This was the last we saw of Tony Johnson and Top End. They provided much entertainment and some wonderful memories as well as much frustration and disappointment. I hope they are okay.

STEVE NOTT

It was a normal day behind the bar when I heard the unmistakable sound of a horse clip-clop coming along the road. Then I could discern more than one clip clop. So I wandered out the front of the pub to witness four horses heading our way with two riders and it reminded me of a scene from the movie Burke and Wills. As they came closer I could see it was a thin bearded man and a beautiful girl, with two fully laden packhorses following on ropes. The bearded man looked like Ned Kelly and the girl like a super-model. It was surreal. And then I remembered Ivan, the owner of Christmas Creek station, 250km east of us, a few weeks ago mentioned a horseman riding around Australia would be coming our way.

The team arrived at the pub, the riders dismounted and tied the horses to the hitching rail and then the weary bearded rider introduced himself in a deep radio announcer type voice as Steve Nott. He said they rode 200km from Cape Crawford through lancewood forest and rocky country and they never saw a soul. He added, in the last few days they only ate one a snake, which he shot, and hadn't drunk an alcoholic drink for two weeks. Steve and his girlfriend looked very tired and hungry so we took them inside for a drink and meal. We also offered them a motel room and a hot shower, they eagerly and gratefully accepted.

Around Australia horseman Steve Nott and girls in front of the Daly Waters Pub

Our pub was licensed as a Public House license, we were expected to stable horses and so I offered for Steve to stable his horses at the rodeo ground behind the pub. Steve was into his fourth or fifth beer when I made the offer and he appeared to have already forgotten his horses, who patiently waited out front. I thought this may have happened to those horses many times previously. So we moved them to the yard where he gave them some water and feed before going to their own room in the motel.

A few hours later Steve and his girlfriend came into the bar looking refreshed but still thirsty. It was obvious Steve liked a beer but he loved a rum. That evening the bar was entertained by Steve Nott telling the story of his ride from Merrygoen in NSW to Cape Byron, Australia's most easterly point and then to Cape York our most northerly and now he was about half way to Steep Point in Western Australia, the most westerly point and was then heading south and then east to Wilsons Promontory in Victoria, the most southerly point of the mainland before going north and home in NSW.

Conversation uncovered the fact Steve's girlfriend wasn't all that enamoured with the outback before joining him two weeks ago and the past two weeks, one snake diet, hadn't changed her mind. Fortunately, with our help, Steve was able to book her onto a Greyhound bus and she left the next day.

Steve stayed with us for a couple of weeks. During his time with us, his girlfriend left for home as he settled into doing some work on his Second World War pack saddles and gear plus letting his horses slowly recover from their long torrid trek from the Cape. But for most of the time, Steve lazed around the pub telling stories to anyone who'd listen whilst enjoying a few beers. We all enjoyed Steve's company and it was a sad day when he decided to ride out of town.

Steve moved his horses to the rodeo ground for stabling

On the day he left, we all stood in the street and waved goodbye. Our yardie Grant decided to ride half the day with Steve and the two of them departed, with Steve dragging his three packhorses whilst riding his pony and with Grant next to him on his mare Bella.

A few hours later, Grant returned and said Steve was already past Sunday Creek and going well. It was two or three hours later, when I saw a lone packhorse gallop through town with its packsaddles dragging on the ground. The horse was covered in foam and obviously scared out of its wits. It didn't stop at the pub nor at the rodeo yard that had been its home and instead, kept going at a tired but full gallop into the bush. Grant and I tried tracking the horse but it was well gone. All of us worried about Steve and decided Grant should ride into the bush and try to find him.

However, less than an hour later, as Grant was ready to leave, Steve came into town with only one packhorse and nursing a badly injured hand. It transpired, the packhorse took fright at a snake and bolted with Steve holding on by the lead. Steve took off in pursuit but unfortunately after some distance, the packhorse went left and his pony went right, leaving Steve to crash into a tree and split the webbing of his hand between the thumb and forefinger. He wrapped it up as best he could and then he tried to find the missing horse, with no result. When we told Steve, his packhorse galloped through town an hour ago, he thought he would be able to find him.

Grant took Steve to Mataranka to get some stitches and they returned later in the day. Steve had way too many drinks that night whilst telling everyone in the bar his story.

After surfacing late the next day he headed into the bush in search of his missing packhorse and gear. Steve rode back into town that afternoon, with a couple of dented packsaddles and some ropes and leather belts ... but no packhorse. Over the next few days, Steve looked far and wide. The boys from Kalala Station gave a hand when they could but his horse was gone bush. Steve's horse was never found and it's still a mystery what happened to it.

Steve kept looking for a couple of weeks and during this time he also mulled over the importance of the decision he needed to make very soon as the wet was approaching fast. If Steve didn't leave immediately, there was every chance the seasonal wet weather would arrive before he crossed the vast wilderness of the Murranji, Duncan and Buchanan tracks forming the combined stock routes Steve needed to follow from Daly Waters in the NT to Kununurra in WA.

If the wet arrived whilst Steve was on any part of the remote stock route system it could be a disaster. These stock routes are crossed by many streams and creeks and whilst empty in the dry are potentially raging torrents turning vast areas of land into lakes during the wet.

After taking advice from a couple of local station people Steve decided it would be wise to wait for the wet to pass. This would mean a wait of about three or four months. He thought he would need to leave his horses with the station and go home to NSW but I could see it was not his preferred option and so I offered him a job working behind the bar and he gladly accepted it. We worked out a deal where Steve would live in a pub caravan and eat whatever he wanted in return for working about twenty hours a week. Any drinks would be put on a tab and he would work the extra hours needed to cover his drinks. This arrangement worked out well. Steve drank plenty, so he worked long hours. He preferred night work as he was a famously slow starter in the mornings.

Steve was a very funny and entertaining barman, and whilst our pet kangaroo Daly didn't like him, everyone else did. Steve liked nothing better than a good laugh and a few beers and rums. He also displayed some strange behavioural habits including eating anything alive for a bet.

He would regularly find a cockroach, an insect not a pest in the NT, and would bet all at the bar he'd eat it. He always collected a mountain bets and never failed to eat the insect and collect the bet. One of his more memorable bets occurred when a huge rain moth, the size of a bird, flew into the bar. Steve leapt the bar, caught the moth in mid-flight, and never one to miss an opportunity, he asked for a hundred dollar bet he couldn't eat it. Now whilst no one individually took him on I did convince everyone, by placing ten dollars on the bar myself, to match my bet. No-one welched and next minute we witnessed one hundred and fifty dollars on the bar and Steve holding a very angry moth. I'm sure Steve would never have eaten one of these monsters before and I wonder if he'd ever seen one, because he took a long time to decide how to attack it. But Steve being Steve and not one to ever payout on a losing bet he started from the head ... maybe his first mistake. He recoiled in disgust as he bit thru the crunchy head. A vile smell hit us all and we realised this moth held a few secrets within. Steve retched and went white as a ghost. We thought he was beaten. I was sure he was beaten. But then in a moment of clarity and reasoning, he asked me to pour him a large glass of rum and proceeded to use it as a dipping sauce and marinade. He slowly but surely ate the huge flapping moth. He really struggled with the wings. He said it felt like eating dusty cotton wool but added it tasted like urine. And in the end, he finished the moth and declared "that does it, never again will I take a bet to eat … a moth".

"I will never … eat a moth again" … Steve Nott

Steve also received a few bonuses by offering his services for horse rides late at night. I won't go into detail but "Steve's Midnight Horse Ride Tours" always seemed to attract the ladies and his rides were in demand.

After about three months Steve was ready to leave. He recruited another packhorse and trained it during his break. His gear was repaired and all his leather straps and ropes were in top order for the rest of his ride. So after way too many beers and rums one night he left the next morning. As he rode out of town part of me hoped he'd be back. He was fun to have around and a great worker.

Steve Nott never rode back into town. But we did catch up with Steve in 1989 whilst driving through the south of Western Australia. In his unique and laconic style, Steve rode into the town where we were staying and we had a long night of drinking and telling stories.

Footnote: Steve Nott went on to become the first person to ride a horse around Australia and visit the four extremities of the continent.

TAFFY and SAM

During our first season, we had regular visits from several coach line (tourist coach) services. They included the famous names of Australian Pacific Tour, Evergreen Coachlines, Wollongong Coaches, Premier Coachlines and ATT Kings. Due to the increased demand for tourist services to the NT several negotiated rates for the entire next season for the pub to serve them a sit-down lunch. Several simply wanted to visit and let their guests wander around, get a drink, buy souvenirs and take photos and a couple of others like Contiki wanted to overnight in our camping area. It was a great blend for us and things were looking good for 1987 ... except we lacked staff.

For most of 1986, we survived with me, Leonie, Phil, Toni and Grant plus the odd backpacker. It was obvious we were going to need more staff to get through 1987.

One of the regular fun coach visits was from an ATT Kings off-road adventure small off-road bus driven by Taffy, a long haired long bearded larrikin of Welsh descent and hosted by his tanned girlfriend fiancée Samantha (Sam). They made an odd couple as Taffy was short-necked and short in stature, loud and funny and whilst he certainly couldn't be described as handsome he did have a "bad boy" appeal to the ladies. On the other hand, Sam was tall with fashion model looks and a keen sense of humour. Together they made a great team and they certainly seemed to get on well with their guests and definitely were liked by everyone around them.

Each time they called into the pub Taffy would relate incredibly funny stories of his detours and exploits to everyone within earshot at the bar. One of his most famous was when he entered the ATT Kings coach into a famous outback mud rally. The trouble was a video of the clearly branded coach powering through the mud hole made the national news and was seen by his bosses. Taffy was definitely going to be sacked but somehow he convinced them they couldn't have bought the national publicity and saved his job. But he was on a lifetime warning not to do another bad thing. For Taffy that was impossible as he took great pride in finding off-the-beaten-track, not on the itinerary, experiences for his guests and they loved it. Other coach drivers hated Taffy but I think they were jealous of his carefree attitude and zest for a good time.

Taffy and Sam's AAT Kings "rally car"

As mentioned before, Taffy displayed a habit of shocking people with his stunts. On one occasion when Taffy and Sam dropped in I mentioned the Daly Creek horseshoe waterfall was flowing in all its glory. This was a rare event to see and they were keen to view it. So leaving their guests at the bar we jumped in the pub Nissan Ute and raced to the falls. As we were powering along the rough bush track I noticed a huge Brahman cow resting on the track. I honked the horn but it didn't move so I hit the brakes hard and turned the wheel but the track was wet and slippery and the ute kept going full pace straight into the poor huge sleeping beast. However, it wasn't sleeping. It was dead and was dead for quite a few days. A strange phenomenon occurs inside a dead cow. The contents of the four stomachs immediately start to ferment and much methane gas is created. This causes the cow to expand to enormous proportions until it finds a weak point and leaks out, or until a car hits it and it explodes … and so when we hit the cow it exploded. The ute was an open-topped vehicle and it exploded all over the three of us. The other phenomenon with the gases and stomachs of a dead cow is the unbelievably bad smell of the rotten maggot infested flesh and stomach contents. Flesh exploded all over the car and us. The hide was stuck to the bull-bar and was under the car. I couldn't believe the smell and we were all dry retching. I kept driving as fast as I could to the creek. As soon as we reached it Taffy leapt out of the ute and stripped naked before running and diving into the water. Sam quickly followed and before long we were all in the water rinsing our bodies, hair and clothes but we couldn't wash the car. The drive back to the pub was a fast but smelly affair. Taffy and Sam's guests couldn't believe how bad they both smelled when they entered the bar and therefore saw no issue with a slightly longer delay in departure as they both took a long soapy shower. But before going to the showers Taffy insisted on telling the story to everyone who'd listen. Both Taffy and Sam laughed the event off as like this happened every day and when they left everyone was still laughing as Taffy described what happened for the tenth time.

The beautiful Daly Creek Horseshoe Falls

Leonie and I decided Taffy and Sam would make a wonderful addition to our small team and so, during their next visit, we offered them a job. They both looked very interested but said they needed time to think it over. A week later we received a call saying they accepted our offer and would join us at the end of the season.

Taffy and Sam joined us soon after Steve Nott arrived. With the addition of these three identities, it was going to be a very funny wet season. Having Taffy and Sam along with Steve and Grant around gave Leonie and me an opportunity to get away a few times. Since moving into the pub we hadn't experienced anything more than the odd day off. Taffy and Steve instantly became great mates and wonderfully entertaining barmen whilst Sam was a terrific help for Leonie. Whilst I know Sam would have preferred more bar work and front of house activity, it was really important Leonie had great back-of-house help and another girl to share the massive load of motel, meals and office work. Sorry, Sam.

We all enjoyed great times together and we loved all of them. We shared our second Daly Waters Christmas together at the Pub and it was great times.

Christmas Day 1987 with Leonie, Andrea, Taffy, Sam
and Steve

Great times never last and unfortunately for us, but better for her, Sam decided to leave and work in Darwin, where she got a great job managing the busy Avis Car Rental franchise for the Bailey family, with whom we became very good friends and still are.

However on the other hand Taffy struggled with Sam's departure. They were engaged for some time and he found it hard to enjoy life without his constant companion. But in time and with Taffy flair, he shrugged it off by purchasing an MG Sports car and burying himself in work, booze and women.

The new combination was Taffy and Steve and together they entertained our visitors and locals with great stories and crazy antics. When Steve started doing his late night horse rides for ladies, we had dubbed "rides with the Midnight Cowboy", Taffy started rides of his own, and we dubbed "rides with the MG Cowboy". It was great fun and we all shared many laughs.

Taffy was not only a great entertainer but was a very good help to me. I was cooking our now famous Beef and Barra BBQ for well over 100 people every night of the week for month after month and it was starting to tell on me. I needed a break every now and then, particularly if I tied a big one on the previous night and Taffy quickly took to it and was an excellent fast cook on the BBQ. At last, there was someone else who could help me with the BBQ job.

Our pub didn't close until the last few people went to bed. This ensured many late nights at the bar. In those days drinking with the patrons was part of the job in the NT. I did it myself and encouraged the staff to do so as well. Unfortunately, it meant late nights and early mornings with many hangovers so with Taffy helping me to get some regular early nights it was a real blessing.

Taffy on the job in his Daly Waters Pub "uniform"

Taffy eventually decided it was time to move on. We enjoyed some great times but it was obvious he needed to get on the road again. Taffy went on to manage Mt Hart Station in WA for many years.

DAVE, DALLAS and BRETT

The first Kalala workers we met, were a well-mannered lad named Dave, a young cheeky boy Dallas Kuhn and local Brett.

Dave was originally from Texas in Queensland. Dave's main job was as a road train driver moving cattle from station to station as well as taking them to markets or meat works in the NT or Queensland. Dave spoke slowly but you could tell he was intelligent and well read. Dallas was instantly likeable but you could see he was trouble and I quickly (and correctly) guessed I'd better always keep an eye on him. Dallas was a station hand who, according to Dave, rode a horse as well as anyone. Brett was the quiet one, who after a few rums became a bit of a stirrer. Brett also drove a road train.

During one bar conversation, Dave told me he was the only person in the region, he knew, who dabbled in the share market. At that time, I didn't own shares myself, having sold all investments to purchase the pub but I did have an interest. Dave found it comforting there was someone else in the area to share his thoughts on the stock market. Eventually the shares caused Dave a bit of heartache, as he loaded up on Alan Bond companies, including Bond's disastrous airship foray and Bell Resources ... Brett and Dallas found it all amusing.

Within a few weeks of becoming publican at Daly Waters I got to them quite well and I realised how difficult it must be, in particular for Dave and Dallas, as both of them were thousands of kilometres from home. Their life was working on the station from dawn to dusk, six or seven days a week and the occasional night in the pub.

I felt it was my duty to entertain them and for the pub to provide an enjoyable alternative to their work. It wasn't difficult, as everyone in town and the pub loved these easy going lads.

The lads loved a practical joke. One Saturday night, very soon after we moved into the pub, Dallas came in with an injured finger in a white bandage. Whilst they sipped on a few drinks I moved around the bar handing out white bandages to everyone and quietly convinced them to wrap their index finger ... without Dallas knowing. At my nod, we all pointed our bandaged fingers in the air. It was hilarious and was a great introduction to the "Kalala lads".

The Bandage night with Grant, Dave, Dallas, Brett, myself, Denise and Leonie

On another night I decided to introduce them to the game of "Beer Hunter". This game was loosely taken from the movie Deer Hunter where the lead actor sits at a table with a white cloth around his head and plays Russian roulette by pulling the trigger of a pistol with one bullet in the chamber. In this game, we all sat around a table and I wrapped toilet paper around each players head and placed a can of beer in front of each person. Everyone then has to close their eyes whilst I shook one can vigorously and then open their eyes and open their can next to their head. Obviously, in this game, the loser doesn't take a bullet but instead takes a full spray of beer to the face … it became more fun when I shook everyone's beer!!

Dave and Brett (opposite) look concerned as I explain "Beer Hunter"

Dave was an adventurous guy who built his own dirt rally car at the station from old car parts and raced it around the tracks. He talked me into swapping the old slow motor in the pub Nissan ute over to a Chrysler V8 motor, retrieved from a wreck at the dump and gave Grant and me advice on how to exchange the motors. When we came to a dead end, because the tail-shaft was too long, he took it to the station, cut it shorter and welded it back together at the right length and refitted it. When completed, the old ute flew.

In our first year, when the pub became really busy, the lads would come into the pub on most weekends looking for girls. Unfortunately, they always dressed up in neatly pressed clothes and white runners. They were always freshly showered and clean shaven and smelled of cheap aftershave. All this, always resulted in the girls ignoring them. It wasn't because they weren't good looking enough or badly mannered but I put it down to the girls wanting to meet real outback jackaroos but the lads looked like the boring city slickers they were escaping from. After watching this for a couple of months I sat down for a drink with a dejected Dave one Saturday night and said "Dave you're going about it all wrong. Next week jump off your horse or truck and come to the pub in your dirtiest clothes, boots and jackaroo hat chewing a length of straw ... and trust me you'll need to place your swag permanently at the creek next door. And Dave, don't come in next week smelling like a bathroom and grinning at every girl like a Cheshire cat. I want you to strut in the pub as though you own the whole Northern Territory, order a beer and act cool. The girls will be intrigued and they'll be wandering over to you in a few minutes to find out who you are and what you do... I can guarantee it".

Low and behold, the next Saturday night into our pub full of tourists comes Dave with his mates Dallas and Brett looking like they were straight out of a John Wayne movie.

The only trouble was they couldn't stop giggling at each other and whilst Dave tried his hardest to be "cool", the immature ever-cheeky Dallas broke up every time Dave tried. Eventually they settled down and finally, a couple of giggling girls approached the lads. Dave couldn't believe it and when one of them later accepted his invitation to go for a "drive" and he gave me a wink as he strutted out the door with the young blonde in tow. Dave's swag became a permanent feature on the creek not far from the pub and his new swagger replaced his previous embarrassed shuffle.

As mentioned, the lads loved a practical joke or two. One day I needed to drive a parcel to Kalala Station, about ten kilometres from the pub on a dirt track. Whilst driving out there I went through a closed gate. In the country, it's an unwritten law to leave a gate how you find it. As I came to the gate I noticed a large white painted rock about fifty metres before the gate. I thought nothing of it. I opened the gate, drove through the gate, closed the gate and drove off. As I drove off I noticed another large white rock over fifty metres past the gate. I wondered what they were there for.

As I was driving to the station it came to me. Years ago when working in the far north east of South Australia road train drivers used similarly placed rocks either side of gates, to let them know where to stop after they opened and then went through the gate. The rock was at the exact distance past the gate to allow a triple road train to just clear the gate and allow it to be closed without going too far past the gate and creating a longer walk than necessary to go back and close the gate. Sound confusing? Well, it works well and the drivers put their trust in those rocks.

On my way back from the station I pulled up next to the first rock and moved it five metres closer to the gate. I then went through the gate and did the same thing to the rock on the far side. As I drove off I was doubled up in laughter. If you don't get why I was laughing, you will soon.

A few days later Dave and Brett rolled through town on their way to the Katherine abattoirs and two days later they came back through town on the way to the station. That night, the three of them came into town for a big night out. During the evening Dave said, "you wouldn't believe it Mark but some bastard moved our rocks". "Rocks", I said, "what rocks". Brett then joined in "we have rocks either side of the gate to show us when to stop so we don't have to walk any further back to the gate than we have to. Someone moved them back a few yards and when I walked back to close the gate I saw the end of the last trailer was still in the gateway. So I walked all the way back to the truck to move forward a few yards and then walk back to close the gate and then the fifty yards back to the truck to take off. Can you imagine how pissed off I was ... after driving for twenty hours straight".

"Rocks. What a clever idea" I said smiling "why would anyone would move the rocks"? Dave started "because some bastard is playing a joke on us ....." And then he realised the joke was played by me and in chorus, they said "you rotten bastard". I said "surely this has been to you before"? They looked at each other and said "nope, never. You got us, you bastard" as they laughed and laughed. Dallas couldn't believe it and would not stop laughing for a week. For the next month, every time he came into the pub, he looked at me and broke up.

The funny end to this joke is about two months later Brett and Dave admitted to me they couldn't trust the rocks anymore and each time they drive through the gate, they would go at least ten meters past the rocks, just in case they'd been moved. It was my last laugh, that time.

This may sound like frivolous stuff but when you live in the outback, these minor practical jokes meant a lot. For them and for me. It kept it fun.

Dave earned the last laugh one night, though. It was late at night and he returned from a long haul to Mt Isa and back. It has taken four days and he was obviously very tired when he came into the bar for a cool drink. Whilst he sat at the bar and chatted, Taffy unbeknownst to us, snuck out to Dave's road-train and unhitched the third (last) trailer and came back inside the bar. After a drink Dave said he was heading home, Taffy winked at me and said, "come with me and watch this". So we wandered out with Dave.

Dave walked across the road and climbed the steps up into his huge Mack prime mover, engaged low gear and drove off. Within one hundred metres he turned hard left and so he steered out very wide to make the turn to not cut the corner and demolish our fuel pumps. In doing so, he looked back to see his last trailer still sitting beside the road. Dave didn't miss a beat. He stopped and then reversed, on exactly the same line, back around the corner and with great precision the second trailer clicked into the joiner hitch Taffy had left propped up, after unhitching. Dave then casually walked back to the third trailer, engaged the hitch and raised the prop before going back to the prime mover and driving off ... whilst grinning at us in the pub doorway and giving us a middle-finger salute.

Definitely, the last laugh went to Dave.

Late in our second year, I was lucky enough to get invited to the Adelaide Grand Prix by Fosters Brewery and the invite said I could take someone with me. Normally it would be with Leonie but she was needed to mind the pub. So I took Dave. We flew to Adelaide. He'd never been to Adelaide, let alone any capital city or a Grand Prix and as he loved fast cars, he was rapt. We were given corporate passes, including a VIP lunch in a beautiful marquee and we were fortunate enough to be seated next to famous Australian golfer Ian Stanley. Ian was a great bloke, who was incredulous Dave drove triple road-trains on a million acre cattle station and that I owned a famous outback pub. We had a terrific day but hardly saw the race ... and we didn't care. Dave and I revelled in a wonderful time in Adelaide and for me the break from the pub couldn't have been timelier as I returned full of energy and ready to get into work again.

After we left Daly Waters Pub, Dave received his helicopter pilot license and eventually moved to Victoria River Downs where he became manager of helicopter mustering for Helimuster, a huge company with choppers all over the north of Australia.

Footnote: many years later Leonie and I were at home one night watching a documentary series about a remote NT station owner, Sara Henderson and the trials and tribulations of a woman running a huge cattle station. In one scene, set at her kitchen table, she is instructing the

helicopter pilot on how she wanted her cattle mustered ...
and you guessed it, there was Dave.

BILLY TAPP

The extensive Tapp family and stations, with the
infamous patriarch Bill Tapp, were based at Killarney
Station but there were sons and daughters spread around
the territory. Bill's siblings were talented horsemen and all
performed, at least, semi-professionally at rodeos. Ben
Tapp managed a station on the Roper River and Daniel
managed another. Daughter Toni married a Coutts and was
on another station, whilst another son Billy Tapp, managed
Maryfield Station only about an hour drive north of Daly
Waters. Billy was a semi-regular and would drop into the
pub with his girlfriend Donna or with his workers. We
really liked Billy and Donna. They worked hard and loved
life in the bush. Their workers were all good lads and I
wished Maryfield Station had been closer to us than
Larrimah, so we could have seen them more often.

Billy invited us to a BBQ one day and said just bring a
few drinks and he'd kill a nice beast and would supply the
food. So when the day came out we went to enjoy a day at
Maryfield Station. When we arrived the boys weren't
anywhere to be found. Donna said there was a bit of work

to do and would be back soon. It all seemed a bit disorganised but hey, that's life in the bush. So whilst I cracked open a cold beer, Leonie shared a bottle of white wine with Donna and together they put on a nice salad. It wasn't long before Billy and the station lads returned from moving a few head of cattle to a holding yard. Billy and I grabbed a beer and chatted, whilst the lads lit a large fire, in an area not far from the station homestead.

Billy's BBQ area was pretty basic. An open yard between the house and sheds housed a rudimentary stone fire pit. The BBQ plate above the fire appeared to be a steel disc off a very large plough but I must admit it made the perfect BBQ plate. The disc naturally sloped down towards the centre and in the centre was a hole where it would normally be affixed to the machinery. All the fat and juices would drain perfectly off the meat, as it cooked. The disc was smoking blue-hot and I reckoned we needed to get something on there soon before it melted.

Before long we all gathered around the BBQ and watched Billy lift huge pieces of marinated rump steak out of a plastic tub and drop them on to the plough disc where they instantly sizzled. Each steak was the size of a large dinner plate and was only sliced about 1/4" (6mm thick) but this didn't stop Billy from filling the disc with about a dozen huge steaks and turn them over and over for at least twenty minutes.

In the Territory, some beef cattle are known to carry brucellosis. Brucellosis can be transmitted from cattle to humans by eating undercooked meat from infected animals.

So even though my preference for steak is medium-rare and Leonie's is rare and even though the beast came from a herd declared free of brucellosis, Billy would ensure every piece of steak to come off the BBQ that day would be crucified to well done.

Finally, after Billy and the station hands were satisfied the brucellosis risk was eliminated by cooking the steaks for well over thirty minutes, we ate. I was starving after consuming a six pack of white cans before and during the cook. Each of the workers placed a large piece of meat on their plate before layering salad over it and moving off to sit under a tree and get into it. When they'd all grabbed their platefuls we were finally invited to get ours. I watched as Leonie scanned the disc for a piece of underdone meat but they all looked the same ... blackened. I didn't get a choice as Billy grabbed a huge piece of steak and lowered it onto my plate. Now I love steak and normally it's the bigger the better but I was seriously concerned this would beat me and I wouldn't look good in front of Billy and the lads. As it turned out I shouldn't have worried about the size of the steak. It was so thin and was cooked so long, there was no volume and weight in it at all. The main problem was the dryness and toughness but what it lacked in tenderness it made up for in flavour. The cooking on a plough disc and the caramelisation through the natural fats and over-cooking gave it an impressive taste. History tells us a station owner normally shoots and eats his neighbour's cattle for the table (named a "killer") and then complains to the neighbour how tough it was. In this case, Billy swore he killed one of his best "killers" and so, even though we didn't say anything bad about the meal as it was really tasty, he would have no-one to blame about the toughness.

We had a terrific experience at Maryfield Station with wonderful bush hospitality and plenty of laughs. Billy and Donna became very good mates during our time at Daly Waters Pub.

Chapter 20. BUSH MEDICINE

Daly Waters Pub is about three hundred kilometres south from the nearest hospital and doctor in Katherine and one hundred and fifty kilometres north of a Health Centre with a nurse in Elliott. Whilst our pub held the "locals" flying doctor medical cabinet it certainly didn't help much if anyone was badly injured ... inevitably that occurred from time to time.

BUSH NURSE

My first recollection of the need for medical help occurred when I was walking near a cattle yard at the rear of the hotel. I trod on a plank with a protruding rusty nail and it went straight through my safety boot (blue thong) and into the sole of my foot. It went deep and hurt like hell but a more pressing problem was the real danger of getting tetanus. Tetanus is a bacterial infection commonly found in soil, dust and manure and I was in a shitty dusty cattle yard ... comprehend my position? I did.

We were instructed to call Katherine Hospital or the Elliott nurse depending on the severity and urgency of the situation. The decision was made to call the nurse in Elliott. She understood what I needed and said to jump in the car and drive to her "for a quick jab". I'm not good with injections at the best of times, so when someone casually says "a quick jab" I worry.

So, as we were busy in the pub, I drove myself the hour and a half to Elliott. Elliott was not a pretty town and the pub had a poor reputation, so as I was keen to get jabbed and get back to the pub, I pulled up at the Health Centre. Basically it was a small house, and I knocked on the door. A friendly lady greeted me and took me inside a relatively normal looking home to the kitchen table. She then opened the fridge where she moved a dozen or so cans of beer aside to expose a box of medical phials. After finding the phial she was seeking and then drawing the contents into a needle she found in the cutlery drawer, she turned around and in one quick calculated move, more befitting a careless jackaroo than a careful nurse, she ripped my shirt up to the shoulder and jabbed the needle into my left bicep. One rapid push on the plunger, withdrawn just as quick and thrown with netball accuracy into a half full waste bin followed by a strong thumb placed over the puncture wound whilst the other hand peeled off two inches of Elastoplast tape and then just as fast she swapped the thumb for the tape ... it was over in a blink and I was in agony.

I went to get up but almost fainted. She rolled her eyes. I asked meekly, "a glass of water please". She rolled her eyes again. I said "I'm not good with needles" and she replied "don't worry, there was a lad in earlier who was worse than you ... but he was only three and a half".

I left and went to the famously bad Elliott pub. My mouth was dry and I thought a beer would help. The beer was hot and the barman was rude and it didn't help, so I drove back to a nice friendly pub at Daly Waters.

MAD DASH

It was a normal day in the Daly Waters Pub. Tourists were pouring in and a few locals dropped by. The pub was busy and everything was going well and then late in the afternoon, a Toyota Landcruiser arrived with two workers on their way to Tenant Creek.

One of the guys was a bit loud and obnoxious but he seemed okay. They said they left Darwin in the morning and after enjoying a couple of beers in the traditional pub stops of Mataranka and Larrimah, finally arrived here. It was late afternoon and I quickly deduced they had enjoyed more than a couple of beers before getting to us.

I went into the beer garden to get ready to cook the BBQ and left Darryl in charge of the bar. It wasn't long before I heard a commotion in the bar and saw the obnoxious one doing a German WWII March with arms swinging wildly as he left the bar and went out onto the road. Next minute Darryl has run out to me saying he'd fallen over, he's unconscious and there is blood coming out of one ear.

This was an obvious "ring the Mataranka nurse" emergency. She asked Leonie to describe the injuries and then rang Katherine to plead for an ambulance to be sent to us. In the end, it was agreed we would drive north with the patient and meet the ambulance on the road.

So we loaded the now groggy but conscious patient plus his mate into our car and I drove the patient with his workmate towards the ambulance. This is dangerous stuff. Driving in the territory at night on unfenced roads is discouraged. Cattle like to sleep on the road as the bitumen is warm on cold nights. People die driving at night in the Territory.

On the way north, the bloke started ranting a raving and insisting he was fine. He wanted to stop at the nearest pub and he tried to take control of the car. He refused to go to the hospital and this gave me and the other guy a really tough job to keep him under control. Eventually, we met the ambulance and once again the guy put up a huge fight.

The ambulance finally left with the patient inside and I drove slowly and carefully back to the pub.

A few days later, we heard the guy collapsed in the ambulance suffering from a bleeding attack on the brain and was airlifted to Darwin for an emergency procedure. Apparently he survived but would not have, if not of our quick action. Incredibly, we never received a call or any correspondence from this guy to thank any of us for what we did for him. Blokes like him don't deserve help.

What we did get though, was a subpoena to appear in court in Darwin. Apparently, the guy was suing his employer, the NT Government, for workers compensation for his injuries "incurred during his journey". The subpoena said Darryl and I were required to testify about the events leading up to him getting injured. We drove to Darwin and after a fun night at a local pub, I was severely cross-examined by the guy's legal team. They accused me of being a hostile witness and threatened to have my testimony censured. But fortunately the judge saw through this ruse and after a full day in the stand, the lawyer said "we have more questions for the witness your honour. I suggest we return tomorrow." That night was the longest sleepless night of my life. The next morning I sat in the stand again and the lawyer asked his first question "how far is it from Darwin to Daly Waters and how long does it take to drive"? I replied "six hundred kilometres and about six hours". The lawyer then said "thank you, you can leave the stand now. Next witness your honour ..."I was confused and angry but I was also very relieved it was over. I felt like I was on trial.

Darryl was let off much easier than me. I wasn't able to witness his cross-examination but according to Darryl, they tried to prove he served the guy when he was intoxicated. Both of us were ready for the question and were able to honestly respond "we only served him about four drinks ... we weren't privy to what he drunk before he arrived at our pub and his behaviour was typical of almost every drinker in the territory."

Darryl and I couldn't wait to get back to our pub and drove directly home ... where we threw down a cold beer or three to end the saga.

IT'S A KNOCKOUT

A fencing contractor from Larrimah named Paddy Heatley and his crew spent a couple of months camped in the airport hangar not far from the pub. They pretty much kept to themselves but did come into the pub every couple of days.

We liked Paddy and his boys. They were rough and tough but told funny and interesting stories of working around the territory. Paddy was a large strong man with huge rough hands from years of toiling in the outback.

Paddy had given us baby pigs for Christmas and on another occasion, at about lunchtime, Paddy bought in a plucked and dressed but uncooked bush turkey and asked if we could cook it in our weber BBQ ready for him to collect for his dinner. Obviously, he didn't have an oven at his camp. Naturally, we said yes and so later in the day he collected his freshly cooked bird.

The fine for killing a bush turkey in the Northern Territory was $2,000 at the time and therefore the locals called it $2,000 chook to guard the secret. Each time we cooked a bird, Paddy would let us try a portion of his "chook" and it was always wonderful. A little gamey in flavour but tender and succulent. No wonder he was so keen on them.

One afternoon he came into the bar and declared it was his birthday. I offered to shout him a beer, so he took a seat at the bar and proceeded to drink quite a few beers. This was most unlike Paddy who would normally only ever have a couple then he'd go to his camp. As the afternoon progressed Paddy became a little drunk but he seemed fine.

Close to dusk, he said to me "shit, I forgot, I have something in the truck for you. Come on, give me a hand to get it". So, with me thinking we were going to get a "chook" or two we walked outside and down the dusty track towards his 4WD. At about half way there he said, as he walked, "bugger it, I'll give it to you now". I turned my head to find out what he was talking about just in time to see a huge fist thrown from a big right hook crash into the side of my head. I went over like a nine-pin. He was towering over me as I tried to get up but he kept laying into me with kick after kick to my body and head. All I could do was cover my head up with my arms. I thought I was going to die there until I heard a male voice scream "enough Paddy, enough". Paddy stopped his attack and stared down at me with a really evil stare before giving out one last kick to my stomach. He then jumped in his Toyota and left.

I didn't know who called him off me, as I tried unsuccessfully to drag myself to my feet and crawl back to the hotel. Within minutes, a couple of locals helped me up and took me to the rear of the pub where Leonie and others tried to patch me up. I hardly remember any of this. I was in a bad shape and my whole body was awash in pain.

The next thing I remember was waking up the next day with a black and blue face and body. I sported a few cracked top front teeth and a very sore jaw, one black eye and a fist scrape across my head. I really should have gone to a doctor as my head injuries were quite terrible and there was no doubt I was concussed. But it's simply not easy when you live as remote as where we lived.

I was told I should ring the police and press charges but I decided to just let it be. I simply reckon Paddy went over his limit and like so many I've seen since, the grog turned him into an angry man and a fighter. I was in the wrong place at the wrong time when he cracked.

A day or so later Roy from Kalala Station, where Paddy was working, came into the pub and informed Leonie he sacked Paddy and told him to leave town. We never saw him again.

The only thing I ever said, to anyone, about the incident was how disappointed I was Paddy hit me without warning. It was a cowardly act from such a big strong man. He would have beaten me to a pulp even if he had warned me but his reputation was sullied by a cowardly king-hit and I believe it was the reason Roy moved him off the station. If it was a fairer fight and even if no-one understood why he hit me, I think Roy would have let him stay without any action and I would have understood.

Fortunately, I recovered relatively quickly from the beating and the only scars I bore for years to come were four cracked and broken front teeth. Thirty years later I underwent a series of painful operations to have the teeth covered by rather large expensive white crowns ... I thought they looked good but Leonie said I looked like the racehorse, Phar Lap.

WHERE'S THE HELP

A man ran into the pub and told me a car had rolled at the creek crossing on the road into Daly Waters and a woman was badly injured. Phil immediately jumped in his car and went to help.

It was morning and the pub was already busy. The boss of the NT Bushfire Council was in the caravan park and after I made him aware of the accident, he also attended the scene. He came back to the pub and rang the Katherine Police and Hospital to report the woman had serious injuries and required immediate help. Carl and Tom from Amungee Station were our local Emergency Services team and they were notified and quickly attended the scene also.

Over the ensuing hours, several frustrating unsuccessful attempts were made, by those at the scene, to convince the

319

authorities to send a Medi-Vac aircraft. The woman could not be moved for risk of her passing away and the waiting game, for an ambulance to attend, started. Leonie delivered much needed water and food to the scene and from her report to me and from my position at the bar, it seemed an unreal situation had developed. In addition to not sending an aircraft, no matter how much they pleaded, the authorities would not allow the Bushfire Council to take the patient to Katherine in their aircraft, which was only several hundred metres away and the team were told to wait for the vehicular ambulance to arrive from Katherine … three hundred kilometres away. Reports coming back to me suggested the woman's condition was deteriorating and she was in need of urgent doctor assistance. More calls were made by angry frustrated emergency services and government personnel and finally, after a few hours of the poor woman lying on the roadside, the authorities agreed to send an aircraft.

In the afternoon, after almost four hours of unacceptable delays, the Medi-Vac aircraft finally arrived with professional medical help. Unfortunately, this help proved to be too late, as the poor woman passed away as they were transferring her to the aircraft. An unbelievable, unacceptable occurrence.

The ensuing hours were difficult for everyone who assisted at the scene, including the woman's family. Their anger was palatable and understandable but there was nothing any of us could do to help. In the following weeks and months, an enquiry was held but we were never made aware of the results. Hopefully it was critical of the authorities. This most unfortunate tragedy highlights the perilous nature of living and travelling in the Australian outback. What makes me angry is the death of this poor woman was completely avoidable.

Chapter 21. GETTING SOME AIR

As we lived right next to one of the more historic airfields in Australia naturally a bit of our life involved the goings and coming related to air travel. In the spirit of original publican Bill Pearce, what follows is some of the more interesting of those flights, comings and goings.

CRASH COURSE

One night late in the bar, Kalala Station worker Dave who I have mentioned several times in the book, told yardie Grant and I he owned an ultralight aircraft and wanted to sell it. Now this wasn't a good thing to say to Grant and I who were quite adventurous spirits at the worst of times BUT to tell us at the bar, whilst having a rum, made our reaction even more predictable, "what ultralight, where is it, how much do you want for it" came out in quick excited words from both of us almost in unison.

Dave went on to explain it was a two-axis joystick, aluminium and cloth, Australian made Scout MK11. It was located in a shed at the station and he wanted $1,000 for it. He also explained he crashed it during its last flight but Dave failed to mention it was also its first and only flight. In the crash, he smashed the propeller and did some damage to a wing but he replaced the damaged parts. For good measure, he added he broke his nose in the crash and the plane scared him so much he didn't want to fly it again. This last part should have raised alarm bells for us but all we heard was Dave saying "okay then, it's a deal, I'll drop it in next week".

Dave came into town the next week with our plane on a trailer and asked, "where do you want it"? Grant and I decided to store it across the road under my house whilst we rebuilt it and then, appropriately, take it to the old plane hangar at the historic WW11 Daly Waters airfield. So we accompanied Dave across the road from the pub and took the plane, in about one hundred pieces, off the trailer and onto the dirt floor. It looked a mess with its broken right wing and splintered propeller and unrecognisable aluminium pieces but at the same time it looked like it could one day be a flying machine and we were excited.

Grant inspecting the Scout as it lays in pieces on the
floor

From memory, the paperwork Dave gave us was limited
to a small booklet with a hand drawn sketch of the plane in
the air on the front some rudimentary plans and
instructions inside. Alarmingly there were no instructions
on how to fly it other than "only fly in low wind" and
something about "do several runs up and down the runway
before taking off to accustom oneself to the feel of the
aircraft". Other than some commentary, we didn't
understand, about how the two axis system of flying works,

that was about it. Surely now alarms bells were ringing ...
nope.

So in our rare spare time, Grant and I would slowly and carefully put the broken aircraft back together. Our first milestone achievement after putting the fuselage together and having replaced the propeller was when we started the engine. Amazingly it fired the first time and we could feel it wanted to move even at idle. At this stage, we hadn't put the wings on so it was a tail with an aluminium frame to a plastic seat, two wheels and an overhead motor with a dangerous spinning propeller. Grant and I couldn't resist taking it for a run and so each of us took turns racing down the road in front the pub. Our only control, being the rudder to turn, that didn't really work well. The only other minor issue (hmmmm maybe not so minor) was the fuel bowl, located just above our head. It was leaking fuel over our face, not only causing burning eyes but a bit of a risk of fire. Grant fixed it by cutting a new fuel bowl gasket from a piece of leather. Other than those issues, the plane certainly plenty of power and it was great fun.

I'm in the pilot's seat taking a run in front of the pub

At this stage, we decided to move the plane from my under croft to the hangar where we would bolt the wings on. The replacing of the wings proved to be the most difficult part of the rebuild. No matter what we tried we could not get the wing "tensioners", running from the end and middle of the wings to the undercarriage, to fit. If we pulled one wing down and fitted the tensioner cable then the other was quite a few centimetres short. The tensioners employed no adjustment mechanism and this was a problem. I can't remember what we did in the end but I can safely assume it was a bit shoddy and probably should not have been done on an aircraft. From this point, it wasn't long before it was together and it was ready to test on the runway.

The Daly Waters historic airport hangar

So one night Grant and I decided the next morning was the time to fly. Leonie, Grant and I drove to the airport at 6am having done all the yard work and bar preparation the night before. We entered the hangar and realised there was a problem. We both wanted to be the first to test it. To settle this we decided to toss a coin. Next problem, we didn't bring any money. So I grabbed the nearest flat object, a Sidchrome spanner, and asked Grant to call Sidchrome side or blank side. Grant called Sidchrome and I tossed it spinning into the air.

It came down Sidchrome and I was gutted.

A jubilant Grant wasted no time putting his goggles on and telling me to spin the propeller to start the engine. I gave the propeller a flick and, as always, it started the first time. After little warming up Grant headed out of the hangar onto the apron and proceeded down the taxiway towards the runway. Leonie, and a disappointed me jumped in our car and followed as close as we could get.

Grant was instructed to go up and down the runway several times, faster each time, without actually taking off, but going fast enough to get the feeling of almost leaving the ground. Take off speed was, according to Dave, about 30kmh. We agreed I would then do the same before Grant would get back in for the first "flight".

The Daly Waters airfield was Australia's first international airfield, was just over a mile in length and very wide and therefore plenty of time to settle the aircraft for Grant to complete his short runs, without any surprises. Yeh, famous last words.

On his first "run" down the runway Grant went faster and faster, as he went through 30kmh I said to Leonie "he's going too fast" and then with no warning the plane took to the air. Whether Grant pulled back on the yoke cannot say, but he quickly went to about ten feet into the air and then immediately started sliding away to the right. I knew he was in trouble when he didn't appear to shove the yoke to the left to compensate but simply and slowly he slewed to the right and lost altitude before leaving the runway apron and then a wing clipped the bare ground and he cartwheeled to a dusty inglorious stop.

It only took a minute for us to get to Grant. Amid the dust, he jumped out of the plane and could not stop apologising. We only wanted to know if he was okay … and it appeared he was. Looking over the plane we could see a broken rear wing, a few broken wires and a torn cloth wing and rudder. It was a mess but at least Grant wasn't hurt.

In silence, we tied a rope from the car to the plane and dragged it back to the hangar and we all went to work. We didn't talk about it much during the day but that night over quite a few beers we recounted the events and eventually were able to laugh about it. Grant was quite convinced the action of "pulling" one of the wings down too far to get the tension cable to meet the fuselage caused the plane to slew but I reckon there was a very slight side wind above the bushes bordering the runway and as soon as Grant was above them, the effect of the side-wind pushed him sideways and without any practise or experience he couldn't arrest it.

The plane sat in the hangar for over a year, as there was no interest in fixing it … I think we both believed it was a death-trap.

A recent article I found on the web said "in the 80's Scout ultralights earned a reputation as pilot terminators for those venturing to fly higher than ground effect flight (about 10 feet)".

In 1988 a few mates from Adelaide stayed at the pub for a few days. When they saw the Scout it was too much for them to resist and they wanted to fix it. So, with some plastic sheet and fishing string, they put the wing and rudder together so they could run it up and down the runway … thankfully, the plastic was not strong enough to support lift-off and it never flew again.

When we sold the pub the Scout became the next publican's problem and I have never harboured a desire to be a pilot since the experience, and the air is a safer place for it.

DELAMINATION DILEMNA

One of the Territory's more celebrated helicopter pilot's was Steven Stiles. Steven called in occasionally for fuel and he made a habit of landing right next to the pub. One morning Steven landed in his usual spot and I refuelled him from our sealed drum of helicopter fuel and said I'd see him in the bar for payment. Steven came into the bar and asked if I'd like to go for a quick joy-flight … an invitation

I could not resist. So I told Leonie I would be gone a short time whilst she looked after the bar.

Steven removed his swag from "my" seat and tossed is on the ground next to my door before we hopped in and belted up. As he started the chopper he said we'd go looking for some of Roy's cattle and have some fun. I should note here Steven's prowess as a chopper pilot preceded him. Almost everyone in the Territory knew of his supreme flying skills and as we took off I hoped I was in for some fun.

As we sped, just inches above the tops of trees, he moved the joystick violently from side to side and in circular motions causing the chopper to spin wildly, duck and weave and go over and around trees faster and more vigorously than I ever experienced. He took it vertically and then seemed to stall and dive towards the ground before he arrested the fall at the last moment and dropped to the ground. It was exhilarating and scary at the same time and I didn't know whether I wanted to get out or enjoy some more.

About to enjoy a "joy-flight" in Steven's chopper (on
the left)

The flight only went for ten or fifteen minutes and when
he landed he dropped the chopper so close to his swag I
could have reached out and touched it. As I jumped out,
slightly shaken and well stirred, he thanked me for flying
with him. This completely surprised me and I think I
replied "I'm the one who should be thanking you … it was
… ummm, incredible" to which he responded with
something like this … "nope I need to thank you, Mark. On
dusk last night I clipped a tree with the rear rotor and
needed to land, in an awful hurry. The rotor was badly
delaminated and I couldn't fly so I was forced to spend the
night in the bush. Fortunately, I possessed some good glue
and was able to bond the laminated rotor together but I
wasn't sure if it would hold under extreme mustering type
pressure. So I needed to get some extra weight and do

some pretty wild flying to really test it out. After you fuelled me up and I discovered you were the only one in the bar, therefore you, plus the full load of fuel, was the extra weight I needed. So, as I said ... thanks".

I walked back into the pub in shock ... I don't think he could have flown the chopper any harder and therefore his glue job proved itself. I am glad he didn't tell me first BUT I am really pleased I had an experience flying like that first hand. It was definitely much more exciting than any show or fair ride I could ever go on.

FLYING FLICKMAN

The Northern Territory is vast and the time taken to travel around can be expensive and wasteful. The Territory is also full of pests that either eat homes, or people, and therefore pest control in important. Their advertisement said "get a Flickman, that's your answer, remember one flick and they're gone". The Northern Territory Flick Company, overcame the problem of distance by contracting a man who held a pilot license and owned a plane. The man wore the nickname "ACE".

ACE flew into Daly Waters one day and announced his arrival with a loud and very low pass over the pub roof. The low flyover was pilot talk for "I am here and I'd like to be picked up from the airstrip when you can". So I jumped in the pub ute and headed to the airstrip where I met a friendly ACE. He rattled off several questions including "do you have rooms, can you refuel me tomorrow morning, is the beer cold, do you have meals tonight …". Every answer I gave him was YES and so he grabbed an overnight bag, locked the plane and we headed to the pub.

That night was a fun night at the Pub. ACE really enjoyed himself and entertained everyone by telling some great yarns about his escapades flying around the territory. He even offered to take Leonie for a quick joy-flight in the morning and promised to do a very low pass over the pub and said, "get your camera out and be ready".

So the next morning, after filling ACE's plane with fuel, he took off for a quick circuit with Leonie on board as I raced back to the pub to take a photo. I stood in the middle of the road waiting and waiting, with about twenty others to take a photo. Whilst waiting there and (unbeknown to me) Doug, the old hermit from down the road, wandered up and asked some tourists what they were doing. They said "the Flying Flickman is going to fly low over the pub and we want to take a photo. Doug raced back to his house and returned with his video camera.

Without visual warning and little noise, the plane suddenly appeared only just above the roof coming straight towards us. It scared the daylights out of anyone who wasn't looking in the direction due to the incredibly loud sound following it. My guess was it cleared the roof by ten feet (3 metres) but it could have been less. It was amazing and I took a great photo of the plane directly above the tin roof.

Ace almost taking the roof off the Daly Waters Pub.

I then jumped in the ute and went to pick up Leonie. We said our goodbyes to ACE and then returned to the pub for the day's work. Little did I realise the old bugger Doug was about to ruin ACE's career.

A month or so later I received a phone call from someone in Civil Aviation Authority. They asked a few questions about the morning "the Flickman flew over the pub" and I responded as well as I could without putting ACE in a poor position. The Aviation official obviously possessed good information and a video of the incident. When I asked him how he received it, he let slip "Doug dobbed ACE into us". I was furious and feared ACE may lose his licence if the enquiry did not go well. My fears were founded as some time later we heard ACE's license was suspended and lost his ability to trade in the Northern Territory.

AIRSICK

We received a phone call from a company in Perth asking if we refuelled aircraft and if their Aerial Magnetometer Survey Team could stay with us for a week or so. "Yes we do and of course they can" I replied. A few weeks later the team arrived. Two in a vehicle and two in an aircraft. That night they requested me to refuel the plane in the morning and asked if I could be on-hand each morning at the same time to refuel.

The team kept to themselves most of the time and seemed to have paperwork to do each night after being away all day every day. Each morning when I refuelled the aircraft they would place an object on the tarmac under the wing and go inside the cabin to do I didn't know what. I did know the object on the ground displayed a triangle symbol on it and two words "DANGER RADIOACTIVITY". I didn't ask any questions and no explanation was forthcoming, but after a few days my inquisitiveness got the better of me and during the refuel, I asked them what they were actually doing. Their response was immediate and simple "magnetometer surveying. We are taking readings from the air to see what's under the surface. That thing is used to calibrate the instruments. Boring stuff really ... do you fancy coming for a run?" "What do you think" I replied.

In essence, this was a normal twin-engine aircraft with two front seats but the rear seats were removed and replaced with a pile of computers and machines. There was a third seat, my seat, facing backwards and directly behind the pilot. All windows behind the pilot were blacked out and as I was belted in by the navigator, who somehow turned around to do this almost impossible task, I started to think "this will be fun". As we started taxiing towards the runway the pilot shouted, "sorry you can't see much and my apology we don't have a headphone or microphone for you but it's not really made for a passenger." He added "we will be doing a series of straight lines following the contours of the land and we are flying very low so it's going to be bumpy. I keep it at the right level and my mate keeps it on track. At the end of the line, we'll bank hard and come back parallel to it and then repeat it and repeat it for an hour before we return. All good, you ready". It wasn't a question.

As we took off I realised why aircraft do have windows and don't have rear facing seats like trains or trams. It's bloody scary when you can't see a thing and all physical sensations are in reverse. The acceleration felt like braking and the normal nose-up as you gain altitude was nose-down for me. It wasn't a good feeling at all but pretty soon we were cruising at the level and it wasn't too bad. I could hear the two up front discussing what they were about to do "okay Jack, see the beacon there, down now, and yep left a little, okay I have the height, you are go, okay we start ... and NOW". It all felt the same to me as we bumped along and the plane shuddered a little for about five minutes and THEN all hell broke loose. I heard something like "okay peeling off NOW" and immediately the plane seemed to roll over on its side, the motors screamed and the shuddering was intense and then we flattened out and "okay I'm on the line, height is good ... and starting NOW". It was about now I noticed how damn hot it was back there and how little air. We repeated this a few times and then I heard the pilot ask "you okay back there (it wasn't a question) … the next few could get bumpy as we go over the hilly section". I thought "bumpier … how". And then I felt sick. I don't get airsick or seasick … "I am gonna be sick".

After a few of these "really" bumpy passes the pilot asked "you okay … Jack check on him will ya. It's getting hot, he may need some air". Jack turned around and looked at me … "shit are you ok" and as I obviously wasn't, he looked around and finding what he was looking for he removed a large air breather hose from one of the computers next to me and said "hold this towards your face, it may help" and then he was back to his flying. I don't remember much after then. I was feeling terrible and all l wanted was to get on land and go back to my pub.

As promised, we landed an hour later. It was the worst flying experience ever. There was not one good thing about it and I didn't even thank them for offering me the opportunity. And that is not like me.

BURBANK … WHAT'S IN A NAME?

A good mate from Adelaide was given the nicknames of Burbank or Banks. He possessed a real name but it was never used. Frustratingly for me now, I never found out where the name Burbank came from but knowing Banks, he probably gave it to himself. Burbank was a true character, with a pilot's license and a light plane. He was an air traffic controller, helicopter pilot, helicopter instructor and a stunt pilot and at one time, he was head pilot for the NT Police force. Burbank was also incredibly clever. He was an expert on a rare species of tortoise inhabiting the Coopers Creek near Innamincka and he owned a property in the Mallee, where he discovered a new species of lizard still bearing his name. He was the most unusual and gifted person I knew and he was exciting to be around. Banks always ran several pursuits at once. Raise any subject in conversation and Banks knew of it. He was a living Google, well before Google's time.

As a young man, Banks was employed as the chief pilot for the NT Commissioner of Police. He once flew the commissioner from Darwin to Gove in the Gulf of Carpentaria and then 600km south to Tennant Creek. Whilst the commissioner held meetings in Gove, Banks decided to top up the tanks but on testing the fuel, he found it contaminated and not safe. He did some quick sums and worked out there was enough fuel to make it to Tenant Creek. However, after taking off and to Banks surprise, they encountered strong headwinds. As they flew further Banks realised, with some shock, they weren't going to have enough fuel to make it. He also knew there were no airstrips in the area and so he decided to, in his words, "drop it gently onto the single strip of bitumen that was the Stuart Highway". He probably should have given the commissioner, who thought they were on approach into Tennant Creek airport, some warning but instead, he waited until the last minute and said "sorry boss, we're out of fuel. I'm putting it down on the road. You might want to brace" as he dodged trees and almost flew head on into an oncoming road train. After "hopping" over the road train, he executed a near perfect landing and was even able to find a truck stop, to park the plane in. The boss however, was not impressed. In fact, as Banks hopped the plane over the road train, he panicked and pissed himself and on landing, sacked Banks on the spot. Hero of the moment Banks, was forced to flag down a bus, whilst the boss waited for a replacement pilot and fuel.

Banks was stunt pilot in the internationally released Australian movie Silent Reach starring Robert Vaughan and Helen Morse. A great mate of mine, Peter Brown, flew to Queensland to catch up with Banks and was immediately hired as an extra, to appear next to Banks in a scene of a light plane taking off from a beach. Brownie wore a wig to look like Helen Morse and Banks was stand-in for Robert Vaughan. Brownie retold the story "each time we took off, a dashboard buzzer would scream at us. On take-off number three I asked Banks what it was and he said, it's the stall warning buzzer. Bloody annoying thing it is" and Brownie thought "Oh bloody great, we are about to stall. Thanks Banks".

Banks was also impulsive and as with the rest of his personality, when he decided to pursue something, he did it immediately and dived in headlong.

An early example of his impulsiveness occurred in the early 1980's, when he decided to go to outback Queensland, to fossick for sapphires in a remote area named Tomahawk Creek. One day, at a party, Banks said "I'm off fossicking". He told us all the story of huge sapphires to be found and as he was about to drive away, I said "Banks, we are going to Queensland in a month. We will look you up". He said "that'd be great. I'll send you the details after I get there". About a week later we received a call and he said "go to the Rubyvale post office. There will be a letter for you with directions to my camp". A month later we were the general area in our Combi van and went to a supermarket to stock up with supplies. We assumed

342

Banks would be doing it rough on the creek and might enjoy lamb chops, vegetables and a few cold beers. So we filled our little fridge with meat and the esky with beer and headed to Rubyvale Post Office.

The Rubyvale area was barren and dry and we couldn't imagine how Banks was coping in the heat. We went into the post office and I asked if they were holding a letter for Mark and Leonie Venable. "Two" the woman replied, as she handed two letters to me. We returned to the Combi van and opened the first letter. It was a rudimentary mud map of how to get to Tomahawk Creek. The next letter simply said "had a gutful of this place. Gone home. Banks". We noticed the stamp on the letter was postmarked "Culleraine, Victoria" and was dated two weeks before. So it was obvious, Banks lasted two weeks and went home, leaving the two of us in the middle of nowhere with two kilos of lamb, two kilos of fresh vegetables and two cartons of cold beer. To say we were disappointed was an understatement. To say were we're surprised would have been incorrect. That was Banks.

Fast forward four years and I received a phone call from Banks. He asked "you told me it was quite scenic around Daly Waters. I'm thinking of flying up to do joy-flights. What do you think"? Before I could respond with my answer, "mmmm, not sure", he said "perfect. See you soon".

A week later the pub was "buzzed" by a low flying aircraft. I jumped in the ute and went to the airstrip, to be greeted by a beaming Banks. All Banks possessed was a light duffle-bag and his plane. I asked him "errr, have you thought this through mate"? He shrugged his shoulders and said "shouldn't be too hard. I'll sit out the front of the pub, with a sign of course, and Bob will be my uncle". Then he added "first up, I need fuel. Can I book it up"?

That night, Banks sat at the bar, booking beers up and asking all the tourists if they wanted to do a scenic flight the next morning. Unfortunately, he didn't understand the style of tourist who visited us were caravanners, who historically spent little, or backpackers who spent less. After a frustrating night Banks said "Vennas, tomorrow morning you are coming with me for a flight, to show me what's around here to see". "Okay" I said "but if you'd listened to me you might have heard me say "mmm, not sure about this mate". Banks being Banks, he shrugged his shoulders and said "it'll be what it'll be. Let's go flying".

Burbank's plane was a tiny, four seater at most, Grumman Cheetah. It was fast and agile and only needed a couple of hundred metres of runway before it was airborne.

So Banks, in his typically cavalier fashion, took off on the two hundred metre strip of bitumen connecting the tarmac to the airstrip almost clipping the trees at the far end. When I looked at him questioningly, he said "I saw it when I landed. It looked long enough and it was ... just". We bounced our way, at low altitude, around the local area and flew over the dry Daly Waters lagoon, the dry waterfall, the dry creek bed and the even drier Kalala Station. "Shit it's dry" said Banks. My response of "If only you'd listened" was ignored.

After only taking one, semi-satisfied couple for a scenic flight during the day, Banks said "I reckon I'd get more business if I landed on the road and parked the plane right about ... about there" as he pointed to the roped off area in front of the pub. "That ain't gonna happen Banks" I replied. He shrugged his shoulders and wandered outside with purpose. I saw him disappear up the road taking deliberate one metre strides. "Oh no" I thought.

When he returned he said "mmmm, the length is marginal and there's a few power lines. The bloody buses may give me some grief but I've landed on a road before you know". "Yeah, remind me how it ended up Banks", I said and we both laughed our heads off.

345

After three or four days of waiting around Banks flew only a couple of customers. Banks drank a few more beers after work than normal and at about 11pm he declared to everyone at the bar, "it's been fun but I'm off tomorrow". I took it with a pinch of salt, thought he'd sleep it off and book some more fuel up the next day.

I awoke the next morning at my usual time of 6am and cleaned, then opened the bar. At about 9am Leonie came in and said "I see Banks has gone, what time did he leave"? "My God, I had no idea he left already. It must have been very early". I replied.

At about 8pm that night, Banks rang and said "just letting you know, I made it home safely. It was fun Vennas but also a pity it didn't work out as well as we'd hoped". I replied, "how can you be home already. You only have left here about twelve hours ago". "Ahhhh make that fifteen hours mate", he said. I flew out at four am this morning. I refuelled twice on bush strips, from Jerry cans and once at Alice Springs airport. The flight was a dream. Tail winds the entire way". I think Banks may have set a world record for a Grumman. To travel 2,000 kilometres in less than fifteen hours, including three fuel stops, would take some beating. Particularly as two hours were in darkness, when the plane wasn't approved to fly, even if Banks was.

In a twist of fate, several years later, Banks was involved in a serious helicopter accident at Parafield Airport in South Australia. He was tutoring a student pilot when a catastrophic failure of the main rotor shaft occurred, causing the chopper to fall like a stone to the ground. It then bounced and toppled to its side with the main rotor blade disintegrating and flying in all directions. Somehow, Banks took over and helped the student reduce the force of the crash and incredibly, Banks and his student managed to escape almost unscathed. What Banks did next amazed me and scared me at the same time. With an injured wrist, he took his shocked student to the office, grabbed the keys to another chopper and took him for a fly. Together they flew the chopper for an hour and talked about the incident. The entire time Banks was convincing his student to "get back on his bike" and ensure he would continue his dream of being a chopper pilot. Incredible but typical Banks.

Unfortunately, this final paragraph for Burbank is a sad one. Michael (Burbank) Hyde, passed away, a few short years later, from illness. Far too short a life for someone so full of life.

Chapter 22. WHEN IT RAINS IT POURS

CYCLONE IRMA ... January 1987

We experienced our first major rain event in mid-January 1987, when Tropical Cyclone Irma crossed from the Gulf of Carpentaria onto land north of Groote Eylandt and headed in a south-westerly directly towards Daly Waters. As it approached the midday sky turned inky black, dogs barked and our birds screamed. Local tour guide Andy came into the pub and declared "I've seen a sky like this before. Batten down the hatches mate, it's gonna get real wet".

That afternoon it poured. It was eerie, as there was little or no wind but the rain drops were huge and it came down in buckets. Fortunately, it was the wet season and therefore were only a few tourists in the pub with a handful of locals. Some of us went out the front and danced in the rain. It was bloody cold but other than the drops being so large they hurt, it was very refreshing and a great relief from the oppressive humidity of the month. That night it didn't stop raining. The locals guessed 12" in 24 hours but, as Larrimah 90km to the north officially recorded 409mm (16.1") in 24 hours, it could have been much more. In the afternoon the last bus to get into Daly Waters came through a rising creek.

The last coach to get through the Daly Creek in flood

The next morning the Greyhound bus didn't come in to deliver or collect the mail and we couldn't work out why. So Phil drove to where Daly Creek crossed the Pub road and came back to declare "there's at least five feet of water flowing across the road. No wonder the mail bus didn't come in". We all immediately drove to the creek crossing, half way between the Pub and the Stuart Highway, and stared in awe at the amount of water flowing north in the creek. As we stood there the water kept rising and before long it was obvious if it didn't stop rising soon, it was eventually going to break its banks and overflow. Phil decided to get his tinny so we could take a boat trip down the swollen creek. This was fun but in retrospect a little dangerous, as we couldn't see what was below the surface and if the boat tipped over it could have quickly turned into a disaster. After the boating we all ran around pointing and shouting "look, it's breaking the bank here and there and, oh look, it's flowing towards the pub ... oh shit, it's really moving fast. Quick ... to the pub".

Putting the tinny in a flooded river was probably
foolhardy

We sped back the 2 kilometres to the pub and along the way were surprised to see water flowing in the earth gutter alongside the road. The water was almost to the pub front door. It was incredible to see this and as much as I wanted the water to stop, part of me wanted it to keep coming, I suppose from interest as much as to see something special.

350

And the water did keep coming, eventually covering the road and then it came in the front door of the pub. The next morning Leonie ran into the bar, where I was serving a couple of the local cattle station lads in a goggle and snorkel, and said "Mark, there's water in the motel. It's like a swimming pool in there". I found this hard to believe, as just earlier the water seemed to have settled an inch or two below the top step at the door. When Leonie opened the door I was shocked to see an inch of muddy water covering the floor and mini-fountains of water spurting about 6" into the air coming up through all the concrete expansion joints in the floor. It became obvious to me the water table was now above the floor level. This caused the floor to "float" and for water to seep in through any opening. This was very worrying as I instantly realised the pubs septic tank would be overflowing and it couldn't be good news. The rest of the day was spent lifting everything above the floors of the pub and the motel. It was hard hot sweaty work in the oppressive humidity but we needed to get it done before we lost stock and furniture. Inside the bar was a different matter as the previous publicans obviously experienced this before. The amazing bar fridge, reputed by Territorians to be the "coldest beer-box on the track" was already on solid feet keeping it above the high-tide level whilst the rest of the bar was "water-proof" and couldn't be affected by the water … after all, that's how we cleaned it on a daily basis.

The floodwaters are just about to come inside the pub

The next pressing matter was how to get our supplies and mail across the creek. It was the wet and therefore the quiet season but we still needed supplies and whilst it was clear the trucks couldn't get to us. Fortunately there was an old railway bridge crossing the creek adjacent our road. The railway bridge was constructed in the 1920's Daly Waters when was subdivided into a town to service the much anticipated and promised railway line. Bridges, similar to the one at Daly Waters, were built throughout the Territory but as the Government ran out of funds, the railway never extended past Birdum and the bridge was never needed. Driving across the bridge wasn't an easy feat as the bridge was only inches wider than the wheels. The slightest lack of concentration would have seen a wheel dropping off the side but we needed supplies and so when the truck arrived that day we were able to load the pub vehicles with the liquor and food and get it back to the pub safely.

The pub ute crossing the flooded Daly Creek on the railway bridge

Another man-made feature at the creek crossing was an old flying fox strung high up between two old gum trees. We wondered why this was here and it became obvious when the creek flooded. We were dying to give it a go and somehow we convinced Leonie to jump in and take a ride across the creek. At the halfway point Phil and I stopped pulling and walked away to let her hang … a panic-stricken Leonie screamed until we came back and pulled her across … it was so funny but at the same time reminded us how many locals and travellers would have been pulled across the river in the fox in the past. Grant jumped in next and we decided to give him the ride of his life, so Phil and I grabbed the pulling rope and ran as fast as we could thereby dragging Grant at high speed across the swollen creek … it was like a show ride and we spent a fun hour or so revelling in the "new to us" flood waters.

Grant flying like a fox across the Daly Creek

Grant was feeling playful after the flying fox ride and when we returned to the pub he came into the bar where I was serving, carrying a toilet door, some rope and wearing a grin from ear to ear. "What's the matter with the door", I said and he replied "it's not a door anymore … let's go water-skiing". I immediately knew what he was talking about so we quickly fired up the pub ute, tied a rope to the tow hitch and I proceeded to drive, slowly at first, down the main street with Grant being towed behind whilst kneeling on the door. It was my turn next and I did a run on my knees and then I decided, to do it properly, I should stand. And so on the next run, with Grant driving quite fast I came past the pub and went around the corner standing up on this very wide single slalom ski. We enjoyed a great day of relaxation, fun and laughs. In the afternoon the lads from Kalala Station came into the pub and when they heard of our day's fun, they all wanted to try. The youngest, Dallas, had the time of his life but never having skied before he took tumble after tumble on the bitumen road and took a large amount of skin off his knees and elbows. It was one of the funniest days of my life and a great way to break the work routine.

Yours truly skiing behind the ute, past the pub.

Soon after the flood waters came inside the Pub a journalist from the NT News rang, as they did occasionally when an "event" happened in our area. The reported rang to ask what affect Cyclone Irma had at Daly Waters. I went into an explanation about the water in the bar, me serving customers in a goggle and snorkel and the local station hands skiing down the road on a toilet door dragged behind the pub ute.

When we opened the pub the next morning, we were still inundated with water, showing no signs of receding. We unanimously agreed it was time to go skiing again but this time Grant decided to make a pair of "real skis" by cutting the toilet door we used earlier in the year, into two planks. With the pubs circular saw, he went across the road and proceeded to slice into the door. Unfortunately, the saw kept grabbing and stopped, so he wandered into the bar and asked me if I could hold the plywood apart. This worked fine until the saw "grabbed" again and flew backwards out of his hands. It was coming straight at my hands so I quickly moved them out of harm's way ... but I wasn't fast enough and the saw flew across the back of my left hand. I knew it cut me and I didn't want to look at my hand ... the look of horror on Grant's face said it all.

When I did look, I knew it was not good. My index finger was slashed with a huge cut across the top knuckle and I could see bone and tendons. There was blood everywhere, so I wrapped my hand in a dirty rag, we were in the work shed across the road from the pub and wandered over to the pub to find Leonie. I wasn't in a huge amount of pain yet but I knew I needed some professional medical help. Leonie said "what have you done now" and when I unrolled the rag and showed her the wound she mumbled something like "you idiot" before getting back to her work in the kitchen. Not unexpectedly, that didn't go down well.

Grant said he heard a doctor was working as a handyman at the Hi-Way Inn Roadhouse a few kilometres

357

away. So we jumped in the Nissan and headed there to find "Doctor John".

Doctor John was found mowing the lawns, so he was immediately interrupted. He came into the bar and asked to see my hand. He didn't show any reaction when he saw it and simply said "it'll need a bloody good clean out and a few stitches. I don't have any anaesthetic for an injection ... are you up to it?" I didn't appear to have an option, so I said "gulp, yep I suppose".

John went and delved into his "medical bag" then set up at a table in the bar area. He asked what I drank ... I said "beer" and he replied "nah, you'll need hard liquor. Do you drink whisky?" I said "I like the odd Bundy rum" and so a bottle was bought to the table. John also requested and received, a toothbrush from the store and some clean tea towels from the bar. He took the cap off the rum and took a swig ... and then I took a bloody big gulp. I was shitting myself. He rolled a tea towel up and put it in my mouth and said "bite down as hard as you can. This is gonna hurt like hell." Then he took my injured hand, unwrapped the rag and placed my hand palm down on a tea towel on the table before pouring a couple of nips on the now gaping wound. I could clearly see the large knuckle bone with a saw-cut through it and a white nerve and a tendon both exposed, the nerve hanging in the air ... and I saw sawdust deep in the cut. John said he was pleased the tendon wasn't cut, mentioned a nerve was damaged, took the toothbrush and looked at me seriously before saying "NOW bite real hard" as he started brushing in the wound whilst liberally pouring the rum over it. I almost passed out from the pain. Grant was told "hold him down" and so he put a tight bear hug grip around my shoulders. The gripped relaxed a little after a few minutes, so I looked up at Grant for support and I swear he was about to faint, which for some strange reason helped me feel better about my situation. I kept thinking "I can get through this. If this is as bad as it gets I can get through this." I took more gulps of rum in between John pouring it over the wound. And somehow I pushed through it. I don't know how I did it and I'm not sure if it was the rum or me seeing Grant falter.

The next part really rocked me. John removed his "sewing kit" from the bag. It was a curved suture needle and what appeared to be fishing line. He poured rum over the fishing line and sterilised the needle with a cigarette lighter and then told me to bite down hard again on the towel. I don't know when the suture needle was last sharpened but I bet it wasn't recently. It also looked about four sizes too large for the job. Each time he pushed it into and through the skin it hurt heaps BUT when he pushed it through the other side of the wound and tried to pull the stitch through the hole it really hurt ... really hurt. The pain was ridiculous and it went on and on ... and then it was over. I think he inserted about ten stitches. I can still see the marks of eight of them thirty years later.

John wrapped my hand in a clean bandage and said, "keep it raised to stop the bleeding ... and if you need to, take pain killers for the pain". I didn't need convincing to take the pain killers. I thanked him, we left and I went to bed.

Two days later I was in agony. On the third day, I couldn't bear it anymore. Leonie unrolled the bandage and what we saw made us feel sick. The red wound was severely infected and yellow liquid was oozing thru the stitches. This wasn't good. Grant again drove me to Doctor John, who this time was cleaning the caravan park toilets. John looked surprised when he saw the wound and said, "what the hell have you been doing". I was almost left speechless. "Nothing but lying in pain in bed. Just what you bloody told me to do" I said. He looked confused and worried and said, "I'm going to have to open it up and clean it out again and this time it is really gonna hurt". I was in shock. Grant went green and said, "you can't be serious".

But John was serious and we did it all again. The stitches were cut and the wound fell open to display a horrible red infection oozing yellow liquid. More liberal pouring of rum ensued and more cleaning. John insisted there was some sawdust he missed, causing the infection and he stitched it back together once again. I was an exhausted mess by the end of this second operation without an anaesthetic and after I returned to the pub I slept for nearly two days. After two more days, the wound appeared to be getting a bit better. I was still in pain but it was bearable but there was a little yellow leakage again and three of the stitches opened up, exposing the wound again. I said to Leonie I couldn't go to Doctor John again and I was worried about losing my finger. I needed to go to a hospital. So Leonie rang the Katherine Hospital for advice. We should have done this in the first place.

The hospital suggested leaving the wound open and liberally and regularly dose the wound with Betadine antiseptic powder from our medical kit. Then ring them in two days and if it wasn't any better we would need to go to Katherine. They were also very concerned about who this "Doctor John" was and they decided to investigate. They came back to Leonie a couple of days later and said Doctor John wasn't a doctor at all. At best they suggested he may have been a nurse in Vietnam but they couldn't even find evidence of that. They added I was probably lucky not to lose a finger or my hand. The first infection could easily have become gangrene, wrapped up as it was in the heat and humidity of the territory.

Fortunately for me, and everyone at the pub who took on extra work whilst I was off, I was able to go back behind the bar in a few days. Grant made a new toilet door, the flood waters began receding and the event became history. Doctor John departed from the Hi-Way Inn, exactly as he arrived, without warning and everything was back to normal.

After about a week, the floodwaters had fully receded and the rest of the team commenced cleaning up and we went around inspecting the pub and motel for unseen damage … and that is when we saw an unexpected problem. One of the 5,000 litre fuel tanks next to our garage "popped" out of the ground and was floating, half in the air and half in the ground, with the connecting pipes, ripped up with it. As soon as we saw it Phil said "we should make sure the tanks are full when it rains in future". A few days later the owner of the Cape Crawford Roadside Inn came into the pub. It was my first day back on deck, after the hand injury and as I pointed to the fuel tank, he said "that's nothing, I was about to clean the swimming pool but it popped out the ground. I reckon it's buggered now". We heard similar devastating stories over the next few weeks.

I felt useless during the clean-up, as my injury meant I could only serve in the bar but there was no way I could help. Without doubt, the worst of this mud was in the motel units. The water had gone back down through the expansion gaps leaving the floors covered in about 50mm (2") of mud and getting it out proved difficult hot sticky work. And when the mud was gone we realised the paint on the floors had peeled so a repaint was required. The mud found its way into every nook and cranny of every building we owned. It took days to clean it all. Imagine the entire area covered with a few inches of muddy water and then the water goes but the mud remains. The sun baked the mud dry and it left a cracked "moon-like" surface.

A week or so later we received a copy of the NT News in the mail with a cartoon of the Pub showing a moustached me, serving in my diving gear and in the background a lad with a jackaroo hat water skiing in front of the Pub. It looked great and immediately the cutting went onto the wall of the pub with the other memorabilia.

CYCLONE JASON ... February 1987

Incredibly, a second major storm event occurred only a few weeks later. Leonie and I had booked local fishing guide Andy "Crocodile" Hind to take us on a three-day fishing trip in early February 1987 to Borroloola (the Loo). It was to be our first days off in over six months and coincided with our wedding anniversary ... how romantic. The Loo is about 300km due east from Daly Waters and set about twenty kilometres inland from the sea on the MacArthur River. It is famous for barramundi fishing and large crocodiles. Andy took us on a drive along the river to Blackjacks Landing where we set up camp and went fishing from the banks of the river. We didn't catch any fish and were just settling down to make a fire and cook some of our Pub rump steaks, when we were approached by a local driving a council vehicle. He wandered over and asked if we were camping there that night. It all seemed a bit strange to me until he said, "you do know there's a cyclone heading this way don't you" ... "Cyclone", Andy said, "we're from Daly Waters, just arrived, we had no idea". The local said it was expected to be a bad one and suggested we should head into the Loo and seek shelter at the power station building as "it is cyclone proof". So without hesitation, we packed up, drove back into the Loo and went straight to the pub knowing we would be guaranteed to find out what was really going on.

In the mid-eighties, the Borroloola Pub was one of a few Australian pubs still operating a white's only bar and a black's only bar. We pulled out front of a full "white" pub carpark and wandered in. The bar was full of locals and we wandered in almost unnoticed. Fortunately, the barman was friendly enough and when we asked about the cyclone he pointed to a corner, where a few men in uniform were sitting in front of a large map pinned to the wall, and said, "ask them, they should know". We made our way across to the table and asked what was happening. An American replied, "Cyclone Jason was expected to arrive early in the morning and at this stage was on track to cross the land near here". It transpired these guys were US Airforce personnel coordinating a US research plane flying through the eye of the cyclone taking measurements and forwarding them to the ground. Amazing stuff but not a flying job I would like.

After a couple of beers, we decided to seek shelter at the electricity sheds where we were greeted by an NT Power Service maintenance guy who had previously met us at Daly Waters. He kindly offered us two rooms in the workers quarters and said he "thought they were cyclone proof". That night the wind howled and it poured with rain, heavy rain, but it never reached the levels of Cyclone Irma or the strength feared. The next morning everything was back to almost normal. It was heavily overcast and the wind was strong but it wasn't too bad. It turned out the cyclone kept a westerly course and crossed the coast near Groote Eylandt a few hundred kilometres to the north where it destroyed all the buildings in the aboriginal community of Baniyalla. Jason then did a u-turn and moved back over the Gulf before heading south and crossed land again near Burketown … we were very lucky this time, as those in its path took a hammering and big drenching.

I learnt to expect the unexpected at Daly Waters Pub. One of the great aspects of pub life is you never know who was about to walk in the door to surprise you, or what we might do to surprise our visitors.

CROC ATTACK

NT Wildlife Officer Jeff Angel, who advised us on how to care for our joey Daly, regularly dropped into the pub. He was a great bloke, who loved sharing some of his great stories of life in the bush with anyone who would listen.

On one occasion Jeff dropped in and said he was on his way to Borroloola to catch a large rogue crocodile, living too close to the settlement. Apparently, it was responsible for killing a few local dogs and a few near misses with locals. He added, if he caught the croc he would need to relocate it to a Darwin crocodile farm and would bring it to the pub for all the tourists and us, to see.

A week later, late in the afternoon I saw Jeff's car pull up near the pub and after ten minutes or so, he came into the crowded bar. It was clear to me he wasn't well and he was bleeding profusely from the side of his head around the ear. I asked him what happened and he replied, "I was just attacked by that damn crocodile". "What croc", I asked. "The croc on the back of my bloody Toyota. Come see" he replied. So everyone in the bar at the time, went outside to his tray top Toyota and on the back was a huge crocodile of probably thirteen feet or more. It was tied to a long timber board and its mouth was tied closed with gaffer tape and it stunk. Photos were being taken by everyone.

I asked Jeff "c'mon mate, how could a tied-up crocodile attack you out here"? He pointed to the broken rear window of the cabin and explained he was speeding along the Carpentaria Highway coming towards the pub from Borroloola with the croc safely on the back when a huge Brahman bull wandered onto the road just in front. Jeff hit the brakes quickly but not quick enough to stop before hitting the bull dead centre of his substantial bull-bar still doing about sixty. This caused the Toyota to stop with a crash, which in turn caused the crocodile to fly forward on the plank. The plank was tied to the vehicle and couldn't move and therefore the croc kept coming forward and came in through the back window into the front (and only) seat of the car. The croc then started thrashing its head from side to side, smashing into the left side of Jeff's head, which explained his injuries. Jeff said he then leapt out of the Toyota, grabbed the croc's tail and pulled it back out of the rear window and onto the tray where he re-tied the croc to the board and drove to the pub.

Jeff was quite shaken by his ordeal, so we moved his Toyota into the camping ground and put a tarpaulin over the croc, after hosing it down. We then put Jeff into a motel room and the girls attended to Jeff's injuries with antiseptic, to ensure the wound didn't get infected. Jeff came into the bar later for a feed and a beer, but desperately wanted a very early night after such a harrowing experience. I also think he needed to get away from the attention and questions, as when everyone found out he was the crocodile hunter, who was attacked by the croc, they all wanted photos with him.

The next morning, a much healthier Jeff displayed the croc for more photos for the tourists and he headed for the Darwin crocodile farm, where you may even find this croc today.

Daly Waters is nowhere near the sea, nor is it near any crocodile infested rivers. Jeff caught his croc 300 kilometres away but that didn't stop the tourists from being very wary about their choice of camp site. What didn't help either was the confusion between our town of Daly Waters and the crocodile infested town of Daly River, about 500 kilometres away to the north-west. It wasn't uncommon for campers to ask if it was safe to camp in Daly Waters because they heard of big crocodiles inhabiting the river. One guy actually asked to be as far away from the river as possible. I would reply "you're absolutely correct, Daly River has huge crocs but its 500 kilometres away so you'll be safe anywhere here" and I would explain there are two separate towns. The whole experience added to their trip to the wilderness and you could see the excitement and sometimes fear in their faces.

POSITIONS VACANT

When I needed a tradesman it was simply a matter of putting a sign on our notice board out the front of the pub. It would read "ELECTRICIAN REQUIRED ... PAYMENT IN BEER ... APPLY AT BAR". In most cases, I would have the tradesman found and the job was done within a couple of days.

On one particular occasion, I needed a sign writer for a small sign-writing job so I put a sign out the front and within the day a bloke came up to me and asked, "what do you need doing". I showed him the job and we agreed on a payment of lunch and beers whilst he did the job. His job was simply to write "COMMUNITY NOTICE BOARD" on a blank blackboard out the front plus a couple of small pub signs.

So our sign-writer retrieved his paint box and stool and proceeded to paint this very simple sign. My dad would have knocked it over in half an hour. He took his time however and devoured a complimentary pub lunch whilst his fluffy little dog "Floppsy" wandered around his feet and eventually fell asleep on the pub verandah. A bit later, neighbour Steve Atwell returned to home from Hidden Valley station with his station hand Lockie and his big dog Boss.

Whenever Steve returned home, Boss executed his daily habit of patrolling his territory to make sure no male dogs encroached on his area ... and part of his territory was our verandah. I saw Boss cross the road to do his sniffing and pissing on every post and tree in front of the pub before I heard the unmistakable commotion made by a small dog in great pain. It was the sound of pain of being trod on by a person, run over by a car, or mauled by a much larger dog and I knew it wasn't caused by either of the former.

By the time I ran out the front, Boss released the little white dog and was retreating across the road to Steve's screams of "Boss, get your ass over here NOW". Boss received a kick up the arse and was shoved into the shed under Steve's house. Steve came over and looked at the small dog on the ground, mumbled something like "he's okay, he's still breathing" and came in for his habitual, after work, beers with Lockie. I wasn't sure if Steve was relieved the dog was still breathing or disappointed Boss hadn't killed him. You never could tell with Steve.

Our sign-writer carefully picked up "Floppsy" and placed him on a towel on the front seat of his van and then he sat in the front for some time making sure his dog was okay.

Sometime later the sign-writer dropped a postcard in our post-box, gave Steve a very wide berth and said goodbye. I asked about Floppy's condition and received an "I think he'll be okay. I'm taking him to a vet". I was going to mention our town stock inspector Pat Barry was handy with animals but thought better of it, as Pat owned a very angry blue cattle dog named Blue.

The next morning I performed the customary post box clearance prior to the Greyhound coach arrival. Whilst doing this one of the postcards dropped onto the ground. I picked it up and accidentally read "Hi love, DID A SMALL JOB AT THIS PUB AND FLOPPSY WAS EATEN BY THE PUB DOG". On way to vet now. Love Bill".

I went to grab my pen and write "it wasn't the Pub dog" but then I thought better of it.

BLIND DATE

I decided we needed to do something for the single guys who worked and lived around Daly Waters and to do it I needed a girl, to be one of the lucky guy's blind date for a night.

As Leonie and Toni were both married, I needed someone single and as luck would have it Sam and Taffy were staying with us on holidays and I managed to convince Sam it would be "good clean fun". However, Taffy wasn't so happy about it.

I spoke to Dave from Kalala and two of the boys from Telstra and they all agreed to be contestants in "DALY WATERS PUB BLIND DATE" and it was true to name, with the contestants having no idea who the date was.

On the Saturday night, we set up a stage in the beer garden and with Toni in her black suit and tie acting as MC and Leonie as the glamour assistant, the show was ready. All the locals came in from town and the stations and there were also about twenty tourists in attendance. It was a terrific show with plenty of hilarious answers to the questions posed by Sam and many laughs and eventually,

Dave won Sam, as his date, for the night. The date was such a funny affair. First it was drinks in the bar, served by Taffy, followed by dinner in the beer-garden, served by Taffy and finally dancing until the late hours. Taffy and Sam were both great sports and Dave, shy as usual, had a great night. All the locals asked "when is it going to be on again" and all I could reply was "as soon as we find another blind date".

Blind Date stage with from left, blind date Sam and then Leonie, Telstra #1, Dave, Telstra #2 and Toni

MY SHOUT

A previous publican rigged a bell, on a post in the bar, for customers to ring if there was no-one in attendance.

However, possibly in a state of drunkenness, he wrote the sign "RING THE BELL" on the wrong side of the post.

When I saw this I thought the mistake was hilarious and then I decided to include my own sense of humour to it by adding to the sign with "SHOUT THE BAR" and added my part on the wrong side of the post as well.

From then, whenever anyone rang the bell, the locals and pub staff would all shout out very loudly "SHOUT THE BAR". The poor unsuspecting person would ask "why" and we would all point to the other side of the post. It was hilarious to most but every now and then the offender would get upset and storm out from the pub.

RING THE BELL - SHOUT THE BAR

Occasionally, when I felt the customers deserved a treat, I would ring the bell myself and cry out "MY SHOUT" to great applause and cheering. Depending on my mood, occasionally could become, quite a few times a week. One night, Steve and Lockie heard me, from across the road and came running in with cheeky grins claiming "YOUR SHOUT".

THE SINGING MECHANIC

An army truck with a four wheel drive on the back rolled into Daly Waters late one afternoon. A couple of friendly army guys came into the bar and settled into drinking quite a few beers. One of them, mechanic Bruce Caterer, who seemed to be the ringleader asked, "if I play the guitar and sing tonight can we get a room and drinks on the house"? I took my time answering this because, based on their current drinking form, it could have become quite expensive ... so I responded "here's the deal, I'll shout you and your mate a room. And dinner, breakfast and beers for you ... but your mate has to pay for his own beers and meals. Unless he can perform too, which I'm guessing he can't. If you get booed and I have to ask you to stop playing, then the deal is off"! Bruce almost knocked me over accepting the deal.

Bruce laid them in the aisles. He was funny, rude and clever and could really hold a tune and belt out a number. He knew all the favourites and sang quite a few of his own. We took a huge amount over the bar and even though Bruce drank more beers than I'd bargained for, it was worth it and was all due to Bruce keeping the patrons entertained. The next morning I said to Bruce "if you're ever coming this way let me know in advance. You'll stay for free and the rest will be on me too".

Bruce looking a little pensive with some groupies

One month later Bruce rang and said, "I have to pick up a broken down vehicle from Elliott this Friday so book me and my mate into a room and if the deal is still open I'll entertain your crowd for the night". "Deal is on definitely mate, see you Friday", I said and we made plans for Bruce to play by ringing all the locals and placing signs in chalk on the notice board in front of the hotel. On Thursday I received another phone call from Bruce but this one didn't have such good news. "Sorry mate", he said "but my boss, the Colonel, has cancelled my trip. He said it was a waste of money to pick up just one broken down vehicle and we needed to wait for another before we can go" … the expletive-filled phone call wasn't what I hoped to hear and Bruce finished with "but I'll get the bastard back … you can be sure".

A month or so later Bruce did come to the pub and play again and it was another memorable event. He was at his naughtiest and funniest and his repertoire contained a few more songs. As we enjoyed a beer together after his show he said to me "hey, I got that bastard Colonel back you know". I said, "you did, how"? "Well, his staff car was in for servicing. It's a big green Statesman and he'd complained the air-conditioning wasn't working very well. I told him I'd fix it, and so I removed the fuse out of the air-conditioner to ensure it didn't work at all and also removed the fuse from the electric windows to keep them in the up position. Do you have any idea how bloody hot a dark car in Darwin can be with no air-conditioning and the windows jammed up? Bugger him".

Bruce entertained the patrons of the Daly Waters Pub quite a few times whilst we were there. He would bring his wife and family to the pub on some weekends and stay for free as he kept everyone enthralled with his jokes and songs. Whilst Bruce was a joker and very funny man, he was an accomplished musician with a wonderful voice. We became great mates and loved having a beer together. I'll never forget one night in particular. Bruce was playing to a packed crowd in the bar and I was serving. During one song I saw a couple of ladies blushing and laughing whilst their husbands tried holding their hands over their wives eyes. I couldn't work out what was going on until I looked towards Bruce to see if he knew what it was about ... and to my shock I saw Bruce sitting on his bar stool, strumming his guitar and singing at the top of his voice with his legs apart and ... and a testicle hanging out of his shorts. It was hilarious and shocking at the same time. I didn't know how to bring it to his attention without embarrassing him but then I experienced a brainwave ... I grabbed a piece of paper and wrote on it "LOOK DOWN ... YOU HAVE ONE HANGING OUT". I tied it to the end of a fishing line, hanging on the wall behind the bar and then I went around into the storeroom, to the left of Bruce and dangled the note over the wall from the fishing rod. As I was behind the wall I couldn't see what was going but I heard a roar of laughter, Bruce momentarily stopped playing, the rod bent like it hooked a fish and Bruce said "oops ... sorry ladies ... slight wardrobe malfunction" and returned back into the song, to loud hoots, whistles and applause. When I came back into the bar Bruce was looking at me with the widest grin on his bright red face and gave a wink. It was, without a doubt, one of the funniest events to happen at the Daly Waters Pub in my time there.

In 1988 Bruce was booked to play at Newcastle Waters Cattle Station, owned by Kerry Packer, as part of the official National Bicentennial Celebration's and the National Cattle Muster happening around Australia. We took a drive down to Newcastle Waters to see Bruce play and the old Newcastle Waters Pub, was re-opened for the event. Bruce was booked to appear on-stage immediately before outback legend entertainer "Ted Egan" and whilst any gig is a good gig, the pressure of performing before the "famous star attraction" would have been difficult for anyone but Bruce, as he slayed the big crowd of over a thousand people. They were eating out of his hand with his natural humour and songs. They loved him so much, when he finished his set they wouldn't let him leave and screamed for encore after encore. Finally, Bruce left and on came Ted Egan. Ted started playing but the crowd, spoilt by Bruce's wit, charm and pace, ensured Ted couldn't crack the restless crowd of Bruce converts. Ted was very good even with the lukewarm crowd. It was a great night and we enjoyed quite a few cold beers with Bruce after the gig at the bar in the Newcastle Waters Pub which closed again forever the next day. Not many people can say they've downed a beer in there.

As a footnote, a couple of years after we sold the pub, Bruce managed and then purchased the Daly Waters Pub, for himself. A more fitting owner and manager of the pub I couldn't imagine.

PAR FOR THE COURSE

One day, as I wandered past the pub, down the dirt track that is actually a government road no-one uses, I looked into the distance to a group of trees and I thought "if it wasn't out here in the outback that would make a beautiful golf hole". Then I thought it could be a golf hole. All I needed to do was grade the dirt fairway to make it flatter and get rid of the weeds and saplings, bore a hole at the far end just in front of the beautiful gums, spread some fine gravel around the hole and pour diesel over it to make a "scrape green", build a small teeing platform at the pub end … and then my imagination really took over and I thought, maybe get a flag for the hole and a ball washer at the tee and produce an official looking golf card and name it the "Not So Royal Daly Waters Golf Club".

So I rang my dad in Adelaide and asked him to see if he could get hold of a golf flag and a ball washer. Dad approached his best mate Ken Ellis, who could procure anything and who happened to be a member of Glenelg Golf Club. Within days the flag and ball washer was organised and as dad was coming up to visit soon he'd bring them with him.

A few days later a grader driver contracting to the Commonwealth Main Roads Department arrived in town to grade the Government owned dirt roads in the area. He set up camp at the rear of the pub campground and that night, as I shouted him a beer, I conveniently asked for a couple of favours. "If I let you stay here for free and gave you a carton or two of beer do you reckon you could use the grader of yours to make me a golf hole and extend the caravan park"? Without hesitation, he said "I'll get onto it first thing in the morning. Where's my first carton"?

Some mates watching the golf course fairway being graded

By lunchtime the next day, and exactly to instructions, we were proud owners of a one-hole golf course and a caravan park, double its original size. Next, I convinced Dave from the station to bring their post-hole borer to the pub and drill some holes. The first hole was the golf hole and the extras were for electricity poles in the caravan park. Another carton well spent.

The fully extended Daly Waters Caravan Park

When my parents arrived, one of the first things we did was put the flag in the hole, about 300 metres from the pub and we installed the ball washer next to the tee. Before I played the hole, and I really wanted to be the first, yardie Grant belted a ball down the fairway. We all followed him to the ball and he belted it again and again and again until he finally hit on the "green". Three putts followed and finally he was in the hole for a score of seven, to which Grant declared "that's a par". I was stunned, "what did you say" and he replied "I'm the first to play the hole. I scored a seven ... so it's a Par 7". Grant's logic was lost on everyone except himself and, whilst the score card and the tee sign both said "300 metres PAR 4", Grant never conceded it.

Golf never became as popular as hoped and therefore we never held a Saturday or a midweek ladies competition but every now and then a few lads from NTEC (electricity commission) would play the course and therefore I held a set of clubs and a few balls behind the bar. The course did come with its hazards but instead of the expected bunkers, trees and water they were replaced by helicopters, cattle, snakes and scorpions. It turned out the hole we bored into the ground was an enticing home for snakes and scorpions and therefore we warned the golfers to take care when "putting out"! Golf etiquette promotes the furthest player from the hole putting first, so it was very important to get close to the hole to ensure your opponent would have to putt first and risk the bite. As an additional surprise, we drilled the hole a metre deep, ensuring the ball was impossible to retrieve anyway.

SAFE NOT SECURE

I wandered into the bar at 6am one morning and proceeded to open up and clean just as I did almost every morning. Grant was already outside raking the gravel and Lockie was sitting next to the "donkey" having his morning coffee fix. At around 6.45am Leonie would normally come into the bar with the till float for the day but on this particular morning she came into the bar and asked me if I knew where should could find the key to the safe.

Our little office was directly behind the rear wall of the bar and contained a desk, two storage cupboards and an old floor mounted safe. The room was secured by a door but it couldn't be locked. Daly the Kangaroo slept in the office in a pillow case hanging from the door knob. The normal procedure in the morning was for Leonie to get into the office at around 6.30am, reach to the top of the cupboard next to the safe and grab the old six-inch long iron key and open the safe. Then count yesterday's takings, put $100 into the till in mixed denominations and another mixed $100 into a float tin and bring it to the bar. She would then replace the takings into the safe with any other day's takings and replace the key to the top of the cupboard. In anyone's language, this is not rigorous security, but it was Daly Waters Pub in the 1980's and it was our security. If you looked at how unsecure the pub was, it is probably best to start at the outside.

The front and side, and therefore the main entry doors, were timber bottom half with a flyscreen top half and both were "locked" by latches normally found in a public toilet. There was no glass, in fact, there were no glass windows in the entire hotel. It was all flyscreen and to break in would only require pushing on any of the flyscreens with your hand. The rear door of the pub, entered into the kitchen and was a simple lock and key affair. The office door didn't lock and the safe was not bolted to the ground. We knew this because we moved it a couple of times to re-arrange the office. So it could be said security was lacking. We were told by several locals and by the police that stealing from a business on the Stuart Highway between Katherine and Tenant Creek was foolhardy as there was one road north, one road south, one road east and a police station at the end of each. We simply hoped would-be thieves knew of this.

Anyway, Leonie hadn't found the key and so I went to the office and searched everywhere with her. After fifteen minutes I said I'd go and wake Taffy who closed up very late the night (actually early in the morning) before. I finally woke Taffy after banging on his caravan door and windows for at least ten minutes. By this time customers were already in the bar. Grant served them but couldn't give them change as Leonie cooked breakfasts. I dragged Taffy into the office and in his weary hung-over state he said in his slightly Welsh accent "well I'll be buggered, I locked them in the safe". "That's impossible", I said. He replied "nope it was simple. I unlocked the safe with the key, tossed the takings in the safe, with the key, closed the door and turned the lock. Simple mistake". Oh shit, we have a problem. "Surely there's a spare key", said Taffy. My look was enough to let him know there wasn't and he also knew he wasn't going back to bed. He went to work.

Later in the morning, after we served all the breakfasts and were enjoying a less busy period, I grabbed Grant and said "you ever broken into a safe". He replied "do I look like the sort of guy that would have"? So we loaded the heavy safe onto a sack truck normally used for moving five cartons of beer at a time and trolleyed the safe across the road from the Pub to the front of our little fuel station shed. We then laid it on its front and rolled out the oxy-acetylene hoses and attached the cutting tool. Grant put on the welding mask and proceeded to start cutting into the back of the safe. The plan was to cut a hole just big enough for one of us to put his hand inside and retrieve the key.

The action of two guys, with sparks flying around a safe on the ground in a small outback Pub with about thirty tourists, is sure to attract attention and before too long there was a growing crowd asking questions and taking photos. Grant made reasonable headway and completed about half the hole when I noticed something looking like sand inside the safe. I exclaimed "What the …", and a Pommy guy from the crowd said, "its sand. Safes have two walls and the gap between the two walls is filled with sand". Before I could ask why someone else did. "To stop anyone from cutting into them with an oxy-cutter. Shake the safe a bit and the sand will settle and make it easier to cut" the knowledgeable safe-guy replied with a cheeky grin. "What are you a safe-cracker", someone else said. It became funny and everyone enjoyed a laugh. "It's Ronnie Biggs", said another. Grant and I shook the safe and he kept cutting until the outer wall hole cut was complete. We removed the 10cm diameter roughly circular piece of metal and then rolled the safe over to empty the sand out before rolling it back onto its door as instructed by Ronnie Biggs, as we now named him.

Grant commenced cutting the inside wall through the hole and then I thought I heard something strange coming from within the safe ... "STOP", I said and we all intently listened and then we saw smoke coming, slowly at first, from the hole in the safe. "It's the smell of burning money, bloody hell get a hose and be damn quick", said Ronnie Biggs. So I rushed to get the hose beside the shed, turned it on and returned to the safe as quick as I could and I proceeded to spray water in through the small hole Grant created. It took about a minute to fill the safe until it couldn't take any more water and we noticed the smoke stop. "Now you have a problem", said Ronnie Biggs. "What now" we all wanted to ask. "You've filled the safe with water and water will have a worse effect than sand. You need to empty most of the water before you can finish cutting it open" and so we did as Ronnie instructed. I was now seriously wondering about this guy's background as a coach full of Japanese tourists arrived. As they disembarked they naturally wondered what the attraction was across the road and so now about one hundred shutter-happy tourists were watching our every move and jabbering away in Japanese.

After emptying most of the water Grant commenced cutting again and before too long the next circular piece of metal fell into the safe with a clunk. We then cooled the inside metal wall down with a bit more water and there was a collective hush as I slowly carefully pushed my hand into the safe. I needed to get my arm into the safe past my elbow before I reached anything and then I moved my hand around searching for the key. I could feel wet mushy paper and not much else until in the farthest corner I grabbed it. I knew instantly it was the key and slowly retracted my arm to avoid cuts from the sharp edges before triumphantly holding the key in the air like one would a world championship trophy. Everyone cheered and backslapped and I turned around to offer Ronnie Biggs as many free beers as he wanted but couldn't see him anywhere. He was gone …

I thought, if I opened the safe now, fifty people would see how much money was in the safe. I didn't want them to see anything and so I said to Grant we needed to get it back into the office. And so we lifted the safe onto the sack truck and said to everyone "the show is over folks, see you all inside" and wheeled the safe back into the office where we finally opened it. The crowd still talking about the Great Daly Waters Safe Break, but at least they were back in the bar.

When the safe was open we realised how costly a disaster we narrowly averted. Almost every monetary note was singed in one way or another. Some on ends, some along the sides and many just to the corner but the biggest problem was they were made of paper and they were soaking wet. I went back into the bar whilst Leonie and Grant removed every note and hung them individually with clothes pegs and paper clips from strings they erected all around the office. When I entered the office later in the day it resembled a Chinese laundry.

It took two days to finish drying all the notes before Leonie carefully packaged them together into a postal box and sent them off to the bank in Katherine with an explanatory note. We were eventually told every note was accepted by the bank and therefore we didn't lose a dollar from the extraordinary event.

Footnote: I still wonder who the man was we nicknamed Ronnie Biggs. If you're reading this book I owe you one mate. There was ten thousand dollars in the safe and it would have gone up in smoke if you hadn't been there to give advice.

JOIN THE DOTS

I closed the bar after midnight and wandered across the road from the pub and was in bed. It was a hot balmy night and therefore the shutters on our upstairs territory home were open to encourage any breeze to flow through the room. At about 3am I was woken by the noise of a Greyhound Bus stopping in front of the pub with the air brakes hissing. This was most unusual as the south heading Greyhound Bus did not stop at Daly Waters Pub but instead dropped any freight to the Hi-Way Inn.

I went to the bedroom window expecting to see the driver drop a package at the front door of the pub and depart, as they rarely but sometimes did. This normally occurred if they were running early or sometimes a passenger could convince the driver she or he needed to see the historic pub. Normally it was only a "woman" who could get the male driver to take the diversion.

In this case, the driver opened the bus door, opened the luggage compartment under the bus and then unloaded a suitcase. He then went to the bus door and helped a young woman get off with another large bag. He pointed to the pub and drove off leaving the woman, with her luggage, standing on the side of the road. There was no-one waiting to collect this person and I realised I was going to have to see what was happening here.

Reluctantly I dressed and headed over to the pub find a young female, maybe in her early twenties, standing in front of the pub with two large pieces of luggage. It was very dark but I could sense she was scared and confused. I asked what she was doing here and who she was waiting for. She said in a thick English accent "I think I am in the wrong place. I am supposed to be staying in Daly Waters and the driver said this is Daly Waters but this can't be it". I told her she was definitely in Daly Waters. "There must be a mistake", she said "this town doesn't even have street lights. This can't be Daly Waters" and she started to get teary. I asked, "why are you so sure this isn't Daly Waters"? She looked straight into my eyes and replied "on our old map at home, the biggest dot in the Northern Territory is Daly Waters. It's bigger than Darwin's dot and so it must be a bigger town". It didn't take much time to convince her to not worry about it until the next day and the best thing to do was for me to show her to a room in the motel so she could get some sleep and we'd talk about it in the morning.

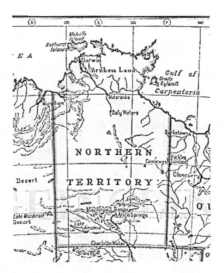

A 1930's map showing Daly Waters as big as Darwin's dot

The next morning, an hour after most people had eaten breakfast and left town, our English guest appeared in the bar. "Okay", I said "I think I know your problem and it goes like this. In the 20's and 30's all the international flights, including those from London, landed at Daly Waters for refuelling and passenger breaks. Then in the Second World War, it was a major air-force base and after, until the early 70's, it was a stopover for QANTAS and TAA. I think it was a larger dot because it was a more important airfield than Darwin and I think your old map reflected the importance. Now, what say you relax with a cup of tea and have some breakfast and we will talk about what you do from here.

After enjoying a hearty breakfast Leonie and I sat with our guest and discussed her next move. It turned out she planned on getting to her next stop Alice Springs, where there was a room booked for her, until a week from now. "Okay then", I said, "what say we introduce you to the local cattle station lads and they can show you around. Roy is always looking for extra hands". She then mentioned she "could ride a horse". I contacted Dave at the station and explained the poor girl's predicament. The first thing he asked was "what's she like" to which I could honestly reply "well, she can ride a horse".

Our girl settled into the Pub during the day by wandering around the grounds and checking out the Pub's memorabilia and asking heaps of questions. She seemed genuinely interested in the history of the Pub and the town and even took a long walk to explore the historic airfield that caused her to be here. Dave called into the Pub late in the afternoon and I introduced him to our guest. They hit it off immediately and it wasn't long before they jumped into the station ute and headed out to meet Roy. That evening she came in for dinner and declared "can I book my room for a few more nights, please? Roy has said I can do some mustering and yard-work with them for the next few days". So for the next week, we hardly saw our UK friend. But when she did make an appearance each evening she wore a smile from ear to ear and was obviously really enjoying her time. She told us she mustered cattle on horseback and motorbike and took a chopper flight. Roy took a shine to her and showed her around the "big house". We hadn't been in there. The station lads all loved her natural style and preparedness to mix it with them at work and at play.

When her time came to an end we booked her a seat on the Greyhound Bus to Alice Springs, leaving from Hi-Way Inn at 3am the next morning, and offered to take her there. She replied "thanks so much for everything. This has been the experience of a lifetime and I am so glad I made that stupid mistake with the map … but Dave has offered to take me to the bus tonight and I already accepted". Good one Dave.

I believe our English maiden enjoyed her stay more than anyone else we met during our time at Daly Waters. She experienced more of the "real" territory and came closer to "real" working men, horses and cattle than anyone. She drank with them, partied with them and was accepted by them. Very few others, particularly English lassies, could lay claim to that.

TRAIN TRACKS

Until 2004 there was no railway line connecting Darwin to the rest of Australia. Therefore the Stuart Highway carried almost all the freight needed to supply Darwin with food, beverage and other hardware plus general life necessities, and it was all carried in long, appropriately named road trains.

These road trains were over fifty metres long and weighed well over one hundred tonnes and the prime movers were powered by huge diesel motors developing over 500hp and were capable of doing over 100kmh. The drivers in charge of these massive units drove at speed on roads sometimes only one lane of bitumen wide with rough dirt verges. Cars coming up behind these beasts experienced a difficult time passing and coming from the opposite direction wasn't fun either. Whilst the road train may be fine tracking down the centre of the highway, when the driver dropped off the centre line onto the verge to allow a vehicle to pass, the rear trailer would become its own worst enemy by snaking and weaving as if it was a wagging dog's tail. This was most unnerving for an experienced driver but for a poor elderly caravan-towing tourist it could become hazardous. Many caravans were destroyed along the track by these huge beasts wagging tails while some vans simply "exploded" or "flipped over" when passed by a road train coming the other way due to the incredible turbulence of the air created by the monster.

Dave jumping into his triple road train on the Kalala track

The drivers of these road trains were expected to do long hours behind the wheel to meet the appropriately named deadlines set by the trucking companies. Our freight company was Gilbert's of Strathalbyn and they'd take full trailers the 3,000km from Adelaide to Darwin and backload to us on their way home. We received our freight each week and it was delivered by two drivers, Banga and Claude, in weekly rotation. As an example, Claude would leave Adelaide on a Monday and arrive in Darwin on the Wednesday. He'd then be back to Daly Waters on the Thursday and home to Strathalbyn on the Saturday. He'd then have a day or two off before heading to Melbourne and back the next week and the Monday after, he'd be back up to Darwin. Banga would do the opposite run thereby giving us a delivery each week. One can't begin to imagine how tiresome and stressful it would be to do over 6,000km in less than six days and then do 1,600km the next week before backing up to the 6,000km once again.

Fortunately for us, Claude and Banga were great blokes who looked after us well and never experienced a crash or major incident whilst we were in the Pub. Late in our first year, Claude said he was taking a month's driving holiday and may drop in to see us. I couldn't believe what I was hearing and said "Claude, you drive for a living, surely you don't want to drive here on your holidays mate. Go overseas, fly somewhere but don't bloody drive mate". But Claude said he wanted to really see the territory and show his wife all the sights along the way that he never previously stopped for. So about a month later a nice couple walked into the bar and said a friendly "hello Mark" and shook my hand. I said "hi there, nice to meet you, what can I get you" and the guy said, "Mark, what's wrong with you, I'm Claude mate". I took another look and said "sorry … errr Claude who" before I realised I was looking at our Gilbert's driver Claude. Seriously, I couldn't believe it was the same man. Road-train driver Claude was pasty coloured, wore truckie shorts and singlet, sported large bags and dark rings under his bloodshot red eyes, was non-shaven and looked over fifty. Whereas holidaying Claude was tanned, neatly dressed in a casual polo shirt, clean shaven, clear blue eyes and looked about thirty-five. I was stunned and told him so, before running out to get Leonie … "come see this, Claude is in the bar with his wife, you won't recognise him" and she didn't. They stayed the night, dined on the beef and barra BBQ and we all had a great time, relaxing. If we ever needed evidence of how hard a job long distance road train driving was then we saw it that day.

Road-train accidents were bound to happen when so many of them moved up and down the highway and eventually one was going to be not far from our Pub.

The first occurred early one morning whilst we were asleep. The first we knew of it was when a policeman came into the bar and asked if Noel Davis was in town. Noel lived diagonally opposite the pub and was a heavy machinery and road plant contractor. He owned a grader and an old bulldozer but he was away grading at the time. The policeman said it was a pity, as they needed his bulldozer to push a road-train that rolled over off the highway, as it was blocking the entire road. Phil offered to drive it there and he surprised me by offering. I didn't know how to drive the old thing and whilst Phil didn't either, I knew he was good at machinery stuff and would work it out. So Phil and the policeman went to Noel's yard and started working out how to get it going. Get it started was the easy part. In the territory hardly any locals lock their house let alone shitty old bulldozers. Therefore the key was in the ignition and it started immediately. It only took Phil ten minutes to work out the gears and lift the bucket and he was ready to go. I decided it would be wise to follow behind him along the highway to the crash scene ten kilometres south. The problem with Noel's old bulldozer was its age and its condition. It was a very big front end loader that swivelled in the centre to steer but the centre pivot was badly worn, causing it to wobble along the road. It required Phil to keep turning the wheel from left to right to fight the wobbling. The faster it went the more severe the wobbles and the harder it was to keep it straight. After about five kilometres Phil pulled up to stop and waved me over before saying "I'm absolutely stuffed. You're gonna have to take it from here" which I did. I couldn't believe what a beast this machine was. It bucked and weaved and tried everything to throw me out of the chair as I tried to get it over ten kilometres per hour. Finally, we arrived to a scene of carnage. It looked like a war zone. There were two trailers laying on their side on the road and one trailer plus the prime mover in the ditch on the side of the road. Somehow they were all still connected. Police were on either end of the scene diverting traffic down a little side ditch opposite to get past. Phil jumped back into the dozer and under instructions pushed and shoved the trailers off the road into the ditch. The machine was powerful and the job was actually rather easy and over in quick time. Taking time to get a look inside the rear trailer, I was surprised to see it was full of food and alcohol and at least some of it was still intact. The police said they'd get the road cleaned up and the trucking company would then be responsible for removing the road-train and destroying or removing the damaged contents whenever they could get down there. We raised our eyebrows and the policeman winked. So we returned to Daly Waters and dropped the dozer back to where we found it. That night Phil and I jumped in the pub ute and drove back to the accident scene to remove some of the contents that, according to the police, were going to be destroyed anyway. There was no-one around and so with torches on we entered the trailers and discovered someone beat us to the loot. I knew the rear trailer contained some unbroken boxes of food and liquor but it was already entered and some of the goods were gone. However, we did manage to find some bottles of tequila and other spirits as well as some packaged food. The two front trailers were locked up tight and so we didn't dare enter them. Two days later we received a visit from the police accusing us of stealing electrical appliances such as stereo players from one of the trailers. We protested our innocence and said we didn't know who took the electrical equipment but it certainly wasn't us. And it wasn't. Later, I was told who stole the goods. It didn't surprise me to hear who it was and whilst I would love to expose her, after all these years, I fear a lawsuit may eventuate.

The next road-train incident occurred a few months later just prior to Melbourne Cup Day. This time it was two reps from the unfortunate trucking company who came into the pub and they weren't requesting a bulldozer but instead asked for a carton of beer. It turned out they needed to stay at the accident scene for a day until a salvage company from Katherine came there to clean the mess up. During the conversation, they said one trailer exploded on rolling over and spilt the contents all over the place and we were welcome to see if we wanted anything as it would be buried or set fire to anyway. When I asked what was there they said simply "clothes". SO once again we drove, in daylight this time and with approval, to the accident scene. It looked like a cyclone ripped through the area. There were clothes scattered everywhere but unfortunately, most of them were of no use to us or were damaged beyond hope. I did find an intact large cardboard box full of something and put it in the ute. That afternoon we went thru the box and discovered heaps of zany colourful board shorts of varying sizes and so I put a sign out the front for the local station hands saying "FREE BOARDIES". Over the next few days, all the lads from the station helped themselves to free boardies. They looked so funny I decided to hold a MELBOURNE CUP DAY event with "board shorts required for entry". On Melbourne Cup Day the lads all arrived in their board shorts and we all wore boardies on as well. It was colourful and hilarious and the tourists thought we were all mad. As the jump time for the race came closer, I turned on the only radio we owned, so we could listen to the race. Unfortunately, reception at Daly Waters was poor and with about five hundred metres to go the signal faded out and we missed the finish ... but no-one really cared as we couldn't place a bet anyway and the sweep results could be declared anytime in the future. An hour or so later a vehicle came into town with the results we were after. During the afternoon the phone rang with a journalist from Darwin, as they occasionally did, this time asking what Daly Waters Pub did for Melbourne Cup Day. A day or so later a visitor showed us the front page of the NT NEWS with a cartoon depiction of the DALY WATERS PUB MELBOURNE CUP DAY with me behind the bar in board shorts and customers in jackaroo hats and board-shorts swilling beers and Bundy and me shaking the radio as it faded out. The artist would have been proud to know how visually correct his cartoon was.

The most culinary enjoyable highway story occurred when a truck broke down a few kilometres from Daly Waters. The driver sent a message to the Pub with a passer-by tourist. The note read "truck broken down on the highway. Please come to see if you can fix". Grant immediately grabbed some tools and took the ute to see what he could do. Grant wasn't a mechanic but like Phil, he was very handy with motors and all things mechanical. When he arrived at the truck he found the Asian driver in a state of panic. The driver told Grant the truck was full of freshly caught mud crabs from Borroloola and he needed to be in Darwin that night otherwise they'd all be dead and so would he. His slight exaggeration and the mood of the driver led Grant to believe the haul wasn't exactly legal. Grant tried to fix the truck but he admitted defeat when the motor wouldn't even turn with a full battery pushing the starter. He explained to the driver the motor was seized and the truck was not going anywhere. Grant offered to tow him back into Daly Waters but the driver wouldn't have any of it and instead, he told Grant to take as many crabs as he liked as payment for his help and to ring his mate in Darwin to explain where he was and what was wrong with the truck. He gave Grant the phone number and said he would wait with the truck until his mate came to rescue him. So Grant took a dozen fresh mud crabs as payment and we cooked them for a special staff dinner that night … they were sensational. I sent Grant back to the truck the next morning to see if the guy was alright and to hopefully get some more crabs but when he arrived, the truck was nowhere in sight. A bemused Grant returned half an hour later empty handed and our plans for serving mud crab to the tourists and making a healthy profit were scuttled.

Chapter 24. STRANGE BEHAVIOUR

During our time at Daly Waters, we regularly witnessed strange behaviour from tourists and from locals alike. I believe the uniqueness of the pub encouraged the uniqueness in people to be more apparent … certainly to me. I looked forward getting out of the bar through the day to get some fresh air and the opportunity generally presented itself when a car would pull up for fuel. The pumps were across the road from the pub and a sign above the pumps read "FUEL – ASK AT THE PUB" and so it would normally go like this. A car would come into town and pull up just short of the pumps. The driver and the passengers would read the sign, look to their right to the pub and then back to the sign, before slowly driving forward to the pumps. On many occasions, I would be too busy in the bar to get to them quickly. The wife or husband would then get out of the car and slowly walk to the pub, stop at the door and peer in, even though the door was always wide open. They'd ask "is this where I get fuel" and I'd be smart and say something like "the only fuel in here is beer mate" before giving them a wink and saying "see you over the road, in a tick".

OL' BERTY

I went to serve fuel to a very old and odd couple travelling in a pickup truck style camper van one day. When I arrived to the passenger door, a short bald old man sat there with his door open and the fuel-cap off the diesel tank just behind it. As I moved to get the diesel nozzle from the pump a huge woman in the driver's seat started with "its diesel you know. Bert make sure he puts diesel in it. Remember what happened last time Bert. You, yes you sonny, you just make sure its diesel"! I turned around to look at Bert and there he was staring at me with a pleading look of "get a gun and shoot her please". So I pretended to grab the petrol hose and gave him a wink. His lips started to create a smile but the wife jumped back in with "and make sure you fill it to the top ... the last place half-filled it and we almost ran out of fuel getting here". I took the diesel hose and started filling the tank. All the time poor Bert was staring at me and then to the tank and back to me and not looking anywhere else. I kept filling and looking at Bert and nowhere else. Not even at the tank. She continued "keep going, it's not even half full yet, I don't care what it says at your end I'm looking at the fuel gauge, keep going". And so I kept going until I heard the diesel foaming and coming up the filler pipe, as diesel does. Normally I would slow the flow down to a stop to allow

409

the diesel foam to dissipate, allowing more diesel into the tank without having it spill over the top but she kept on with "don't stop, its only three quarters, keep going, I don't want to run out again. Keep going" and so I kept going. Bert was looking even more pensive than before, as he shifted his glance from me to the tank, now oozing diesel foam over the lip and down the side of the truck and then looking back to me. I didn't even bother looking at the tank but kept my stare on Bert. I had filled hundreds if not thousands of diesel vehicles and I knew exactly what was happening down there. Diesel foam now became pure diesel and it was flowing over the side of the vehicle and onto the ground and STILL, Bert said nothing! Not a word but glancing from me to the ground as the diesel flowed towards the front wheel and looking back to me and she went on "keep going it's nearly there … don't stop yet, keep going keep going. It's full … STOP NOW. See I told you Bert, that's why we ran out last time. It was all because you didn't keep an eye on him". And I stopped. By now there were at least five litres of diesel flowing down the street past the front of the truck and around the corner and Bert watched it flow and then looked at me with a look of "how can you let me go through this, please poison her or do something". I gave him a wink as I took the filler cap from his little old wrinkled hand and said "I'll look after this for you Bert. Wouldn't want you getting into trouble for not doing this properly would we" as I replaced it as well as putting the diesel nozzle back in the bowser and said "that'll be seventy-three dollars and sixteen cents, thanks lady. Pay in the bar" and walked back into my sanctuary.

MATES GAMES

On another occasion, two almost identical Nissan four wheel drives towing caravans pulled up to the bowsers. The guy in the first one said "fill her up please mate" and so I did exactly that. I then said, "pull up over there mate and I'll see you in the bar for payment". His mate then pulled up to the bowser and said "how much did he take" to which I replied "he took forty-two dollars neat". So the guy says "in that case put thirty-eight dollars into this baby". I did and said to him "pull up over there and I'll see you and your mate in the bar". I locked the bowser and wandered back into the pub. The first guy and wife were waiting for me at the bar when the second couple wandered in. The first guy asked me "okay, give it to me. How much did he take"? This took me by surprise but I replied, ""ah, he took thirty eight-dollars and you took …". He threw his cap on the bar in disgust and exclaimed to his friend "no bloody way. Again. You bastard, how do you do it"? I said "what's going on"? The first guy answered, "we have exactly the same cars and same vans and I have tried everything on this trip to conserve fuel and he always takes much less fuel than me and I'm bloody over it". It was the best I could do to stop bursting out laughing. Particularly when the second guy said "so it's beers on you again pal. We'll have two VB thanks" as the first guy's wife stared at her husband with a look of disappointment. A bit later I said to the second guy when he came to the bar "hey great trick mate, but you know you are going to have to fill up first eventually" to which he replied "way ahead of you mate, the bet stipulates the loser has to lead all day and fill up first".

LOCKJAW

I was serving in the bar one day when a Victorian registered station wagon pulled up out front and in came three guys aged in their early twenties. After having a glance around the bar one of them approached me and ordered, "three cans of Carlton Draught please and can I have one with a straw". I looked at him and said "a straw"? He replied, "yeh a straw, my stupid mate over there broke his jaw playing footy a week ago and needs a straw to drink his beer". Now, we've all heard the rumour, drinking beer through a straw gets you drunk faster but it only took a glance towards the poor lad to show me he was serious about his injury. The poor guy was still getting over two black eyes and his jaw was still swollen to about the size of a football. The lads proceeded to knock down a few beers before deciding they needed to spend the night in the caravan park and so they paid for a tent site and headed to the camping ground to take a break before dinner. In the evening they wandered back into the bar and asked what was on the menu for dinner. They must have been blind (literally) as the Beef and Barra BBQ signs were plastered everywhere around the pub ... but on reflection, I know what I was like when I was their age. I explained the menu to them and they all ordered the barramundi. I didn't even consider how the lad with the broken jaw was going to eat his meal. They ordered the usual three beers, with one straw and went out to the beer garden. At the normal time of 5.30pm I started cooking the BBQ for our guests and eventually I called out the names of the three Victorian lads and "you're three barramundis are ready boys". When they came to me, to collect their meals, I said to the injured lad "if you can't drink without a straw how the hell are you gonna eat this mate"? He responded by showing me what he held in his left hand, he hid behind his back. It was a blender. Then through a wired-shut jaw he mumbled "drop the barra in here please mate", which I did. With a small crowd of intrigued diners looking on, he then went to Leonie's buffet salad table and selected his salads by spooning them into the blender on top of the barra and then came back to me and quietly asked "have you a handy power-point mate"? As it happened there was a power point in the little room next to the BBQ and so I showed him where to find it. With about fifty spectators now watching his every move he plugged the blender in and WHHRRRRR it went. In about thirty seconds the barra, lettuce, tomato, coleslaw and mayo was blended into a liquid Barra smoothie. He then walked over to the table where his mates were eagerly tucking into their fillets of barra and sat down. Then in a well-rehearsed theatrical style move, he reached into his pocket, elegantly withdrew and then wiped clean a large diameter straw and proceeded to drink his BBQ barramundi. Later that night he explained to me, after he broke his, he said to his mates "there is no way I am going to miss out on the trip of a lifetime and so he worked out his own way to "do everything on the trip my mates do". Well, he certainly did that at Daly Waters Pub.

DODGY BROTHERS

An old Ford drifted into town one morning and into the bar came four lads. "Gidday mate, we're the Dodgy Brothers from Victoria and we heard this pub's alright", one of them said. "Mate we don't let Mexicans up here, how'd you get past the border police" I replied. "Easy, we told them we have a job here at the Pub" said another. "Well, in that case, you'd better get to work. What'll it be boys"? With formalities over the Dodgy Brothers settled into a forty-eight-hour drinking session that became legendary.

The lads sat at the corner of the bar all day and into the night. They drank beers and then rums like no southerners before them. The pub was very busy, and even after the last tourists and locals went to bed, the Dodgy Brothers pace stayed the same. At about 2am one of them said to me "you can go to bed boss, we'll put the money in the till. Honestly" but they were funny guys with plenty of stories and I was happy enough to keep serving them.

At 6am Leonie came into the bar and was in shock to see me still there. I said, "these boys have spent up big and wouldn't let me close up, you'd better ask Grant to take over from me for a few hours".

At 11am I came back into the bar to ensure I was ready for the coach lunches and was surprised to see two of them still at the bar. "We checked into a room boss but it only has two single beds, so we've decided to rotate the sleeping and drinking into four hour sessions, before we get serious tonight".

At 10pm, all four of the Dodgy Brothers were at the bar, drinking every bit as quick as they were the night before. I looked at Leonie with pleading eyes and she said "okay, I'll look after them tonight".

At 6am the next morning I came into the bar to start cleaning for the day's trade. I found it immaculately clean and the four Dodgy Brothers sitting at the bar with Leonie, and looking very happy with themselves. Leonie obviously had put them to work.

At midday, the Dodgy Brothers, after four hours rotation sleep, drove out of town.

The Dodgy Brothers about to leave Daly Waters … with beers in hand

As they left one of them said "we're going to Mataranka, then Katherine, then Darwin and Kakadu and we'll be back to see ya in a couple of weeks". Phew, at last we could all get some sleep.

Less than a week later the Dodgy Brothers drove back into Daly Waters and declared "Darwin was boring, so we left early". I went "argghh no, not so soon". The first night back in town the lads did a full repeat of last week's performance by staying up all night but fortunately this time they decided one night was enough and the middle of the next morning they headed for home. We never heard directly from the lads again but several tourists called in over the next couple of days and said "the Dodgy Brothers say hello from Alice Springs" or Tenant Creek or wherever. I hope you made it safely home lads.

IT AIN'T CRICKET

Telecom workers were regularly doing work on their transmitter stations dotted all across the territory. Therefore we constantly had Telecom workers staying or drinking at the Pub. They were great guys and loved nothing better than a good time. Phil and I decided we should put on a "Daly Waters All Stars" versus "Telecom Terrors" cricket match. So we arranged it for Australia Day in January 1987 as we knew the Telecom and cattle station workers would get a day off together.

The day arrived and we somehow managed to put together some stumps, a cricket ball and importantly the two teams. We measured out the 22 yards for the pitch on the road just past the pub and painted the crease. It was decided this was the best place for the pitch as it was flat but more importantly, it was close to the bar. The Daly Waters Pub team was made up of Publicans Mark and Phil, Yardie Grant, Dunmurra Publican Robbie, Tour Operator Andy, Cattle Station lads Brett and Dallas, Fencer Paddy and his boy, Grader Driver Noel and Stock Inspector Pat.

418

The rules were the same as any fun cricket rules including, on the roof of the pub is six and out, and you must always have a beer when fielding. When I came out to bat I wore a motorcycle helmet in Tony Grieg fashion.

Yours truly opening the batting in my Tony Grieg helmet

The day was going well until a mustering helicopter landed on the pitch to refuel. Whilst I looked after this job, the players decided to refuel themselves and it wasn't easy to convince them to leave the shade of the bar and come back out to finish the game.

We, "Daly Waters All Stars", eventually defeated the "Telecom Terrors" and collected the "stump" trophy made from stainless steel stumps and a wooden block. It was a long day and if it went on much longer we would have needed to turn the car lights on. In the end, it was a day, and night, we will all remember.

The victorious Daly Waters First Eleven with the "stump" trophy which can still be found in the pub. Back Row Standing: 2 of Paddy's kids, Robbie Knight, Andy Hind, Brett, Paddy Heatley, Noel Davis and Pat Barry Front Row Kneeling: Grant Wood, Paddy's lad, Me

A MAN AIN'T A CAMEL

In late 1987 the NT Police embarked on a camel trek from Darwin to Adelaide. It was named the Bicentennial Police Overland Camel Expedition and was organised to celebrate the extensive use of camels in Northern Territory Police history. The expedition arrived, as planned, in

Adelaide at exactly 1 minute past midnight on January 1st, 1988.

The small group of hot and thirsty cameleers arrived at the Daly Waters Pub mid-afternoon and they needed a beer. So after tying their camels to the front of the pub, next to a big water trough, they came inside. I said to them "like a drink" and in unison they replied, "a man ain't a camel".

Leonie greeting the cameleers with the promise of a cold beer inside

Whilst they skulled beers, one of the camels was obviously more interested in the beer than the water and became very vocal out the front. His handler went to calm him down and before I could blink he came back into the bar leading the camel. The camel wasn't the first four legged people carrier to enter the bar, as a couple of horses previously walked in for a look, but it was at the drunken urgings of a few jackaroos not because they wanted to. Horses, being shod with steel shoes, were very scared of slipping on the shiny concrete floor, let alone the unfamiliar environment of a bar. The camel on the other hand, was soft footed and calm and took it all in his stride. It even became inquisitive and curious at the sights and smells of the bar and attempted to drink from the cans of beer the officers were holding, but the camel's curiosity all came undone when it raised its head a bit too high and its ear was clipped by a fast spinning overhead fan. Fortunately, the camel simply lowered his head again and was turned around and led back out the front … curiosity cured.

The camel could smell the beer and refused to stay outside

The police and their entourage set up camp in our caravan park and put their camels in a yard behind Pat Barry, the stock inspector's, house just around the corner. It was planned they would only stay the one night but the next morning one of the officers came into the pub with distressing news. One of the camels was seriously ill through eating the bark off a tree in the yard. A tree hiding a toxin deadly to camels. Apparently, most camels won't eat the bark because it tastes funny but some find it irresistible. The police decided to move the camels to the rodeo ground yards and delay leaving for a day just in case others came down with similar symptoms. After walking the camels for over six hundred kilometres I think the police needed a rest day anyway and they enjoyed it by spending the day in the bar and beer garden having a few beers and putting their feet up. After all, a man ain't a camel.

Unfortunately the sick camel did not survive the day and the police were forced to amend their roster of walking and riding. We received a letter, a few weeks later, from the head of the camel trek thanking us for our hospitality and informing us the full team arrived into Adelaide exactly on schedule on the 1st January 1988. What a great feat.

LIVE BAND COLOURED STONE

In 1987 a dirty old van pulled up at the pub and out of it poured several aboriginal lads. They came into the bar and introduced themselves as members of rock band Coloured Stone and said they were on their way to be the support act for a Darwin concert featuring Midnight Oil. They seemed like great blokes and they loved the pub. I remember one of them saying he grew up in Ceduna, and as Phil and I knew the area quite well from our surveying days, there we had a bit in common to talk about. They were experiencing problems with the van and were short of money, so Phil spent a fair bit of time across the road trying to fix it for them. The van was chock a block full of their equipment and the overloading was causing the van motor to overheat. In the end, the lads stayed overnight and ate a counter meal at the bar. They were great lads, with almost no money, and so we didn't charge them and filled their van with fuel for free. The next morning as they left, lead singer Bunna said to me "Boss we want to repay your generosity by playing a free gig in the beer garden on our way back down south". I leapt at the offer and arranged for it to be the next Saturday night.

During the week we made preparations for the concert by clearing an area of the beer garden for the band, creating a small dance floor and sending word to all the cattle stations in the area. Stock inspector Pat Barry said he'd make some posters and take them up and down the track to put in the pubs and cattle stations he visited. It wasn't until after he left I read the poster and it read "COLOURED BAND ... LIVE STONE". It was too late to change it but nobody cared.

We prayed the band would remember their promise.

On the Saturday at 4pm there was no Coloured Stone and we were getting worried as the bar was filling up with expectant locals, tourists and cattle station folk. Finally, just on dusk, the lads arrived after again experiencing problems with their van and that night played one of the best concerts you could imagine. I reckon there were about two hundred people in the bar and beer garden. The band were brilliant and the local aboriginal kids had a ball dancing and singing all night.

Coloured Stone went on to be one of Australia's best aboriginal bands with several chart-topping hits including the wonderful Black Boy as well as Dancing in the

Moonlight. We were incredibly lucky to have them play for us at Daly Waters Pub and I only wish we filmed it.

OPEN AIR CINEMA

A couple wandered into the bar one day and asked if they could screen a movie in the beer garden in the evening. I asked them what was this all about and they said they travelled the outback showing movies for the locals who rarely get to see anything on the big screen. They explained they bought a projector and a large screen and would set them up in the beer garden and take donations. It sounded like a good idea to me but I did say if they gave us some notice we could have sent the word to all the stations. This didn't seem to bother them but I did offer to ring around anyway.

That night a group of about fifty locals and tourists watched The Man from Snowy River on the big screen. The young aboriginal lads from the cattle stations were in stitches laughing at some of the horse riding scenes but were hushed during the famous scene of the horse racing down the almost vertical mountain and what followed was much banter and debate of the rider and the horse and if it could actually have been done in real life.

POLITICALLY INCORRECT

Norm and Fiona Darcy owned and managed Mallupunyah Station about two hundred kilometres east of Daly Waters. We saw the Darcy's each year at rodeo time and occasionally they would drop into the pub if passing through. You would never know these people were millionaires because, typical of territory cattle station owners, they were hard-working quiet spoken unassuming people. When we saw their sons, the infamous Darcy boys, it was completely the opposite, as they drank like there was no tomorrow, and they could fight like no-one I ever saw. I couldn't believe they were from the same family but that said, I only saw them at rodeo time. I think the rest of their "pub time" thankfully was at Cape Crawford's Heartbreak Hotel near their station.

Fiona Darcy was a member the Country Liberal Party and in 1987 she booked our beer garden to hold a regional CLP meeting for about thirty members. On the day of the meeting, we set the tables in a large rectangle with chairs all around the perimeter and a few tables off to the side for interested visitors. Norm Darcy, like most Territory born cattlemen, was a big man who spoke with a slow calm tone. He wasn't a member of the party and so he sat at a table to the side. After an hour or so of the proceedings,

Norm came into the bar and ordered a small straight rum, he skulled it before rolling his eyes to me and heading back out to the meeting. Norm's next rum was poured fifteen minutes later and the rum after came in ten minutes. After five more minutes, he came into the bar, looked me in the eye and said "Mark, if you ever see me at a bloody political meeting again take my gun and shoot me dead" as he walked out the door, jumped into his four wheel drive and sped out of town.

HELLO SAILOR

In 1987 Italy sent two yachts to Fremantle to sail against twelve other yachts for the right to challenge Australia for the America's Cup. After the Gucci-sponsored Italian boat Consorzio Italia was eliminated, the crew took a whistle stop tour around Australia and whilst on tour they spent a night at the Daly Waters Pub.

I had forgotten their visit until I was reminded of it recently by my sister Jules who was visiting us from Adelaide when the Italians came to town.

As I remember it, the Italians booked out all our "one-star" motel rooms and were travelling in a small bus. They arrived late in the afternoon after taking a boat cruise on the Katherine Gorge followed by swimming in the hot springs at beautiful Mataranka. Not having anything resembling an outback pub in Italy, and preferring Peroni to VB, they were obviously underwhelmed with the concrete floored tin-shed Daly Waters Pub. They suffered through a quiet evening in the beer garden and tolerated our Beef and Barra BBQ before taking an early night and leaving at dawn the next morning.

As my sister Jules remembers it, a white minibus pulled up in front of the hotel and in came eight to ten handsome Italians in pressed white shorts and shirts embroidered with the Gucci logo and the Italian flag. They were adorable, talked to and entertained everyone with their world yachting stories, drank heaps of VB, loved barramundi for the first time and loved it, partied hard and sang and danced all night. Finally, when the sun was coming up they drove out of town leaving all the ladies sobbing in the street.

The truth probably falls somewhere in between the two stories. But it did happen.

At the bar with cattle station Dave and my sister Jules …
the Italians shouted us Proseccos

ARE WE AT WAR?

I was in my usual position behind the bar one morning,
serving breakfast to some tourists, when two foreign lads
aged in their early twenties entered the pub. I wondered
how they came into Daly Waters, as no-one had just driven
into town, as they spoke enough English to communicate
but I couldn't work out where they were actually from.
One of them seemed more forthright than the other and he
asked for a word in private. I said "I have customers and
can't leave the bar. Talk to me here". I have to admit I was
curious, but for some reason I couldn't fathom, I was
guarded at the same time. These guys didn't arrive in a car

and they carried little luggage except for a small shoulder
bag each. They appeared tense to me and none of them
would look me in the eye.

The forthright guy said something like "we need some
work please. We have no money and we need to be in
Sydney in two weeks" to which I replied, "I don't have any
work for you, sorry". He looked disappointed and said
"you don't understand, we need work so we can get to
Sydney. We do anything. Please". Again I said, "I just told
you I don't have any work for you". The other guy grabbed
his friend by the shoulder and pulled him away from the
bar where they whispered to each other. By now I was
getting concerned something was not quite as it should be.

They came back to the bar and the non-talker took over,
"Please man, we don't have no money and we need to keep
moving. We've walked all the way here from the Hi-Way
Inn because they wouldn't help us and we couldn't get a
lift", which explained them walking into town. So I asked
what I thought was a perfectly reasonable question "what
the hell are the two of you doing out here with no money in
the first place"? They moved away from the bar again and
whispered to each other.

This time is was the talker who started "okay, this is
how it is. We were flown to Darwin and we were left there

431

with no money and we were told we needed to be in Sydney in less than three weeks". I said "that's no explanation. Where did you fly from"? "Paris", he said after getting a nod from his friend. "Why" was returned, after a shake of the head, with "not allowed to tell you, sorry". "Why can't you tell me" came back with "Not allowed to". So I went next with "are you on the run"? The question came back without hesitation "God no. Do you think we are criminals"? "It did cross my mind", I said and they started laughing and then I laughed. My laugh was from relief. Theirs, I wasn't sure.

Now the ice was broken, I pushed on "okay, so you're not on the run but you're doing something for someone and you can't say. It's not much to go on". This time the quiet one came forward and said "if we told you, would you give us a job" to which I replied, without really knowing why "yes, I'll give you work for the rest of the day and pay you $50". They briefly looked at each other before nodding and replying "okay". "Okay" I said, "out with it".

The quiet one leant forward and said quietly, "we are in the French Foreign Legion".

"Seriously", I said. "Yes seriously" he replied. "Then what the hell are you doing out here … are we at war"? I asked grinning. The forthright one said "no. It's a test. We need to move quickly through Australia without raising suspicion or breaking the law" and the other one jumped in sheepishly "and without telling anyone". Back to the forthright one "if we get to Sydney on time we pass the test and then maybe we qualify and become officers in the Legion" he said with pride.

So I put them to work. They cut down some trees in the caravan park and cleaned out all the gutters around the motel. They slashed the weeds around the fencing and did a few other odd jobs and by the time they finished, the pub and grounds were looking great. Grant was using the Ute so I loaned them my Range Rover to take all the rubbish and foliage to the dump, promising them a beer and their pay when they returned.

Whilst they were on the dump run I went to the kitchen and told Leonie the story. When I finished my story she glared at me and said "so you've just given our Range Rover to two foreigners, who you thought were criminals ten minutes ago. What were you thinking"? "At least I didn't pay them yet" I said, as I made my escape.

Thirty minutes later the French Foreign Legion came back into town.

I paid them fifty dollars and they enthusiastically thanked me, refused my offer of a beer or a lift, and walked out of town towards the Hi-Way Inn where they planned to get on the Greyhound Bus and head as far towards Sydney as twenty-five dollars each would get them

I'd love to know what happened after they left.

TIE ME KANGAROO DOWN

In 1987 Rolf Harris embarked on a trip through the Northern Territory where he entertained locals and tourists in, from memory, Darwin, Katherine, Tenant Creek and Alice Springs. Just prior to the series of concerts we received a call from his agent, asking if we had a couple of spare rooms. Apparently, Rolf had requested to stay at the old Pub rather than Mataranka where the rest of the group was staying. It appeared Rolf had visited the Daly Waters Pub some years before and loved the old pub's charm and hospitality.

Late in the afternoon Rolf and a few others arrived to check-in. Rolf introduced himself to me and he seemed to be a very nice man. Rolf explained he was as crook as a dog with the flu and needed some rest but he assured me he'd be in the bar later for a drink and a meal. On the way to his room he met and fell in love with our kangaroo Daly … and I think Daly, who normally disliked men with beards, was taken by Rolf's charm as well.

To his word, Rolf did return in the evening and enjoyed our Beef and Barra BBQ. And while he was not feeling well he played eight ball with a few tourists, offered to sign our visitor's wall where he signed his name and said hello to everyone and surprised even me when he took on all challengers on the eight ball table … and won. Before leaving he thanked me for not expecting too much from him and for me requesting the tourists to give him space. I think one of them may have told him I did, as I certainly didn't let him know.

As they were loading luggage into the car in readiness to depart Rolf came into the bar and said, "I know you're too polite to ask but would you like a photo taken with me out the front to put up in the pub"? He must have read my mind.

Rolf Harris insisted we have a photo taken out the front
... thanks Rolf

A GREAT ~~PIE~~ PUB

In 1987 John Williamson made a surprise visit to Daly
Waters Pub. He had been touring Western Australia
playing many concerts and was on his way home. John
Williamson was a legend in the bush and two of the most
popular songs in our jukebox were his. We played them all
the time when no-one else was putting songs on.

John walked into the bar, looked around and ordered a
soft drink and a pie. He didn't introduce himself so I said
"welcome John" and held out my hand ... maybe he didn't
see it. He kept to himself with his friend and they sat at the
table in the corner talking quietly. I rushed the order out to

the kitchen and said to Leonie "don't stuff this one up, it's for John Williamson". She went white "no way, really" and I replied "yep, really. My God, John Williamson in our pub".

In ten minutes out came the pie on a plate with chips with a serviette and cutlery. Leonie grabbed the tomato sauce on the way past and delivered her most important meal ever … to one of the most popular entertainers in Australia.

John quickly ate his pie, finished his drink, stood up and was about to walk out through the door and leave and I couldn't believe what I was witnessing. A man who sang passionately about the great outback and who was idolised by every country person in Australia, including everyone in the Pub at that time, was about to leave one of the most famous and historic pubs in the bush without saying thank-you or anything. I couldn't let it happen and so I grabbed a black Texta, held it up and yelled "excuse me John. Could you sign your name above the door please"? John Williamson turned around and looked at me for a moment, with a look of "God, do I have to" but his voice said, "yeh okay, where"?

I came out from behind the bar and pointed to the small section of wall above the front door and as John was too short to reach the wall, I grabbed a seat for him to stand on and said, "how about right there next to the photo of Rolf Harris". John took the Texta, stood on the chair and after a second, to decide what to write, he penned *"A GREAT PIE ... John Williamson"* handed the Texta back and walked out the door.

After John left I reflected on what just happened and decided to give him the benefit of the doubt, by assuming he was either shy or very tired after a long tour and just wanted to get home but one of the tourists wasn't so forgiving and said "bugger him" and immediately grabbed the Texta from me, climbed on the chair and changed the letter I to U and E to B, so the sign now read *"A GREAT PUB ... John Williamson"*.

To this day I believe the Daly Waters Pub, and its thousands of visitors, deserved that much from John.

AUSTRALIA'S PARTY

Australia was settled, or invaded as your opinion may sway, by the English in 1788. To celebrate the event, of two hundred years, many celebrations were held around Australia.

A couple of days prior to New Year's Eve, in late December 1987, a team from Channel Nine, that included well known reporter Ken Sutcliffe drove into town and said they were booked into the pub for three nights. They added "we're here to film an outback New Year's Eve in your pub, to be shown live around Australia, for the Bicentennial celebrations.

I was ecstatic our pub was included in this but at the same time, I must have looked confused as I couldn't find a booking and told them so. The producer said "you must have it. I arranged it a month ago on the phone. I spoke to a woman … let me see here … yes, I spoke at length with, Val. Is she here"? I knew then, we weren't going to be in the program.

I explained Val owned the "service station" down the road and I added "don't worry. I will call her and tell her you've changed you mind and are staying here". The producer looked around the pub and said "this place is sooo cool … but we've done a deal mate. Val has us booked in and we've arranged a satellite vehicle to arrive there tomorrow. I love this place but a deal's a deal. So, she doesn't own the old pub then"? Once again Val cashed in on the fame of our historic pub. The rotten old "so and so".

Ken Sutcliffe came up to the bar and said to me "I'll be back for a beer, as soon as we've checked in" and they left. I was gutted.

439

Ken and a couple of other did come back and all agreed they were booked in the wrong place and the program was going to be shown live from the wrong place but nothing could be done about it. They did take a bit of footage around the pub but I never found out if any of it was ever shown. I did hear Val shouted drink after drink to them to keep them "from coming to the old pub" but I expected her to do exactly that and it didn't surprise me.

A great chance of worldwide exposure missed …

A GOOD DAY TO BE A VEGAN

Steve Atwell invited us to Hidden Valley station for a BBQ several times and eventually, we found the time to get there for it.

The only route we knew to Hidden Valley was to go south to Dunmurra and then west to the station turnoff and then a few kilometres into the homestead, we were told was built in the 1940's by outback legend Dick Scobie, and was one of the more traditional homesteads in the NT. The drive took much longer than we expected but it did take us past an incredibly big sinkhole, which appeared a few years earlier in the middle of the road. Steve told us he almost drove into the hole on the way back from Dunmurra one night. He added it definitely wasn't there when he went to the pub.

Hidden Valley Homestead in 1960 (Ellen Kettle Collection, courtesy of NT Library)

When we arrived at Hidden Valley, Steve's girlfriend Bronwyn took us on a tour of the beautiful huge square homestead that was surrounded by a single long shady verandah. Steve and Lockie then asked us to follow them into the bush for a "bit of fun". We had no idea what was in store for us but knowing Steve and Lockie it would be entertaining.

We drove into the bush for about twenty minutes. There was no track and it seemed to us there was no plan. We finally arrived at a clearing and noticed a few cattle in the distance standing in the shade of some large gum trees.

Steve got out of the car and motioned for us to come over. He pulled a big rifle from behind his seat and said "there you go mate, take a shot at the biggest one". He obviously didn't know I wasn't good with guns and so I politely replied "Steve if you want an angry wounded bullock running around the bush then I'm your man ... but if you want a clean kill then you'd better take the shot mate". It only took one glance towards Leonie and he knew she wasn't interested and so with Lockie approaching blindness Steve took aim by resting his elbow on the bonnet of the ute and "kaboom" one of the cattle, well over one hundred metres away, was dead before it hit the ground.

We hopped back in the vehicles and drove to where the animal lay dead on the earth. Steve and Lockie immediately went to work. Steve produced a knife from nowhere and cut the beast's throat and then with Lockie's assistance they proceeded to pump the blood out before skinning the animal whilst it lay on the ground. We couldn't believe the speed with which they worked and the unspoken teamwork they demonstrated showed many kills they had done together.

After skinning the carcase, Leonie and I were told to tear eucalyptus branches off nearby trees and lay them in the ute. The leafy trees were full of tree ants and their bite hurt, so it was best done in a hurry. While we did this Steve fired up the chainsaw. I thought he was going to cut a tree down to make it easier for us. Instead he walked to the animal with chainsaw revving, and with Lockie pulling on each leg, Steve cut it up into about a dozen manageable pieces. Steve and I then loaded the warm, slippery sections of beef into the ute on top of the leaves. "Why the leaves Steve" I said, still scratching my bites from the millions of ants, and he replied "flies mate. Flies won't come near the beef if we cover it in eucalyptus leaves". "maybe it's because the ants bite the flies mate" I replied scratching. I went to grab one section of meat and it moved. I couldn't believe it. Lockie laughed aloud and said "its only nerves. And I don't mean yours". As soon as we loaded the ute we covered the cuts of beef with more leaves and branches and drove back to the homestead.

On our return, Bronwyn took Leonie aside and the girls went inside to make salads for dinner. Steve, Lockie and I did the men stuff and went to the "butcher shop". I love beef and have never had a problem with handling meat and cooking it but this was different. The meat was still warm as Steve skilfully cleaned the cuts up. All bone ends were trimmed and many of the cuts were re-cut on the bandsaw

443

and we put all the cuts away in the cold-room. I assumed they would hang for a week or so to get tender and then get portioned into steaks, sausages and mince to go into the freezer. Steve said "okay that job's done. Now would you and Leonie prefer ribs, fillet or rump for dinner"? I cooked over one hundred rump steaks on the BBQ every night at the pub so the choice was obvious for me "fillet please" I said. "Okay, let's go shopping" Steve said.

Steve then surprised me. He took me into the cold-room where he selected a section of the beef we had just killed and then back on the bench he proceeded to extract a long eye fillet from the section. The fillet was so fresh it had contractions on the bench as he sliced it up. I thought they would have hung the carcase for a few days before cooking it, as I had experienced at Billy Tapp's BBQ, freshly killed meat was really tough. I incorrectly assumed the killer was for show and not for now. Twenty minutes later the freshly killed fillet steaks were tossed on the BBQ.

With our beers in hand Steve and Lockie started cooking the steaks. The girls set the table and a beautiful couple of salads sat in the centre. We all stood around the BBQ on the verandah and watched as the BBQ cooked. Lockie and Steve are two of the funniest guys we'd ever met and they we were all in stitches laughing as they jokingly abused each other whilst trying to cook the steaks properly. When it was cooked we all sat at the table and the steaks were placed in the middle. Our orders of medium and rare were forgotten and it was grab a steak and hope. Leonie whispered to me "is that the beef we shot today"? My look said it all.

We had a wonderful day with plenty of laughs with great friends but unfortunately, the beef we consumed that night was the toughest we ever ate. My piece was so tough I was only able to eat the salad as I quietly, invisibly, gave my steak to Steve's dog "Boss" who was hanging around under the table. Leonie saw me do it but no-one else did and for the first time ever I thought to myself "today would have been a good day to be vegan".

The next morning Steve said he would take us on a shortcut to Daly Waters. He needed to pick up his mail so he would lead the way. So we followed Steve and Lockie in the Toyota utility in my Range Rover, the car Steve and Lockie previously described as a Toorak tractor, a Snob-car and a four-wheel drive in drag. At one point the track became boggy, and the going slowed to a crawl, until Steve bogged. He got out, came back to me and said "you'd better turn around and go back. That car of yours won't get through this mud". I replied "My car isn't even struggling

445

Steve. Let me get in front and I'll tow you out". His return laugh was loud. I put the Range Rover into gear and drove easily past his bogged ute and asked for a rope. We tied the cars together and the Range Rover, in low range first gear, slowly but surely pulled the Toyota from the bog. Steve and Lockie could not believe it. To rub salt into the wounds I said "you boys go ahead, I'll come behind you to tow you out of any further bogs". I was needed to do it one more time. When we arrived to the pub Steve said "I am going to get me one of those Pommy cars one day. Most impressed I am".

CONTIKI COCKTAIL HOUR

Contiki was a raft expedition that crossed the Pacific Ocean in 1947 not to be confused with Contiki, who were a tour company for under 30's, regularly visiting the pub in the 1980's. It was all about fun and adventure and they didn't take anything seriously. A Contiki tour was, in reality, a pub crawl around Australia and definitely not a scenic tour. If you wanted to embrace nature and historical sites then Contiki wasn't for you.

In October 1986 our first Contiki Coach thundered into town at 11am and stopped in the middle of the road in front of the pub. From the bar I shouted out to Leonie, Phil and

Toni who were doing other tasks around the pub "you beauty, a Contiki coach has just pulled up out front"

The coach door opened and out jumped a good-looking young guy in a floral shirt appearing like he came from the beaches of Brazil. He ran into the pub and introduced himself as Jorge Fernandez, host of Contiki Tours. He then asked "I hope the bar is open, I have forty thirsty travellers. It's 11am and that makes it cocktail time". I replied, "the bars been open for hours and have I got a cocktail for you"!

Jorge ran back to the bus and within a minute there were forty loud young girls and guys looking around the pub with "oohs" and "ahhhs" and "look at that" and many other wild exclamations. One of the prettier girls put a song on the juke box and I ramped up the volume.

Jorge then came to the bar and said, "Where's Bill"? I replied "he left here a month ago. It's us now". We went to the end of the bar and he said "now Mark, last time I was here Bill made an incredible cocktail called a Daly Waters Dust Settler and I've been telling them all about it. Don't let me down, they will spend plenty". Fortunately for us, previous owner Bill, left the recipe for the Dust Settler behind the bar and we expanded the cocktails to include a Daly Waters Snake Bite Remedy. "Mate they are in for the time of their lives, watch this".

Phil, Leonie and Toni came into the bar to help and as I spruiked the cocktails and took orders they pumped out cocktail after cocktail at 11am in the morning. Even Jorge drank a few but not the driver, who I felt sorry for. At about midday, Jorge shouted "okay guys, on the bus. It's Mataranka for lunch" but everyone was having a ball and no-one wanted to go. It took him half an hour to get them out as they kept buying Dust Settlers and an array of t-shirts, singlets and stubby coolers. After they left we cleaned up the pub and counted the takings. One Contiki coach spent more money over the bar, in one hour, than we'd normally take in a day in 1986, so we were eager to see them again.

Jorge and Contiki returned many times over the next couple of years and every time was great fun. Jorge was an incredible host and his enthusiasm never waned. Each time he left I thought to myself "why didn't anyone tell me you could get a job like that when I left school"?

Footnote: Some years later I was flying to Brisbane and Jorge happened to be on the same flight. He told me he had quit Contiki and was now in his own travel agency. Knowing Jorge, I am sure he would be successful.

HUFF AND PUFF AND BURN THE PUB DOWN

For a while Roy Beebe's son-in-law Robert managed Tanumbirini Station about two hundred kilometres east of Daly Waters Pub. Just like Roy, Robert was a big man but unlike Roy, he wasn't very polite and he became terribly angry when drinking. This was never more evident than late one night in 1987 in the Daly Waters Pub.

It was late, on a relatively normal Saturday night. Most, if not all the tourists, were in bed but a few of the station workers were still in the pub drinking, laughing and playing music and eight-ball. Carl and Tom from Amungee Mungee were enjoying themselves but, as was his habit when drunk, Carl found himself in an argument with one of the Tanumbirini boys that developed into a full on fight between the two camps. When a fight like this starts there is nothing to do but encourage them outside by pushing and yelling aloud "get out, take it to the streets and get into it". So, with only Darryl and Leonie there to help me, we managed to get them out into the street in front of the pub where they continued fighting. Eventually, the fight was over and the points were given to the Tanumbirini boys. Carl, Tom and their team left and went home with their tail between their legs. Normally the victors would keep drinking and brag to each other how good they were in the fight but tonight I decided it was late and the pub was shut. It was about now the night deteriorated even further.

I told them through the fly-screen door we were closed and to go home. The lads were wild and shouted profanities toward the pub before Robert came to the door and shouted, "open the f*^#ing door or we'll burn the pub down". We turned the lights off inside the pub and Darryl, Leonie and I were sitting in the middle of the bar. I have to admit I was unsure of what would happen next but I was reasonably confident they wouldn't burn the pub down. They didn't need to do that. If they were really serious about getting more booze they could have pushed the door open with one hand. Everyone knew the pub was easy to get into with its flyscreen windows. It was about now I realised the bowsers were still unlocked and the lights across the road were still on. I said to Leonie "I have to go over there and lock them up and turn the lights off". "Don't be stupid" Leonie and Darryl replied.

By now Robert and his half dozen station workers were standing in the middle of the road, none the happier but at least a bit quieter. So I opened the front door and slowly walked across the road towards the pumps. I walked straight towards Robert, who was in a direct line with the pumps. When I reached him he refused to let me past and so I said "get out of my way Robert, the pubs closed. I am going to lock up my bowsers and go back inside and if you lay one hand on me you'll never drink in another pub in the Northern Territory". I then brushed past Robert and walked the ten metres to the bowsers. I locked each of them, turned the lights off and turned around. Now I needed to repeat the exercise again. I heard a couple of the lads urging Robert to belt me but I was fairly confident he wouldn't. I was confident because I knew Robert knew Roy would back me ahead of him and sack him. He also knew the police would undoubtedly send him to jail and he would be barred from all hotels in the NT if he hit a publican …particularly a publican in a town without a police officer.

So once again I asked Robert to move aside, He reluctantly did, after saying "you'll regret this" and I went back inside and locked the door with the pathetic little a bathroom type latch. We sent Daryl to bed as there was nothing left to do but wait. So Leonie and I sat in the dark for about half an hour whilst Robert and his workers, full of wind, planned to burn the pub to the ground and other crazy things. Eventually they became sick of it, hopped in their car and left a very relieved publican and his wife in peace.

HELD HOSTAGE

In 1988 during a quiet time, early in the tourist season, a Western Australian Aerial Survey Team spent some time staying at Daly Waters Pub. The boss of the small outfit arrived prior to the survey team and after the main job was completed he stayed a few more days to clean up. During this time he spent more hours drinking than working and therefore spent plenty of money over the bar.

One night, at around 9pm, whilst I was still working with Taffy, he came into the bar wearing camouflaged army fatigues and brandishing a knife. He had been drinking in his room and was obviously under the weather. We refused to serve him any more alcohol and eventually convinced him to go back to his room and "sleep it off". Not long after this I finished for the night and went to bed.

As Taffy tells it, later that night he returned again to try to get a drink. Taffy said he refused to serve him and told him to get some sleep. Apparently, he wasn't happy about this and started to rant and rave and carry on in a very strange, drugged like fashion. Taffy said he eventually half carried and dragged him to the motel where the guy was still in a very agitated state, before Taffy went back to the bar. It hadn't been a busy night so Taffy closed the pub just before midnight when the last of the drinkers left. Taffy then went to his staff caravan in the caravan park where he promptly fell asleep.

I am not sure of the time when the banging started on the door of our "donga" at the rear of the pub but it must have been well after midnight. When I opened the door about four of our staff piled in the door shouting "close it quick", which I did. After calming the staff down they proceeded to describe what occurred, causing them to seek refuge with us. They insisted I turn all the lights out in the donga.

Apparently, they were awoken by the sounds of a man banging on Taffy's caravan door and screaming he was going to kill him. After about ten minutes the guy gave up and left and they thought it was over. But then the guy came back in his four wheel drive and started crashing it into the caravan whilst still screaming "get out here Taffy you bastard, I'm gonna kill you". Then they said "after another few minutes he gave up with the attack and disappeared. We decided we needed to get help and so we came here. What are you going to do"? It was about now there was more banging on the door. We all shut up immediately fearing it was the lunatic. Then we heard "open the bloody door, It's Taffy".

Taffy was out of breathe and looked like he saw a ghost. He finally calmed down enough to tell us the guy hadn't been back to the van for about five minutes and so he decided to run for it and warn us. He didn't realise the entire staff were in our donga doing exactly the same. So there we all were, in darkness. We all peered out of the two windows in the kitchen/lounge of the donga into the darkness. We could see the rear of the pub and to the left we could see through a ten-metre gap into the beer garden. The beer garden has some light spilling from the two toilet blocks used by the caravan park and so our view was pretty good. If anyone was coming we would see them.

Within five minutes of Taffy arriving we saw him. He was creeping through the beer garden and then we noticed him carrying a rifle. He stopped and then moved as little and stopped and looked around. It was scary to watch and it felt like we were watching a movie but everything was very real. "Oh my God he has a gun", said one of the girls and the others said "shhhh". It was many years ago now but I can clearly remember the fear in the room. We observed the guy walk around the beer garden and check out the pub in silence. He glanced towards the donga a couple of times but didn't appear interested in coming this way. Eventually, he turned around and slowly headed back towards the motel and caravan park and went out of sight. We looked at each other and waited.

I waited five minutes and then rang the Mataranka Police Station where I woke up Senior Officer Bob Allen. I told him the complete story and when he said "do you want us to attend" I said rather forcefully "bloody oath I do Bob, this guy has a bloody gun and we're holed up in my donga at the back of the pub fearing for our lives". With that Bob said he'd be about two hours and to sit tight. I said "Bob when you get here drive around the pub and pull up at the donga. I'll come out if it's safe".

Two hours later and with no signs of movement from the gunman the police arrived. Bob and his partner sat in the car. I opened the door, went over to them and told them what transpired. Bob asked if I held a key to his room to which I said, "yes, of course". He then said, "okay get the key and let's go". I reminded him of the gun and the knife and the car but Bob calmly said, "I'd say he's in his room sleeping it off, so let's go". I went into the pub and took the spare room key from the hook and the three of us went to the motel units. I crept hunched over in fear. Bob walked through the beer garden like it was a Sunday stroll whilst his partner kept to the rear. We arrived to the motel and Bob asked "well, what room" and I said, "shhhhh" and pointed to the last room on the left. Bob casually walked up to the last door with me following quietly on my toes and he took the key from me.

I expected Bob to quietly turn the key and then crash through the door with his pistol aimed. Instead, he turned the key and walked in with his pistol still in the holster. I couldn't look and hid out of sight. His partner was still behind me. I wasn't sure if he was protecting my back or himself. The next thing Bob's arm comes out of the door holding a rifle vertically. His partner reached around me and grabbed the rifle and Bob said "it's all okay boys. Check this out".

Bob was so matter of fact, I assumed the guy wasn't even in the room but when we entered I could see him lying asleep on the bed with a few knives on the bed next to him. Bob grabbed the guy and shook him vigorously until he woke and said, "okay, you're coming with me". Bob dragged him out of the room and said to me "does the door go to the front road", which it did and added "I don't want to make a scene". He then told his partner to bring the police van around the front. Bob dragged the groggy guy out the front and sat him in the dirt. A minute later the partner pulled up in the car. It was still dark when Bob shoved the guy into the cage on the back of the police ute and said, "okay he's ours now. I'll call you later" and they left.

I went to the donga and told the staff it was safe now and everyone went to their beds. None of us slept. In the morning the bar was full of people complaining about the noise in the caravan park. I didn't tell them a gunman was on the loose but instead said the noise was due to a couple of guests having "a lovers tiff".

Later in the morning Bob rang me and said "we took him to Katherine where he's been charged to appear in court sometime in the future. You will need to fill out an incident report form and statement. I'll send it down". I asked what would happen to him now and he said, "that will be up to him".

Next morning we heard on the grape-vine he was let out of jail and we couldn't believe it. We were not sure how he was let out of jail so quickly, or how he came to Daly Waters from the Katherine lock-up, but some-time during the day we noticed his car was gone and his room empty with the key in the door. We still didn't feel safe but at least it appeared we were rid of him.

Footnote: a year after the incident Leonie and I were travelling through Katherine on a well-earned holiday after selling the pub. We were having lunch at the Katherine

Hotel when a female customer asked, "hey, I know you, you're the owners of the Daly Waters Pub". We explained we'd sold the pub and were now on holidays and she said, "I work at the courthouse and we've been holding a cheque for you for over a year". She didn't know what is was for but said for us to go there after lunch and she'd give it to us. A bit later she gave us an envelope with a cheque for about $600 and a small note reading "Payment for damages to staff caravan" and then I remembered when I filled out the police statement, I declared the gunman caused $600 damage to the staff caravan, when he crashed into it with is car.

Justice at last.

Chapter 25. ITS TIME TO GO

The pub was getting busier and busier each year, the facilities were stretched to the limit and so were we.

We extended the caravan park to the boundaries of the property. We dug extra septic tanks and extended the electrical requirements of the pub to the maximum the town generator could supply. We were consuming so much water the town bore struggled to keep up and we purchased so much food and drink each week we needed extra deliveries and the pub storage couldn't handle anymore. We were selling so many meals the kitchen wasn't big enough … it wasn't in the beginning either. We increased the staff from one when we started to ten and the staff accommodation needed upgrading. We cooked the Beef and Barra BBQ every night and the barbeque wasn't big enough nor was the beer garden. Our refrigeration plant kept breaking down due to the heavy workload and the heat. Some days five or more coaches of tourists would pull up and the old bar couldn't handle that many people at once. We were working eighteen hour days, seven days a week and there weren't enough hours in the day.

One of the many "straws that broke the camel's back" occurred in 1988. I received a phone call from my mum telling me dad suffered a heart attack and was in hospital.

The heart attack occurred whilst they were on holidays at our favourite destination Edithburgh, on Yorke Peninsula in SA. Mum waited a couple of days before telling me so I wouldn't worry. I was in shock, my dad was my mate and I thought he was fit and indestructible. I couldn't believe it and was upset I wasn't told straight away. Mum convinced me I must not return to South Australia as dad would be upset he caused me to leave the pub. I didn't know what to do but in the end after several phone calls from mum and my sister I stayed. Thankfully Dad recovered well and to this day is going great.

Leonie was my rock at Daly Waters and the staff's best friend. She never complained or faltered and continued to work incredible hours day after day. We rarely took a day off in our time in the pub and during that time my dad experienced his heart attack and we couldn't leave the pub to attend her funeral or my father's bedside and we constantly missed our family. Whilst I worked as many hours, or more, than anyone at the pub, sometimes I drank too much, as much as a release to the pressure of running such a busy demanding operation in front of everyone, as anything else. I also think drinking helped me forget how tired I was. By the middle of the tourist season in 1988, I was starting to wish I was somewhere else. I started to dream of somewhere quieter and a place where I wasn't on show to the public every minute of my day. When you are lucky enough to work in a place such as Daly Waters Pub you owe the pub and the customers a good experience and for over two years my sole reason for being there was to please every person who walked in the door. As you have read in this book, I loved almost every minute of our time in Day Waters and I felt very lucky to have the experience, but my interest and enthusiasm waned and I needed a break.

One morning Leonie, Max and I woke to the customary 5.45am alarm. Max was so accustomed to the routine he simply rolled over and waited for us get up and leave. I looked at Leonie and I don't know why I did it but I said "Leonie, I am so bloody tired. Let's sell". We both became teary as we hugged and thought about what I just said. Max joined in purring and reluctantly, as a family, we agreed it was time to go. It was an incredibly hard decision. We loved the pub and hated the thought of selling our dream … but after talking about it all day, that night we decided if we didn't we risked becoming unhappy and may regret not selling more than selling. The time felt right.

The next day I rang hotel broker and friend, Bud Goldsworthy, and told him I wanted to sell the freehold and business of the pub. I gave him our "walk in walk out" price which basically meant everything in the pub stayed and thereby preserved the history of the pub. We considered leasing the hotel to another operator but the pub is made of timber and a serious fire risk. If it burned down during the lease it would not be able to be rebuilt with the history and therefore we wouldn't have a business to lease. So, in my opinion, we needed to sell the freehold. Bud immediately said he there was a buyer in his mind.

The relief at making the decision to sell the pub was instant and enormous. I felt a monkey was lifted from my back. That may seem a ridiculous statement given the success of the business and the profit we would make from the sale but my Daly Waters Pub monkey was never "financial", it was a never ceasing "stress and long hours" gorilla. We hadn't worked for money and in fact, we didn't know how much money was in the bank. We worked hard to please the visitors and locals and whilst we loved doing the job, it took its toll.

Within a fortnight, Bud rang to say a couple of guys were interested in buying the pub and he'd like to send them to us. A week later two country boys from South Australia arrived. Peter and Wally loved what they saw and in quick time made the decision to purchase the pub and within a couple of months we packed our bags and left. We held a couple of big parties to say thanks and farewell to all of our friends and one day after putting almost all of our possessions, including our Combi Van, into Banga's road-train we made an emotional early morning exit.

Max, Leonie, Burke and I drove away from the Daly Waters Pub in our Range Rover with our caravan behind and tinny on the roof. We drove for hours without saying a word until we arrived to Tennant Creek around four hundred kilometres south. Normally we would have kept driving but on that day I turned into a small motel, checked in, closed the curtains and the three of us slept for eighteen hours.

It was about one thousand days since Leonie found the ad for a "historic Northern Territory Pub FOR SALE" and every day since we lived and breathed Daly Waters Pub.

The dream had become reality and now it was over.

Chapter 26. A TRAGEDY

When I decided to write this book I knew I would need mention a tragedy that changed our lives during our Daly Waters Pub adventure.

Chronologically this story should have been appeared much earlier but as this book is a series of short stories with many out of order, I decided to leave it to the end. When we went to Daly Waters, Phil and Toni had been our great friends for over twelve years and Phil was one of my best mates, in our surveying careers and away from it.

In the first few months at Daly Waters, none of us took a day off. We worked non-stop, starting at 6am and going to bed when the bar closed. Eventually, in February 1987 after eight months at the pub, Leonie and I had our first time off and went to Borroloola for three days fishing with Andy Hind, when we were camped on the Macarthur River for our wedding anniversary. We didn't catch a fish but we relaxed with a nice break from work.

A few weeks later Phil and Toni, with our yardie Grant, went fishing to Roper River for their first break. Tragically, they didn't make it as there was a terrible accident whilst Toni was driving on a dirt road. The car rolled over, causing Toni and Phil to be seriously injured and Grant to also suffer injuries. Due to the Toni's injuries and the remote location, in time and distance to a hospital, Toni passed away in the back of the ambulance taking them to hospital. Phil ended up in Katherine Hospital and then was transferred to Darwin Hospital for an extended period, whilst Grant was well enough to return to the pub a few weeks later.

Eventually, Phil returned to the pub but the memories were raw and painful and it was never going to be the same for him without Toni. Eventually Phil asked Leonie and I to buy him out and after some juggling and refinancing, we did.

This was a sad chapter in all our lives. The Territory is a tough uncompromising remote place and it took someone we dearly loved. RIP Toni Thurnam

Chapter 27. OUR DALY WATERS ENCORE

After selling the Daly Waters Pub Leonie, Max, Burke and I travelled home to South Australia and then took almost a year touring through to Western Australia and up to the Northern Territory in our home, our Range Rover, tinny and caravan. We then came back down to Daly Waters to catch up with old friends on the other side of the bar. Billy and Donna came into the pub on our second night in town and we had a great evening reminiscing. During the night Billy mentioned he was doing a muster of a remote bush area of Maryfield Station with helicopters and bull-catchers but unfortunately a catcher rolled injuring a station hand and made him a worker short. He said he was in town hiring. I couldn't get my hand in the air quick enough and next minute I'd been recruited as a "bull catcher assistant". I said, "what the hell does that mean". "What the hell does that mean" would come to haunt me. I was told to report for duty the next day at 8am to the station and warned we would be camping out for two to three nights so bring my swag.

The next day came quickly and whilst nursing a slight hangover from too much reminiscing we drove to Maryfield. Donna said Leonie could stay with her so it worked out well. As soon as we arrived Billy said "okay let's do it". So I jumped in his 4WD and we headed into the bush. After about an hour drive, on bush tracks, we came to an open area where the station hands were building a large holding yards with temporary cattle fencing panels. Billy and I immediately joined in and helped them. One by one the lads I remembered gave me a nod of welcome but it didn't go any further than recognition. No handshake and certainly no smiles. I reckoned they wondered what a bloody publican was doing out there getting in their way.

Our job was to complete the large holding yard that day and to also assemble panels and wire fencing into two "wings" running away from the yard like a V. It was bloody hot and hard work. The panels were not only heavy but they were blisteringly hot from sitting in the sun. By sunset we achieved our aim and Billy made a radio call to Donna and asked her to phone the helicopter pilot, and tell him they'd start first thing the next morning. So on a balmy evening we set up camp under the trees.

Billy's boys quickly started a blazing fire and from the rear of the ute Billy retrieved a large cooking pot and he placed it on the fire, threw in a heap of potatoes and we sat around talking whilst we waited for whatever it was in the pot to cook. Billy kept checking on the pot and eventually lifted something out of it, took it to the back of the ute, placed it on the tailgate and said to me, as the guest, I go first. So to set the scene properly you need to understand it was now dark. I mean seriously dark and our only light source was the fire about five metres away. I could just make out a stack of enamel plates on the tailgate next to a lump of what I assumed was meat and a pile of assumed whole potatoes. There was a knife stuck into the "lump" of meat, so I pulled it out and proceeded to take three slices off the top of the meat. I also grabbed a couple of potatoes and moved away to a tree trunk and took my seat with the plate on my knees. Using my hands, I tried to pick up a hot slice of meat but it was a bit slippery as well as being very hot. Finally, I secured the slice and took a big bite into a horribly jelly like textured salty piece of something vulgar. I winced thinking I'd just eaten something off or rotten and immediately blurted and spat it out in the dust. I looked across to the ute to see Billy and the lads watching me closely and they were all laughing with their hands over their mouths. Billy couldn't control himself any longer and said "Mark you've taken three of the thickest slices of corned beef FAT mate. It's the fatty outer layer, you can't eat that, throw it away and get over here for a few slices of the real meat you idiot". The rest of the meal was wonderful. The slow cooked beef was tender and tasty. Much better than his BBQ ... although I didn't say it.

That night I slept like a baby. I was stuffed from the hard day's work and it helped. The next morning Billy woke us all up at sunrise by honking the car horn. I struggled through some beef again with bread and cups of warming tea before quickly getting organised and getting into the vehicles. I went to hop into Billy's ute but he put up his hand and said "you're a bull catcher now mate. Jump into that one ... and hold on tight."

Billy's three bull-catchers were old Toyota 4WD tray tops with the roof cut off, no windows and the doors removed. There was a roll bar to hold onto and a big bull bar around the perimeter of the vehicle. The entire underneath of the catcher was covered by a welded steel plate. There were leather belts hanging from the roll bar and the dashboard.

I jumped into the catcher Billy indicated. It was driven by the young Craig Mills who frequented the pub when we owned it. I remembered he was a quiet brooding lad but he caused me a bit of grief a couple of times and I know I evicted him more than once during our time. His dad, Dave Mills, also worked for Billy. In his past, I believe he was a legendary horseman who now drove the station truck.

Craig barely acknowledged my presence, which wasn't unusual for any of these lads, before taking off at high speed on a rough dirt track. We drove for a few miles into the scrub before all coming to a halt behind Billy. The lads all seemed to know what we were waiting for. I was about to ask when BRRRRROARRRRR exploded above my head as a helicopter flashed above our heads from behind us, barely above the low scrubby trees we were sheltering under. The chopper was going backwards and spinning out of control but incredibly it was definitely under control. I couldn't believe what I was witnessing ... CRAIG didn't bother to look up as he rolled a cigarette. The chopper disappeared out of sight. Craig smoked his ciggie as I tried to imagine what was going to happen next. Billy slept. And then I heard the distant sound of the chopper. Everyone sat up and listened. Billy stirred into action and said "get ready boys". Craig looked at me and said "I bloody hope you're up to this". I tried to smile but failed.

The mustering helicopter came from nowhere

Next minute the chopper came straight at us before spinning backwards and going back in the opposite direction. "Let's go lads" screamed Billy. The catchers started and off we sped into the light scrub all lined up next to each other and roughly fifty metres apart. We bounced across the uneven ground and then I saw what was happening. The chopper was pushing a group of about fifty cattle ... and I mean pushing. It was flying so low it touched the occasional beast on the rump and then it would rear into the air to clear a tree by inches before diving back down, spinning, urging and edging the cattle forward. The chopper made enough noise itself but in addition to the engine and propeller noise, a siren blared from a speaker. It was surreal. Dust was flying from the chopper and the catchers as together we pushed the cattle along at a fast running pace. Craig took a position on one side near the front. Billy was on the other side in the work ute and behind us were the other two catchers. At the rear was the chopper. I was lost, until I spotted the wings of the cattle yard in front. The chopper guided the group of bull catchers and cattle with amazing precision down the funnel of the wings and into the yard. The catchers pushed the last few cattle into the yard and we closed the gate. It was exhilarating and I thought to myself "job done. That was fun" but I was wrong. The chopper was already gone and was flying back toward where it first appeared. The catchers all fired up and off we went in pursuit. Billy remained at the yard with old Dave Mills asleep in his truck.

A few miles from the yard the chopper came straight at us pushing a huge bull and Craig took off straight at it. He did a long fast turn and as the bull went past us it turned left so Craig turned right and after about a hundred metres started to get on its tail. The chopper moved away and left us alone. His job was completed by bringing the bull to us. We were bouncing across the rough ground dodging the odd tree or mound and eventually Craig hit the bull directly in front of the bull bar when, with a flick of the steering wheel and foot hard on the accelerator, he spun the bull sideways and ran over it!! I mean, seriously he ran over it. The bull catcher was raised in the air on my side with the front wheel above the ground and the bull was under the vehicle. Craig looked at me and said "you're up now. Do it". "Do what"? I said. "Craig grabbed a leather belt off the dashboard handrail and ordered me "grab his front leg and wrap the belt around it and then around the other leg and ... and bloody hurry". Somehow I immediately understood what he expected of me. I leapt out the catcher and saw the bull's two front legs hanging out the front of the catcher near the driver's side front wheel. I bent over and grabbed the top leg just below the knee so I could start to wrap the belt around it and the bottom leg and ... and well it went a bit blurry here. I remember getting kicked in the chin by the bull and staggering backwards towards Craig sitting in the driver's seat ... and I clearly remember Craig saying "the bottom leg. Grab the bottom leg first and lift it up to the top leg and wrap them together at the same time AND put your foot on its bloody head. You don't want it to horn you". Which, to my amazement, I did and I stepped back feeling quite proud of myself. Craig slowly reversed off the bull and shouting at me this time, "hurry up. Jump on the back, there's more" as we sped off towards the chopper. As we flew along I could see the other two catchers doing the same work and the chopper with another bull. We repeated this for about two hours, with me standing on the back of the ute holding on for dear life to the roll bar whilst pointing towards the bull and screaming to Craig at the top of my voice "he's over there ... to the right ... To the right ... yes that way, straight ahead ... can you see him" and that was how Craig rolled them over and I belted three more bulls ... and somehow without major incident. It was insane but exhilarating at the same time and I felt alive.

After getting kicked in the face I learnt how to do it.

(Note my foot on the bulls head so it didn't gore me and me lifting the bottom leg before I tie the belt ... pity I wasn't told earlier)

In the afternoon we drove around to find our belted bulls. The belting together of the legs stops them moving too far but what really impressed me was Craig knew roughly where each bull was located and we found them within ten minutes of arriving where he said they would be found. His dad Dave would then arrive in the cattle truck with Billy in his ute. Then by using the bull catcher as a tow truck and a bit of manpower we would drag each bull up into the truck with a rope tied around their horns that fed thru the front of the cattle truck to the tow catcher. The catcher would reverse slowly and pull the bull up the slide or the bull would stand up and thrash around unwillingly onto the truck ramp and into the cage. It was hot tough work but it was thrilling at the same time.

That night over another corned beef dinner I said "Millsy, you could've told me to grab the bottom leg first so I wouldn't get kicked in the face" to which he replied, "if you hadn't kicked me out of your pub I might have". In his mind we were even. I tended to agree. What a day.

The next day we completed the muster by catching a few more bulls and yarding them but not before Leonie and

Donna paid us a visit and the pilot Leonie took a wild ride in the chopper during which time the pilot did some exciting mustering, low flying manoeuvres to thrill her ... Or more correctly scare the wits out of her.

The whole mustering exercise still rates as one of the most exciting and adrenalin pumping experiences of my long, lucky, adventure-filled life.

The Maryfield mustering team … Billy Tapp is far right

Chapter 28. EPILOGUE ... LUCKY IN LIFE

I've owned quite a few pubs since Daly Waters Pub and I'm still involved in a few. I'm also a partner in 2 Mates Wines and a property development company. During my sixty years I've experienced many exciting jobs, where I've been exposed to dangerous creatures and people. I've dived professionally for pearls, in aptly named Shark Bay in Western Australia and I've collected the deadly blue-ringed octopus in South Australia, for delivery to the Sydney aquarium. In the Northern Territory I swam into one of our prawn-farm ponds to retrieve a "hopefully" dead crocodile and somehow escaped serious injury when I was caught in the path of an out of control territory bushfire. I've been barbed twice in my foot by a stingray whilst crabbing in South Australia and I've been bitten by a Wobbegong shark whilst working on our oyster farm near Edithburgh on Yorke Peninsula in SA. To this day, I continue to dive for scallops in South Australian waters where I recently experienced a close-up viewing of a 17' white pointer. I've wrangled wild scrub bulls during a helicopter muster but as tough as it all may seem, I wasn't a fighter and I was therefore beaten up by a couple of bar-thugs and just held my own against a few others.

But the best experience of my life … being publican of the historic Daly Waters Pub wins hands down.

Enjoying a rum with Lindsay Carmichael. Publican 2000 to present.

2017 and behind the bar again, after thirty years … like we'd never left.

Since selling the Daly Waters Pub, almost thirty years ago, we have lost some of our loved co-workers, neighbours and dear friends. They will be remembered forever by featuring in this book and in our hearts.

Rest in Peace

Toni Thurnam

Grant Wood

Roy Beebe

Annie Harrington

Taffy Abbott

Rossie Robertson

Lockie McKinnon

Burbank

Acknowledgements

I want to thank my business partners and their wives, who over the years have made it possible for me to do so much with my life and at the same time become close mates.

And lastly, a massive thankyou to my family and friends, who I tortured during the final stages of writing my book by asking them to read and re-read and be honest with their feedback, until I was finally satisfied my manuscript was worth publishing.

Made in the USA
Coppell, TX
26 December 2019

13775969R00266